The Washington

D1301711

KID O RAMA

JOHN F. KELLY AND CRAIG STOLTZ

Sports, Theater, Zoos, History, Nature, Art, Games, Science and Lots More To Enjoy With Children in the Washington Region

Published by
WASHINGTON POST BOOKS
1150 15th Street, NW
Washington, DC 20071

First Edition

The text of this book is composed in Times New Roman, with the display in Futura Extra Black and Century Gothic.

Manufactured by Chroma Graphics, Largo, Md.,
in association with Alan Abrams

ISBN: [0-9625971-7-1]

EDITOR AND PUBLISHER: Noel Epstein
GRAPHIC DESIGNER: Robert Barkin
ILLUSTRATOR: Susan Davis
RESEARCHER: Susan Breitkopf

This book can be accessed online at
www.washingtonpost.com,
though it may be in somewhat different form there.

Of all nature's gifts to the human race, what is sweeter to a man than his children?
— CICERO

There is always one moment in childhood when the door opens and lets the future in.
— GRAHAM GREENE

The real menace in dealing with a five-year-old is that in no time you begin to sound like a five-year-old.
— JEAN KERR

CONTENTS

THE PLAY BOOK

HELLO. IF YOU'RE HOLDING this book, you probably have a child, either a recent or somewhat older model. Maybe you have several. Or perhaps you're a grandparent, an aunt or uncle, a teacher or someone else who is responsible at times for shepherding other people's children. Regardless, you're probably hoping to find worthwhile things to do in the Washington area that will excite and engage the kids yet leave your sanity intact or — who knows? — perhaps even enhanced.

You've come to the right place. The two of us — John Kelly is the former editor of *The Washington Post's* WEEKEND section and father of two girls, and Craig Stoltz is editor of *The Post's* TRAVEL section and father of two boys — have spent the last several years checking out hundreds of area attractions with our own and others' children. We've toured the town on solo missions, with spouses and with day care, school and other merry groups. We've done it with infants and teenagers, occasionally at the same time. We present the results of our labors here — the best of things to do with kids, along with the information we suspect you'll find most useful in preparing for visits of your own.

For example, we've concentrated on providing:

❑ **Attractions based on kids' interests, not geography.** Why? So you can easily tailor outings around things your charges enjoy: animals or trains, art or science, go-karts or ballet. You'll find them all here, and much, much more, arranged kid-like in alphabetically reversed chapters, from Z to A. In a metropolitan area like ours, we believe that where an attraction is located is less important than what you get once you arrive. So our primary method of organization is What, not Where. But we're not zealots. We know that commuting time and location can be important factors when planning an outing. So you'll also find all the attractions organized by jurisdiction in **WHERE THEY ARE**, in the back of the book. If you're determined to work through the entire list of kid-friendly things in, say, Prince George's County, hey, we're here for you.

❑ **Planning-friendly categories.** We've also included **CROSS-PREFERENCES** that let you choose places by a wide array of criteria: Free, Good for Rainy Days, for Toddlers, for Teens, for Birthday Parties, for Groups with Strollers or Wheelchairs, for Grandparent Outings, for Pre-Readers, for All-Family Exercise and more. We hope you'll find these a valuable addition to the book.

- **Kid-specific advice.** Many entries include Words to the Wise, or nuggets we wish someone had told us before we went — unusual time or age restrictions, annoying entry policies, hidden costs, poor parking, etc. Our write-ups don't mimic brochure copy or tour guide scripts; they describe how to approach a place with kids of different ages and interests. We also provide numerous notes about nearby attractions, restaurants and other family-friendly amenities. This is in addition to phone numbers, prices, hours, addresses, World Wide Web sites and a ♿ symbol to indicate establishments that identify their main facilities as handicapped-accessible.

- **Wide area coverage.** We've assumed that folks using this guide live somewhere in the sprawling area known as Metropolitan Washington (though we suspect that those in Baltimore or Richmond also will find it useful). To create a target territory for attractions to include, we've drawn a rough circle reaching about 40 miles beyond the Capital Beltway in all directions. Because in practice this can mean 90 minutes or more in the car (for outside-the-Beltway Marylanders contemplating Virginia forays, and vice-versa), we've added this guiding principle: The farther outside the Beltway an attraction is, the more unusual and kid-friendly it has to be to make the cut. In a few cases we've reached outside the 40-mile range to include, for instance, Gettysburg, Pa., and several caves in the Shenandoah Valley. When we list a place outside our range, you can be confident that it'll be worth the trip.

- **User-friendly exclusions.** As a public service, we've left a lot of stuff out. We've omitted some tourist attractions and guidebook staples that, in our view, aren't that well suited to family touring. So you'll find a narrower-than-usual selection of, say, historic houses — but you can be sure those we do list are welcoming and engaging to children. Government agencies are listed only if their presentations are unusually well suited for children. As for museums, we direct you to the areas and features kids are most likely to enjoy. Also, for the most part we don't list attractions that require you to make reservations. Some do (and we tell you which ones those are), but most allow you simply to show up.

GRIEF SAVERS

IN THE SPIRIT of our Words to the Wise, we've also collected advice about outings with children generally, gathered over our numerous kid trips. Think of them as Grief Savers. Ignore them at your option — and peril.

Expect Less, Enjoy More

If there's anything about which we feel strongly, it's our refusal to romanticize outings with children. It's not all gumdrops and puppies out there. Kids can be grumpy. They can demand drinks of water and bathroom breaks at the most inconvenient times. Virtually from birth, the most precocious of them engage in what professionals call "limit-testing" — determining what excesses their parents will abide before punishment kicks in. When your son or daughter is belligerent, whiny or otherwise unimpressed with your loving and wise ways, you may wonder not only why you bought tickets to "The Nutcracker" or decided to check out the art museum, but why you wanted to be a parent in the first place.

We're here to tell you that such feelings are absolutely normal. Frustrating incidents happened to us, and to many other parents we observed, nearly every time we ventured out. Did we have some Kodak moments? Sure. Did we have some Maalox moments? You betcha. Did most of our moments fall somewhere along that all-too-familiar continuum? Of course. Yours will, too. In other words, when things go badly, first of all don't blame us. But don't blame yourself, either.

Don't Let Your Child Grow Up to Be . . . Anything, Yet

Babyhood takes forever, toddlerdom even longer. By the time your child is 3, you're likely to have a serious case of cabin fever. As soon as your son or daughter is toilet trained, you may be tempted to plunge into all sorts of extracurricular activities — especially those you've been deprived of yourself for over three years now. Our advice: Start slowly. You and your junior partner can take in the Dutch Masters at the National Gallery later. Better to begin with a sock puppet. You will have a much better time if you keep in mind the age appropriateness of the activity you hope to undertake (which we've tried to point out in our entries). This runs counter to a parent's natural inclination to believe that his or her 4-year-old is ready for whatever other peoples' 6-year-olds are doing, or that even though Melissa is only 7, she's so mature and "musical" that she'd love a three-hour evening at the symphony. Resist. You will have plenty of time later to explore ever more complicated and grown-up things. Ride the carousel before checking out the Bill of Rights.

High Culture, Low Doses

Hard and painful experience has taught us this: Expose tiny kids to museums and other repositories of high culture in tiny doses. An early trip to the Mall might consist of little more than a session watching the Foucault pendulum in the lobby of the National Museum of American History, followed by a walk across the way to the carousel. Next time out, swing through the Hirshhorn's outdoor sculpture garden and, maybe, take a lap around the second-floor galleries, followed by another visit to the carousel. Some rainy day, push the stroller through the National Museum of American Art, and then take lunch in a Chinatown restaurant. Walk through the East Building of the National Gallery, primarily to get a snack at the cafe and watch the waterfall. Ideally, these small doses of the sights and smells and sensations of art and culture will leave a child intrigued and wanting more. When you find your child asking to go to a museum — or choosing a visit from a list of diverse possibilities — that's the cue that you've succeeded and that the dosage can be increased. Subjecting young kids to a forced march through a crowded museum full of objects aimed way over their noggins is likely to breed precisely what you dread — a child who rejects museums before he or she knows anything about them.

Tours: Proceed With Caution

The guided tour is the bane of young kids everywhere. The George Washington Masonic National Memorial in Alexandria, Va., for example, is a neat-looking building. It'd be perfect for rambling through with your family at your own pace. Problem is, you can't. No offense to the Masons. It's their building, after all. But the only way to take it in is by tour. Surrounded by tall people listening to historical minutiae for 30 minutes or more, unable to break away or linger over something that interests them, children become like milk bottles microwaved with the cap on: primed to explode in an ugly mess. Our suggestion: Until your child is old enough to sit agreeably through a 30-minute presentation — we're guessing that's somewhere between 8 and 10 — avoid guided tours (except those aimed *specifically* at kids' groups).

Get There Early — or Beware

Re-reading our write-ups for this book, we were struck by how often we found ourselves warning parents to get to a place early and avoid crowds. But, darn it, it's true. For all the places we've visited, we can't think of a single one that was better taken in later in the afternoon — when it was inevitably more crowded — than first thing in the morning (okay, there is one: the FBI Building tour). Even the most consistently overpopulated spots (the National Air and Space Museum, the National Aquarium in Baltimore) are possible to enjoy if you're among the first wave of folks at the door. Besides, early in the day kids' minds (and often their parents') are sharper, their moods higher, their baggage lighter. And kids will enjoy just about anything, from a display of old-time dolls to a dinosaur bone, if they have it nearly to themselves.

In retrospect, our best outings have been those when we made it out of the house before 9, enjoyed a full morning of unbothered play, exploration or demonstration and were first in line for lunch at 11:30, before the restaurant/snack cart/cafeteria got packed. We feel sure that our maker intended afternoons for naps, errands and peaceful winding down — not for standing in lines and fighting off fatigue, crowds and foul moods. The choice, of course, is yours. But we are unambivalent fans of early entry/early exit. This book will help you if that's your chosen path. Note the opening and closing times we publish with each entry. And if you find yourself out the door mid-day, try to aim your brood at one of our Least Crowded places. Save more popular places for days when you can arrive early and bright.

Pack a Survival Kit

Having spent several years mastering the field-tripping process, we offer the Kid-O-Rama Survival Kit: a pad of blank paper, coloring books and colored pencils or markers (crayons melt in car seats); a few picture books; dolls or action figures; Ziploc baggies of pretzels, fruit roll-ups, mini-cookies or Pringles; box juices and/or bottled water; a few kid-wipes; a traveling pack of facial tissue. Have a bag full of this stuff packed and by the front door, or hanging in the hall closet, at all times. This makes the out-the-door process a lot easier. Later, when you're stuck in traffic, waiting for the Metro or on line to take your seat at the puppet show, it may save your child's life. Disburse its contents slowly. And if your child does go ballistic in public, the bag is handy for slipping over your head so you are not recognized.

It's the Journey, Not the Destination

We all have heard the story about the expensive present ignored in favor of the box it came in. The same principle applies to field trips. Despite a parent's best intentions, kids enjoy and remember what they *do*, not where they go or what they see. We can almost promise you that kids under 8 will enjoy the staircase at the Corcoran more than any of the masterworks on display there; you may think you're taking your 5-year-old to the Hirshhorn's sculpture garden, but your child sees it only as a chance to chase pigeons. The paddleboats in the Tidal Basin will make much more of an impression than the quotations by Thomas Jefferson inscribed on the nearby monument's walls. This is not failure. This is childhood. Let it happen.

Though we have made every effort to make this book darn near perfect, we can guarantee that it isn't. Attractions may close. Phone numbers may change. Hours may be altered. Try to call and confirm details before you set out on an expedition.

Also, use *Kid-O-Rama* in conjunction with *The Washington Post* WEEKEND section. Every Friday WEEKEND's Saturday's Child column explores a different family activity, and its Carousel listings outline special activities that week.

We wish you many wonderful and memorable adventures with the kids.

— John F. Kelly
and Craig Stoltz

ZOOS and AQUARIUMS

A DAY AT THE ZOO is the prototypical childhood experience. Adults find plenty to enjoy here, too, but it's the child — first in arms, then in a backpack, then in a stroller and finally under his or her own lumbering power — who truly comes alive at the zoo. Washington has one of the best zoos in the country, and your family should be frequent visitors. But there also are other less obvious choices to consider, from Baltimore's especially kid-friendly zoo to privately run animal operations that let you do something you can't at the National Zoo: touch the merchandise. And don't forget how aquariums also can light up children's eyes and minds.

The District

NATIONAL ZOO
3001 Connecticut Avenue NW

HOURS: May-Sept. daily 6-8, Oct.–Apr. 6-6. Closed Christmas. **COST:** Free, except parking. **PHONE:** 202/673-4800. **WEB:** www.si.edu. **METRO STOP:** Cleveland Park, Woodley Park/Zoo. &

This is a great zoo and one with which you're likely to become very familiar. Every child has his or her favorite animal, but some highlights are worth stressing. One is the orangutan exhibit, which permits the animals to swing on ropes and towers above the zoo's walkways, essentially outside of any enclosure. Another is the indoor Amazonia exhibit, which displays rainforest environments and creatures. Others include the cheetah conservation area and the new invertebrate house, which offers a number of hands-on displays and a wonderful, see-through ant colony (the volunteer docents here are especially accommodating to children who show an interest, possibly in an effort to redeem the boring reputation of most invertebrates). Try not to take in the whole zoo in a single visit; that's not good for anybody. On the way in, let each child pick two or three animals to visit, and get a map to plan an itinerary. Or agree to explore just an area or two on this visit. If you don't, you're setting yourself up for some tired and whining kids. You can rent wagons and strollers, and don't be reluctant to procure one for toddlers.

> **Words to the wise:** *With Metro, get off at the Cleveland Park station and walk south (downhill) to the zoo. When you leave, continue south (downhill) to the Woodley Park/Zoo station. If you're driving and plan*

to visit for the whole day, try to park in the lower lot (Lot D). It's an uphill walk to most of the animals, but that means it will be downhill when you're heading back to your car with weary youngsters in tow. Avoid Lot C if at all possible: You have to climb a narrow staircase to get to the animals. Lots A or B, near Connecticut Avenue, are good for quicker visits, providing easy access to the cheetahs, the panda, the elephants and rhinos, birds and hoofed stock. But if you're planning an all-day visit, the top lots require an uphill climb at the end of the day.

NOTES: The animal buildings and Amazonia are open 10 to 4:30 (till 6 in summer, with exceptions posted). Panda feedings are at 11 and 3, and seal and sea lion training and elephant care sessions are at 11:30 on most days. **Food:** Fast-food stands of the hot dog-hamburger-snowcone-and-soda variety are dotted throughout the zoo. Two sit-down restaurants, the Panda Cafe and the Mane Restaurant, have a wider menu. You needn't go hungry at the zoo, but it's safe to say that the really tasty food is reserved for the animals.

NATIONAL AQUARIUM
Commerce Department Building, 14th Street between Pennsylvania and Constitution avenues NW

HOURS: Daily 9-5; closed Christmas. **COST**: $2 adults, 75 cents ages 2-10, under 1 free. **PHONE**: 202/482-2825. **METRO STOPS**: Metro Center, Federal Triangle. ♿

You have to feel for the nation's oldest public aquarium. Overshadowed by its snazzy counterpart at Baltimore's Inner Harbor, the National Aquarium can be excused for suffering from an inferiority complex. But the two are very different. Washington's National Aquarium is cheaper and less crowded and much smaller in scale. Think tropical and freshwater fish, not dolphins. Think frogs, turtles and koi, not killer whales. Washington's aquarium is kind of like a big pet store, but you can lay your hands on critters in the "touch tank" and watch as handlers feed piranha (Tuesday, Thursday and Sunday at 2) and pint-size sharks (Monday, Wednesday and Friday at 2).

Words to the wise: *Don't oversell the visit to the young ones, and try to time the trip to coincide with one of the fish feeding frenzies.*

NOTES: While there is a Commerce Department elevator for the disabled, some aquarium exhibits are not fully accessible. Some small tanks also are too high for small kids to see, so you should expect repeated "Pick me up!" requests from little ones. **Food:** A gleaming new food court is across the street in the Reagan International Trade Center. Just two blocks away is The Shops at National Place, and across Constitution Avenue is the National Museum of American History, with one of the Mall's best and biggest cafeterias. **Nearby:** The White House, Old Post Office Pavilion, National Museum of American History.

O. ORKIN INSECT ZOO
National Museum of Natural History, 10th Street and Constitution Avenue NW

HOURS: Daily 10-5:30. **COST:** Free. **PHONE:** 202/357-2700 (TDD: 202/357-1729). **METRO STOP:** Smithsonian, Federal Triangle. **WEB:** www.si.edu. &

Whether your kids are the type who'd rather die than touch a grub, or the sort who will happily hold a maggot in their palms, they'll love this place, the most lively and interactive zone in this heavily visited Smithsonian museum. Highlights include a climb-inside replica of a termite mound; live, under-glass anthills and beehives; stick insects that are very hard to distinguish from real sticks, and a fat, hairy tarantula that gives everyone the creeps. But the true stars are the spiders, roaches and other crawlies, which museum staff remove from their enclosures and let your kids (or you, if you're feeling brave) "interact" with.

Words to the wise: *Weekend afternoons in this small space can get as busy as an anthill doused with Kool-Aid. If you must visit on a weekend, go directly to the Insect Zoo as soon as the museum opens.*

Nearby: National Aquarium, National Museum of American History, Old Post Office Pavilion.

Maryland

BALTIMORE ZOO
Druid Hill Park, Baltimore

HOURS: Weekdays 10-4:30, weekends in summer till 5:30. **COST:** $8.50 adults, $5 ages 2-15 and seniors, under 2 free; children free the first Sat of every month before noon. **PHONE:** 410/366-LION or 410/396-7102. &

Why should a self-respecting Washington-area family drive to Baltimore for to visit a zoo? Because Baltimore's zoo has two things you won't find in Washington: animals presented in anachronistic, prison-like cages that predate the enlightened, ecologically sensitive zoos of today; and one of the nation's best children's zoos. In the kids' area, visitors can carouse through a scaled-up set of mole tunnels, even poking their head above ground, in a plastic bubble, for a mole's-eye-view of the world. A path invites you to duck into caves, hop on lily pads and indulge in other species' behaviors.

Words to the wise: *The Baltimore Zoo offers a tram to take you to various parts of the premises. If you're with very little ones, use it.*

NOTES: Food service is enough to keep you going, but it's nothing compared to the dinner in Little Italy that you might want to add as a capstone to your day.

Directions: *Take I-95 north to Baltimore to I-395 to Martin Luther King Blvd. Go 2.5 miles to a left on Eutaw St., cross North Ave., and turn right on Druid Park Lake Dr. Go left at the stop sign near the white statue, and follow signs to the zoo.*

NATIONAL AQUARIUM, BALTIMORE
Pier 3, 501 E. Pratt Street

HOURS: Mar.-Oct.: Sat-Th 10-5, F 10-8; July-Aug.: daily 9-8. **COST:** $14 adults, $10.50 seniors, $7.50 kids 3-11, under 3 free. **PHONE:** 410/576-3800 (information); 202/432-7328 or 410/481-7328 (tickets). **WEB:** www.aqua.org.   &

You don't need to know much about Baltimore's National Aquarium other than that it's one of the region's world-class family attractions. You and your kids are likely to want to go there often. From the massive first-floor "Wings in the Water" exhibit (with the nation's largest gathering of sting- and other rays) to the five-level Atlantic coral reef finale (you descend walkways surrounded by a 335,000-gallon tank loaded with sea life, including dozens of sharks), this may be the most spectacular water-life exhibit you'll ever witness. However, you will pay for the privilege, both with cash and, depending on how you plan your attack, crowds and other creature discomforts.

Access is controlled by timed-entry tickets, so unless you plan to arrive by 8 a.m. (for a 9 a.m. opening), we suggest buying your tickets after 3 p.m. the day before through Ticketmaster (and paying the service charge). Otherwise, you'll run the risk of arriving at 10:30, standing in line for an hour, and then learning that the first available tickets are for 3 (or, worse, that you've been shut out completely).

Also, we recommend locals visit on weekdays or winter, spring and fall weekends, as summer crowds can be unpleasant. Finally, each aquarium entry ticket includes a pass for a specific dolphin show held in the Marine Mammal Pavilion; the shows are usually timed so that you have an hour or more to tour the aquarium first. While the shows are good, they lean more toward education and conservation issues than the kind of raw circus-animal thrillathon you might find at Sea World. Small kids may be bored.

Words to the wise: *It may be hard to get kids out of the first-class Aqua Shop with your credit card intact. Discuss spending limits in the car. Also, if you think you'll visit a few times a year, consider a $70 annual family membership. It lets you walk in a special entrance without buying a ticket or waiting in line.*

NOTES: Strollers are not permitted. Backpacks are available to borrow for free for kids under 25 pounds. **Food:** The Pavilion Cafe offers lunch and snacks, though it's predictably crowded at lunchtime. The Inner Harbor's many eateries are nearby, as are the wonderful restaurants of Little Italy. **Advance Tickets:** To order via Ticketmaster, call after 3 p.m. the day before your visit (202/432-7328; service charge). Your tickets will be at the advance purchase window. **Nearby:** Baltimore Maritime Museum, Inner Harbor.

Directions: *Take I-95 north to Baltimore's Inner Harbor exit and follow signs.*

CATOCTIN WILDLIFE PRESERVE AND ZOO
13019 Catoctin Furnace Road (Route 15), Thurmont

HOURS: Memorial-Labor Day daily 9-6, (last admission at 5); closed Dec., Jan., Feb. and in inclement weather. **COST**: $8 adults, $5.25 ages 2-12, $7 seniors. **PHONE**: 301/271-3180. **WEB**: www.fwp.net/CWPZoo. &

This is a kid-friendly stop during family day trips around Frederick, or a side trip for families spending time at Catoctin Mountain Park or Cunningham Falls State Park. The modest, privately operated zoo lacks big attractions and fancy displays, but kids who love animals will enjoy its simple, intimate environment and a chance to see the usual zoo crew in different settings. Highlights include a gigantic Andean condor and an indoor display of reptiles. Scattered around in simple cages and other modest enclosures are the usual array of lions, tigers and bears. A new petting zoo area lets kids get personal with goats, sheep, a llama and several kinds of birds.

> **Words to the wise:** *Admission fees make this a fairly expensive diversion, and the facility is dotted with quarter-munching machines that dispense food for ducks, fish and other small wildlife. Bring a bunch of quarters, since kids love feeding animals. Also, paths are packed earth, so people with strollers or wheelchairs will likely find the going tough after wet weather.*

NOTES: Nearby are Catoctin Mountain Park and Cunningham Falls State Park.

Directions: *From the Beltway, take I-270 north toward Frederick to Route 15 north toward Thurmont. The zoo is on the right (10 miles north of Frederick).*

SALISBURY ZOOLOGICAL PARK
755 South Park Drive, Salisbury

HOURS: Memorial-Labor Day: daily 8-7:30; otherwise 8-4:30. Closed for the Thanksgiving and Christmas holidays. **COST**: Free. **PHONE**: 410/548-3188. **WEB**: www.dmv.com/~zooed. &

This one is best for breaking up a long drive to or from the shore or for a quick escape from the beach when you've had your fill of sun and sand. It's just a nice little zoo, created in the 1950s when the town's department of public works found itself caring for an orphaned bear cub and deer. It's grown to 400 animals. By not wrestling with such "charismatic mega-fauna" as elephants, tigers or hippos, the zoo is free to direct its resources at smaller animals, including waterfowl, prairie dogs, spider monkeys, spectacled bears and bison. Best of all, a system of raised wooden walkways lets children get a better angle on the animals.

> **Words to the wise:** *Try to time your visit between 10 and 3 Tuesday through Sunday. That's when the hands-on area of the visitors center is open, allowing kids to see and handle various animal artifacts.*

11

NOTES: A concession stand sells hot dogs, chips, sodas and barbecue, or bring a lunch and sit at a picnic table. There are also plenty of fast-food spots in the vicinity. **Nearby:** Delmarva Shorebirds baseball team, Delmarva beaches.

Directions: *From Route 50 in Salisbury, head south on Civic Ave., turn right on Glen Ave., and then go left on Memorial Plaza to South Park Dr. and the zoo.*

Virginia

RESTON ANIMAL PARK
1228 Hunter Mill Road, Vienna

HOURS: Summer-fall weekdays 10-4, weekends 10-5, weather permitting.
COST: $9.95 adults, $8.95 for children 2-12 and seniors, under 2 free.
PHONE: 703/759-3637. ♿

This improbably located petting zoo — on suburban farmland, with subdivisions fast encroaching — provides one of the region's best opportunities for kids to interact with animals and observe them up close. A barn here is filled with sheep, goats, chickens, pigs, llamas and cows; most are happy to be petted. Tiny, tame goats wander free, encountering children face-to-face. Chickens and turkeys scratch around the open yards. There are pony rides, a couple of huge tortoises in a central enclosure, and a hayride "safari" to a big open area where you can see zebras and horses lazing on the suburban veldt. A small playground and a picnic area round out the offerings.

NOTES: On Mondays and Tuesdays, admissions is reduced to $7.95 a person.

Directions: *From the Beltway, take the Dulles Toll Rd./Route 267 (Exit 12B) to a right on Hunter Mill Rd. (Exit 14). The park is two miles down on the left.*

ON THE WILD SIDE ZOOLOGICAL PARK
Route 29, Madison

HOURS: Daily 10-6. **COST:** $6 adults, $4 for children 3-12, under 3 free.
PHONE: 540/948-4000. ♿

This is an old-style, privately run zoo that's worlds (and miles) away from the National Zoo. It has more than 200 animals, including antelope, pheasants, camels, snakes, alligators and a brown bear in the same cage as a dog. The zoo is skimpy on the sort of information you'd expect them to provide; many cages have just a number on them, forcing you to look in the brochure to determine exactly what's supposed to be inside. But it does allow visitors to get a little closer to the residents than at bigger, more natural zoos.

Words to the wise: *Call ahead if it looks like rain, since the zoo sometimes closes in bad weather.*

Directions: *Take I-66 west to Route 29 south. The zoo is a mile south of Madison.*

OLD MINE RANCH
17504 Mine Road, Dumfries

HOURS: Apr.-Nov. daily 10-5. **COST**: $4, under 2 free. **PHONE**: 703/441-1382.　♿

The Calpin family is in the pony-renting business. They'll happily unleash a herd in your back yard for a birthday party or other special occasion. Eight months of the year they also open their farm to visitors. Children can see the ponies and horses, feed goats, lambs, ducks, chicks, llamas and potbellied pigs, go through a hay tunnel or take a hay ride, and go on a guided walk down by the Quantico River. Pony or horse rides are $2, and there are places to picnic.

NOTES: For shoppers, Potomac Mills is nearby.

Directions: *From the Beltway, take I-95 south to Route 234 (Exit 152). After turning right on Route 234, go two blocks and turn left on Route 627 (Van Buren). Then make a right onto Mine Rd. The farm is on the left.*

2

VISUAL ARTS (and CRAFTS)

THE FRONT OF YOUR refrigerator should be proof enough that art is important to most kids. Art exhibits can be, too. We know what you may be thinking: The hear-a-pin-drop surroundings, the marble floors, the heapin' helpings of high culture — galleries and girls and boys don't mix. Well, you may be surprised. For the most part, while children care little about art history or art movements or even *artists*, they do like cool pictures. The key is not to overdo an art museum. See what the kids want to see, bail out when they get restless.

Many museums in this chapter have special programs designed with kids in mind. Most require reservations, so call for information. Many also publish free or low-cost family guides. These point you toward specific works, engage you in scavenger hunts and provide puzzles and trivia. While they're useful, we've found that the guides are not the magic bullet you might be seeking. By all means, pick one up (especially if it's free), but recognize that younger kids may not have the patience to work through the suggested activities.

Here's something we've tried with success: Have each child wear a backpack that holds (in addition to snacks) a pad of paper and sharpened color pencils. If they come across masterpieces they like, have them sketch their own versions. That will help them focus better on the art, and other patrons will regard you as the clever parents you no doubt are. And keep in mind other places where they can watch art being made or where they can make things themselves.

NATIONAL GALLERY OF ART
Constitution Avenue between Third and Seventh streets NW

HOURS: M-Sat 10-5, Sun 11-6. **COST:** Free. **PHONE:** 202/737-4215. **METRO STOPS:** Archives/Navy Memorial, Smithsonian. **WEB:** www.nga.gov. ♿

Washington's premier art collection certainly can entertain and inspire children. The secret is to steer clear of rooms of boring paintings of thin-faced saints or lace-collared noblewomen (unless your kids really *like* thin-faced saints and lace-collared noblewomen) and concentrate on kid-pleasing subjects.

To that end, start in the West Building. Yes, the East Building is architecturally more playful, and its generally more modern art is perhaps more childlike. But the West Building has a wonderful way to plan your entire visit: the Micro

Gallery, near the main floor's Mall entrance. It's filled with touch-screen computers you can use to slice and dice the gallery's holdings in all sorts of ways. The best for kid-trip purposes is to search by subject: mythology, literature, family, animals, even sports and games. Ask your kids what interests them, whether Greek heroes, brothers and sisters, historic figures or artists they may have learned about. The computer will pull up tiny images of the works. You can print out a map of the location of the paintings or sculptures and then head off on an art hunt. West Building works that kids might like include "Watson and the Shark," "House of Cards," the Rotunda fountain, the classical sculptures on either side of the Rotunda and the room of dreamy Monets.

When you're done in the West Building, go to the bottom floor and take the underground walkway to the East Building. (You'll pass a nice gift shop with a whole section filled with kids' stuff.) The moving sidewalk (like those at many airports) is a hit in itself, as is the waterfall that splashes against a glass wall. I.M. Pei's angular, airy East Building should appeal to youngsters. The colorful 20th Century art — splotched-canvas paintings, found-object sculptures — may remind them of their own creations. Art can be funny, they seem to say. Art can be beautiful, scary, thoughtful, provocative. Kind of like daughters and sons.

Words to the wise: *When your young art lover shows signs of fatigue, it's time to leave.*

NOTES: For **Food**, the West Building's Garden Cafe and the East Building's Terrace Cafe aren't as good choices for the family as the Cascade Cafe between the two buildings. It has a well-stocked buffet, with items ranging from hamburgers to barbecued chicken. Cheap it's not, but there's something for everyone. Try to get there before noon in order to avoid the crowds. **Disabled Access Points:** Wheelchair access is at Sixth and Constitution for the West Building and at the main entrance of the East Building. **Nearby:** The National Museum of Natural History, the National Air and Space Museum, the Navy Memorial and the U.S. Capitol.

CORCORAN GALLERY OF ART
500 17th Street NW

HOURS: M & W-Sun, 10-5; closed Tu, open till 9 Th. **COST:** Suggested donation: $5 family groups, $3 individual adults, $1 students and seniors, under 12 free, **PHONE:** 202/639-1700. **WEB:** www.corcoran.edu. **METRO STOPS:** Farragut West, Farragut North. ♿

While each Smithsonian museum or wing of the National Gallery seems to specialize in a different sort of art, the Corcoran has a little bit of everything and a lot of some things. There are no single standout collections so far as kids are concerned, though the Hemicycle Gallery is just a neat semicircular space, regardless of what's being shown. American masterpieces are displayed throughout, including Rembrandt Peale's huge "Washington Before Yorktown." Barye bronzes on the first floor include dogs attacking bears, lions attacking horses and minotaurs and centaurs battling Greek heroes. Other sculptures include Hiram Powers' once-scandalous "Greek Slave." Kids who are familiar with the story of Joan of Arc may want to see Boutet de Mouvel's series of paintings about the heroic French girl. They sparkle with gold leaf, as does the Salon Dore, a rather over-decorated room.

"Sunday Traditions" family art programs are held every other Sunday at 2:30 and include a "think" portion as well as a hands-on project. There also is a gospel brunch on Sundays, with local gospel groups providing stirring music to a hearty meal. You'll need reservations for Sunday Traditions but can't make them for the gospel brunch. Kids may be intrigued that the Corcoran also is an art school. Spiky-haired, paint-splattered students often are lounging around the school's New York Avenue entrance, and their work is periodically on display.

Words to the wise: *Be aware that the Corcoran is just out of the easily-walked-with-little-kids range of noted Metro stops.*

NOTES: **Birthday Parties:** One of Washington's little secrets is that the Corcoran has begun doing birthday bashes, with the celebrations including a tour and hands-on activities (call 202/639-1724 to make arrangements). **Food:** The Cafe des Artistes serves little-old-lady fare, and since it occupies a relatively small space in the wide-open atrium, a family with rambunctious children may find it hard to hide. **Nearby:** The Renwick Gallery, the White House, the Washington Monument and the Interior Department.

HIRSHHORN MUSEUM AND SCULPTURE GARDEN
Seventh Street and Independence Avenue SW

HOURS: Daily 10-5:30. COST: Free. PHONE: 202/357-2700 (TDD: 202/357-3235). METRO STOPS: Smithsonian, L'Enfant Plaza. WEB: www.si.edu. &

The Hirshhorn and the National Gallery's East Building are a lot alike. Both have (mostly) modern art, and both are architecturally interesting. The Hirshhorn probably is stronger on sculpture — from small bronzes in the circular hallways connecting various galleries to massive constructions arrayed around the building's stumpy legs. Ideally, you and your children should experience both, though there's no need to try to do it all in the same day. Perhaps it just depends upon which side of the Mall you happen to be near.

Art at the Hirshhorn that might interest children: Robert Gober's playful "Untitled," a wingtip-wearing wax leg sticking out from a wall; Alberto Giacometti's "Dog," one of his trademark droopy sculptures that just radiates caninity; a fish mobile by Alexander Calder; the puppets of Alexandra Exter; and (unfortunately) Nam June Paik's construction of 70 televisions arranged like a U.S. flag. (Such is the power of TV that kids often stop dead in their tracks when they get off the escalator in front of the piece, enraptured by its busy, endless loop of images.) The Hirshhorn Museum has one of the nicest family guides in town. It's a little folder with a dozen or so card inserts. Each card has a photo of a specific work, with details on the artist, how the art was created and fun ways to look at it. It's sort of like museum "Deal-A-Meal": You select a few cards at the start of your visit, then head off in search of the art. The incredibly high-shooting fountain in the Hirshhorn's central doughnut hole lures kids, and youngsters also enjoy romping through the sculpture garden across Jefferson Drive in front of the museum.

Words to the wise: *If you need an extra incentive to instill good behavior, promise the kids that you'll go afterward to the nearby Mall carousel. That often does the trick — and you should take them there anyway.*

NOTES: For **Food**, in summer there's an outdoor cafe, with a menu that includes decent child-size pizzas. Waits, though, can be frustratingly long. **Nearby:** The National Air and Space Museum, the Arts & Industries Building, the Smithsonian Castle, the Sackler Gallery of Art, the National Museum of African Art and the Freer Gallery of Art.

NATIONAL MUSEUM OF AFRICAN ART
950 Independence Avenue SW

HOURS: Daily 10-5:30. **COST**: Free. **PHONE**: 202/357-4600, 202/357-2700 (TDD: 202/357-4814). **METRO STOPS**: Smithsonian, L'Enfant Plaza. **WEB**: www.si.edu. &

With some prompting, children may recognize what's different about the art in this underground museum, besides its obviously unique African style: For the most part, it wasn't made merely to be looked at but to be *used*. Thus the creations have the wonderful patina that comes from being touched by countless hands, and they possess an extra power because of it, especially the ritual objects used in worship. There are many recognizable, utilitarian things here — walking sticks, chairs — but there are also interesting variations on a theme: carved wooden headrests, for example. The permanent galleries are mostly small, intimate and filled with glass cases. Children can press up close and see a fearsome crocodile headdress, enigmatic masks, colorful beaded crowns, carved staffs and lots of figures of women nursing babies. There usually are drop-in workshops appropriate for ages 4 to 8 (free, with no registration required, but an adult must stay).

Words to the wise: *The gift shop has a good book selection for various ages, tiny leather purses, inexpensive jewelry, videos and CDs. But it also has expensive sculptures and ceramics and African musical instruments that must be handled carefully, so keep an eye on what the kids are up to.*

NOTES: For **Food**, the closest spot is at the Air and Space Museum's cafeteria, which gets crowded at peak times. **Nearby**: The Sackler Gallery, Freer Gallery of Art, the Arts & Industries Building, the Smithsonian Castle, the Hirshhorn Museum, the National Air and Space Museum.

NATIONAL MUSEUM OF AMERICAN ART
Eighth and G streets NW

HOURS: Daily 10-5:30. **COST**: Free. **METRO STOP**: Gallery Place-Chinatown. **PHONE**: 202/357-2700 (TDD: 202/357-1729). **WEB** www.si.edu. ♿

This Smithsonian museum is big enough, and varied enough, that random rambling may result in rambunctious kids. Here are some suggestions: Youngsters seem to feel an affinity for folk art. The museum's collection on the first floor includes crudely but endearingly carved animals, a button-studded wall hanging and, perhaps the zenith of this style, James Hampton's "Throne of the Third Heaven," a manic, religiously inspired assemblage of cardboard, light bulbs and tin foil. Also on the first floor are George Catlin's Indian paintings. The next floor up holds numerous paintings, sculptures and stained-glass windows with pictures of angels. Two adjacent rooms on the second floor coincidentally hold some works depicting children (one sculpture, called "Reproof," is of a girl holding and scolding a kitten while a dead bird lies at her feet; a painting called "The Sick Child" exercises a strange power over young viewers, even if it was painted before amoxycillin). Youngsters also connect with the colorful, childlike paintings by William H. Johnson. On the airy third floor are 20th Century works. Some more demanding (and, perhaps to some parents, a few potentially inappropriate) paintings and sculptures are there, along with such kid-pleasing creations as a gigantic jack, shiny sci-fi-esque human torsos, the colorful vertical lines of Gene Davis and the big, splotched canvases of Helen Frankenthaler.

Words to the wise: *This museum is harder to negotiate than the National Gallery. Go with a specific plan in mind.*

NOTES: For **Food**, there's a small, competent cafeteria on the first floor, but it gets swamped at peak times. You are, however, only a block Chinatown's numerous restaurants. **Nearby:** The National Portrait Gallery (they share the same building; see next entry), Chinatown, the MCI Center, the FBI Building and the Hard Rock Cafe.

NATIONAL PORTRAIT GALLERY
Eighth and F streets NW

HOURS: Daily 10-5:30. **COST**: Free. **PHONE**: 202/357-2700 (TDD: 202/357-1729). **METRO STOP**: Gallery Place/Chinatown. **WEB**: www.si.edu. ♿

Babies, parents learn early, love looking at faces. This is a museum filled with them. Most of the faces are famous. Frankly, though, many children will not know that (a minor member of an acclaimed literary movement does not possess the cachet of, say, Michael Jordan). So it's a good idea to keep to portraits of people your kids might recognize. Pocahontas is here (though in the blouse and frilly collar of a 17th Century Englishwoman), and so are numerous sports figures (a good choice for would-be athletes). Every U.S. president is represented, with George Washington taking pride of place with eight portraits, including two by Gilbert Stuart. The building once housed the Patent Office, and in the gloriously decorated Great Hall on the third floor are some models that inventors once submitted along with their creations. Older kids interested in the Civil War should check out the portraits and other material relating to the War Between the States on the mezzanine level.

Words to the wise: *Try timing your visit to coincide with a historical figure your child is learning about in school.*

NOTES: *See notes above for* NATIONAL MUSEUM OF AMERICAN ART.

THE PHILLIPS COLLECTION
1600-1612 21st Street NW

HOURS: Tu-Sat 10-5, Sun noon-5, additional Th hours 5-8:30. COST: $6.50; $3.25 students and senior citizens; under 18 free (voluntary on weekdays). PHONE: 202/387-2151. METRO STOP: Dupont Circle (Q Street exit). WEB: www.phillipscollection.org. &

What children seem to like most about America's first museum of modern art is the fact that it started life as a house. Wealthy Duncan Phillips began collecting modern art (and art that influenced modern art) in 1918. In 1921 he opened two rooms to the public. Nine years later the family moved out completely and the home was turned into a museum. Additions have been built since. The Goh Annex, while pleasant, is your typical high-ceilinged, big-roomed space. The original house, however, is idiosyncratically homey. It's a kick to walk into gallery after gallery and keep seeing . . . *fireplaces*, each one different. Most rooms also have old-fashioned furniture that you can sit in. And instead of bored, uniformed guards, normal people — and art students — wearing regular clothes mind the art.

So what about the art? The most famous work is Renoir's large and festive "Luncheon of the Boating Party." But children also may like Paul Klee's "The Way to the Citadel," Degas' "Dancers at the Bar," William Merritt Chase's playful "Hide and Seek," and a cut-up, tin-can bird sculpture by Alexander Calder dangling from the ceiling. A small gift shop in the basement offers a modest but nicely chosen selection of children's art books and craft projects.

Words to the wise: *Call for a Family Fun Pack, materials with projects kids can do before, during and after a Phillips visit. The kits, which change with exhibits, include games, worksheets, self-guided tour booklets and reproductions of some art on display. You usually can get one at the door, but a family is likely to enjoy a show more if it goes through a kit ahead of time.*

NOTES: There is some street parking. **Food:** A small basement cafe has soups, salads and sandwiches as well as a special kids meal: hot dog, chips and apple juice for just $3.75. You can find more restaurants on Connecticut Avenue. **Nearby:** The Textile Museum.

NATIONAL MUSEUM OF WOMEN IN THE ARTS
1250 New York Avenue NW

HOURS: M-Sat 10-5, Sun 12-5. **COST**: Suggested donation $3 adults, $2 children. **PHONE:** 202/783-5000. **METRO STOPS:** Metro Center, McPherson Square (14th Street exit). **WEB:** www.nmwa.org.   &

Young ladies (or gentlemen, for that matter) who haven't yet figured out that things have been different for girls might wonder at this museum's organizing principle. In our case, a 4-year-old daughter kept asking why there was a museum *just for women artists*. She'll understand soon enough. Until then, a visit here is a good inoculation against the under-representation of female artists that children may encounter at other museums. The collection ranges from European Renaissance oil paintings to Colonial American silver to modern abstracts, proof that women long have been impressive artists, even in the face of societal resistance. There's a comfortable feel to this place — starting with an inviting lobby and curving marble stairways where kids love to scamper. Stop at the Education Resource Center, just inside the front door, for clear, basic displays on different art forms and how they're created. Family programs, one Sunday a month from 2 to 4, combine a tour of the art and hands-on projects. The museum's "Role Model" program links older girls (12 and up) with professional women artists of all stripes (call 202/783-7370 for information and reservations).

Words to the wise: *Bring $1 bills. With admission by donation, kids seem to love dropping bills into the big Plexiglas cube at the entrance.*

NOTES: For **Food**, a museum restaurant serves soup, sandwiches and salads. Across the street is a McDonald's, though, as at any downtown fast-food place, you may encounter a homeless person muttering to himself. **Nearby:** MCI Center.

SACKLER GALLERY AND FREER GALLERY OF ART
SACKLER: 1050 Independence Avenue. FREER: 12th and Jefferson Drive

SW HOURS: Daily 10-5:30. **COST:** Free. **PHONE:** 202/357-2700 (TDD: 202/357-1729). **METRO STOPS:** Smithsonian, L'Enfant Plaza. **WEB:** www.si.edu.   &

Kids may not instantly connect with the Asian art that is the focus of these two museums. Calligraphy scrolls, subtly hued porcelains, intricate jewelry — they can seem a bit rarified. But the Sackler and Freer host one of the most imaginative and valuable learning programs on the Mall: ImaginAsia. More on that in a moment, but first the museums: The Freer displays the idiosyncrasies of its benefactor, with Asian art (Buddha sculptures, fierce wooden carvings and bronzes, brushwork scrolls) coexisting with Asian-influenced Western paintings and other works. Kids should stick their heads into Whistler's breathtaking "Peacock Room." The famed artist created it in a London dining room, with a lavish peacock motif. Children seem to be overwhelmed by the impracticality of it all.

You can reach the underground Sackler Gallery from the Freer. It, too, displays Asian art, with a broader selection. It's also where you'll find ImaginAsia. Children ages 6 to 12, accompanied by an adult, can participate. A typical program might send kids off with a clipboard, pencil and well-written activity guide into the Sackler or Freer to find and learn from specific works. The worksheets are clear and manageable, encouraging children to look at and learn from the art. When that's done, they return to the classroom to create their own masterpieces: scrolls, tissue-paper wall hangings, origami birds. The teachers are attentive and interested in their young charges' progress. ImaginAsia is held Saturdays from 10 to 12:30 from March through October, except in July and August, when it is on Mondays and Wednesdays. Reservations are necessary, and it does fill up (call 202/357-4880, ext. 422).

Nearby: The National Museum of African Art, the Arts and Industries Building, the Smithsonian Castle, the Hirshhorn Museum and Sculpture Garden and the National Air and Space Museum.

RENWICK GALLERY
17th Street and Pennsylvania Avenue NW

HOURS: Daily 10-5:30. **COST:** Free. **PHONE:** 202/357-2700 (TDD: 202/357-1729). **METRO STOPS:** McPherson Square, Farragut West. **WEB:** www.si.edu. &

This Smithsonian museum, an outpost of the National Museum of American Art, focuses principally on crafts: blown glass, fiber creations, art furniture, jewelry and the like. In some respects, this is not an easy place for children to deal with. Crafts tend to be utilitarian objects that become art by virtue of the extra skill and imagination that have gone into creating them. But it's hard to explain to smaller children why they're not allowed to touch the rug or the chair or the desk or some other object. There is some whimsy here, most notably "Game Fish," a mounted swordfish adorned with dice, yo-yos and action figures; "A Little Torcher," a stained-glass creation depicting pyromania (okay, maybe not so whimsical, but kids' eyes open wide when they see it); and the trompe l'oeil tour de force "Ghost Clock," a seemingly shroud-covered grandfather clock carved entirely out of wood.

Words to the wise: *If the crafts don't do it for your children, climb the imposing stairway to the Grand Salon. Once the most famous art-filled room in Washington, it is still hung with 18th and 19th Century paintings, one atop the other, as was the style in those days. It's plush, rose-colored, circular banquettes are perfect for sitting on while contemplating the art.*

NOTES: There is no food at the gallery itself, but if you walk up 17th Street you will find a number of eating choices. **Nearby:** The White House, Lafayette Square, the Corcoran Gallery of Art and the Interior Department Museum.

SPECIALIZED COLLECTIONS

These museums have a narrower focus than those listed above. They aren't necessarily ideal destinations for kids, unless you have a child who shows a special interest in the subject covered.

ART MUSEUM OF THE AMERICAS
201 18th Street NW

HOURS: Tu-Sat 10-5. **COST:** Free. **PHONE:** 202/458-6320 or 202/458-3000. **METRO STOP:** Farragut West.

Housed in a formerly grand residence, this gallery behind the Organization of American States exhibits modern art from the countries of Latin America.

B'NAI B'RITH KLUTZNIK MUSEUM
1640 Rhode Island Avenue NW

HOURS: Sun-F 10-5; closed Sat. **COST:** Suggested donation $2, $1 children. **PHONE:** 202/857-6583. **METRO STOP:** Farragut North. ♿

There's nothing especially kid-friendly about this modest collection on the first floor of B'nai B'rith's national headquarters. But if you dig in you'll find some memorable items to enlighten kids, especially for Jewish families seeking to deepen their understanding of Jewish and Israeli culture. It has some excellent holiday and ceremonial pieces — Hanukah menorahs, ram's horn shofars, elaborately printed torahs from the 19th Century. There is a remarkably detailed silver dreidel, a menorah made of bullet casings and a tiny sculpture garden out back. Most items are paintings and photos, some by noted American Jewish artists, some by Israelis. If your child is not old enough for the U.S. Holocaust Memorial Museum (see p. 126), the Klutznik Museum offers some dark and instructive, but not terrifying, imagery to direct discussion about Jewish history. The gift shop offers many hand-made and artist-made items.

NOTES: While disability access is generally good, ask for an accessible restroom.

MEXICAN CULTURAL INSTITUTE
2829 16th Street NW
HOURS: T-F 9-6, Sat 11-5. **COST:** Free. **PHONE:** 202/728-1628.

You may never get inside the Mexican Embassy, but you can get inside a building that used to be the Mexican Embassy. The mansion boasts a mural that sweeps up along the grand staircase and contains the sort of vibrant, colorful art children seem to like.

THE TEXTILE MUSEUM
2320 S Street NW
HOURS: M-Sat 10-5, Sun 1-5. **COST:** $5 (suggested donation). **PHONE:** 202/667-0441. **METRO STOP:** Dupont Circle. **WEB:** www.textilemuseum.org. ♿

Youngsters may get a kick out of seeing carpets on the wall rather than on the floor, and they may enjoy the vibrant colors and patterns of the fabrics on display. Exhibits draw from a collection of more than 15,500 items, from scraps of ancient cloth to 20th Century Latin American textiles. The exhibits change often and may not always appeal to children. (Kids seem to especially like Oriental rugs and colorful molas.) The second-floor Learning Center does a good job of introducing the concepts of design and construction to young visitors. To explore the notion of pattern, for example, they can rearrange colorful magnets and use stamp pads to ink different designs. There's a loom for trying, magnifying glasses for inspecting fibers and a collection of plants that lend their dyes to rugs and garments.

NOTES: No strollers are permitted. There's no food service either, though you can picnic in the garden out back. While we have noted wheelchair access, you should call ahead.

Baltimore

BALTIMORE MUSEUM OF ART
Art Museum Drive and N. Charles Street at 31st Street
HOURS: W-F 11-5, weekends 11-6; closed M, Tu. **COST:** $6, $4 seniors and full-time students, under 19 free. Free admission on Th. **PHONE:** 410/396-7100. **WEB:** www.artbma.org. ♿

Depending on where you live, a trip to Baltimore might be just as convenient as one to the Mall. And while it's easy to dismiss the BMA as just a smaller version of the National Gallery of Art, it has some features that make it a good family choice. For starters, it's not as crowded as the National Gallery. Except at peak times or with the most popular shows, you can stroll from gallery to gallery in relative peace. The collection is fairly broad, so you can touch a lot of art history bases: Old Masters, French impressionism, modern art. A few things are particular hits with kids: The African, Native American, Oceanic and Pre-Columbian exhibit has a fearsome assortment of masks and other ritual objects displayed and lighted in a way that makes viewing by children easy. The Cheney Miniature Rooms are tiny tableaux showcasing the best in the dollhouse-maker's art, with stools that short patrons can climb to peer inside. One little room is decorated like a Colonial-era drawing room, complete with infinitesimal deck of cards on a table and a thimble-size porcelain planter with daffodils. Andy Warhol's "Silver Clouds" is a metal pipe and fishing wire "room" holding pillow-shaped, helium-filled Mylar balloons. You're allowed to play (gently) with the installation. The collection of the remarkable Cone sisters — works by Matisse, Picasso, Monet and other giants of the Paris art scene — may inspire siblings to devote themselves to a lifetime of collecting. Or maybe not. Compared with the Hirshhorn's sculpture garden, which is more sculpture than garden, the BMA's is more garden: sloping paths through greenery, peppered with sculpture. Youngsters love running there. Finally, the BMA has some of the best hands-on kids' art activities, as part of the free Freestyles events (the first Thursday evening of the month) and on some Sundays; call for details.

Words to the wise: *Bring quarters for the parking meters.*

NOTES: There's a nice restaurant, Donna's, in the museum.

Directions: *From the Beltway take, I-95 north to I-395 (Exit 53) to Martin Luther King Jr. Blvd. Stay on that for about a mile and turn left on N. Howard St. Go two miles and bear right on Art Museum Dr. The museum is on the left.*

WALTERS ART GALLERY
600 N. Charles Street

HOURS: Tu-F 10-4, weekends 11-5 (until 8 the first Th of the month). **COST:** $6, $4 seniors, $3 students 18 and up, $2 6-17. **PHONE:** 410/547-9000. **WEB:** www.TheWalters.org. &

There's a little of everything at this museum, the legacy of a father and son who collected whatever struck their fancy. That turned out to cover items from all over the world, including Old Masters paintings, porcelain, tapestries, coins and more. What might kids enjoy most? For starters, taking the spiraling stone staircase down to a dungeon-like room displaying armor (as in "knight in shining . . ."). Children get a special kick out of the protective gear that horses wore. You'll also find broadswords, daggers, maces and other ancient artifacts of war. Older children can try their hands at a scavenger hunt in this section. Kids can let off steam in the airy Renaissance Sculpture Court. The museum's 1974 building is closed for renovation through 2001; while the full Greek, Roman and Egyptian exhibits thus aren't available, highlights (including one of the museum's mummies) are in other galleries.

Words to the wise: *The collections are housed in different buildings, linked on some, but not all, levels. Navigation can be difficult.*

NOTES: For **Food**, the Cafe Troia serves light lunch fare.

Directions: *Take I-95 to I-395 (Exit 53) to Martin Luther King Jr. Blvd. Turn right onto Druid Hill Ave., which becomes Centre St. The Walters is on the left. Parking can be difficult despite street meters and garages in the neighborhood.*

AMERICAN VISIONARY ART MUSEUM
800 Key Highway

HOURS: Tu-Sun 10-6 **COST:** $6, $4 students (all ages), seniors; under 4 free. **PHONE:** 410/244-1900. **WEB:** www.avam.org. &

This museum displays "outsider" art: art created outside normal art-school traditions, indeed traditions of any kind save the fevered imaginings of its creators. You might call it folk art, though visionary art is edgier, in many cases more appealing and in some cases scarier. From Vollis Simpson's utterly amazing 55-foot whirligig that tops the museum to a stegosaurus made entirely from junk (clocks, license plates, doll heads, binoculars), there's much here that will captivate children. Ours burst out laughing at a group of pigs fashioned from milk cans, hub caps and scrap metal and were delighted by the endless, meandering line of watch faces that decorates a wall. But because visionary art is created by artists who often have a less-than-secure grasp on reality, it can be a window into an unsettled mind.

A temporary exhibit on the Apocalypse had a few paintings that could frighten a youngster (rivers of blood, sinners consumed by flame — that sort of thing). The museum is good at warning you which galleries have graphic works, and that means you can't just blithely stroll through the place. Right behind the museum is Federal Hill Park. It's a steep climb, but it has a wonderful view of the harbor and a nice little playground.

Words to the wise: *Parents should screen the art the way they would screen TV programs. But to avoid this museum just to avoid such decisions would be to miss a cool place.*

NOTES: Food: There's a nice sit-down restaurant, Joy America Cafe, on the top level of the museum. **Parking:** There's metered parking in front of and behind the museum. **Nearby:** Maryland Science Center, Inner Harbor, National Aquarium, Baltimore Museum of Industry, Fort McHenry.

DIRECTIONS: *Take I-95 north to Key Hwy. (Exit 55). At the bottom of the ramp, turn left. The museum is 1.5 miles down on the left.*

WATCHING ART BEING MADE

TORPEDO FACTORY ART CENTER
105 N. Union Street, Alexandria, Va.

HOURS: Daily, 10-5. Closed major holidays. **COST:** Free admission.
PHONE: 703/838-4565. &

Almost 200 artists share 84 studios in this converted munitions factory along Alexandria's waterfront. The problem is, on weekends the place functions more like a commercial gallery than a cluster of working studios: more selling, less making. Still, on weekdays it's a great place to take preschoolers, or others who happen to have a day off from school. Then, through the studios' glass walls, you'll be able to watch potters throwing, photographers printing, painters daubing and weavers warping. Some love to talk as they work. If you do go on a weekend, plan to arrive at 10 a.m. or expect to suffer crowds and less quality interaction with the artists.

Many shops have small, inexpensive handmade items for sale — pins, pencils, sketch pads and jewelry — making the Torpedo Factory an excellent alternative to a mall when kids are looking for gifts for friends, teachers or others. The wharf out back is excellent for strolling. There's a food court right on campus, and the neighborhood is filled with restaurants, shops, galleries and other attractions. You can picnic on either side of the building. Don't miss Studio 327: The Alexandria Archeology Center has a lab where archaeologists investigating the city's history work and explain their projects.

Words to the wise: *Go early. Parking's a bear; expect to park at a pay lot. Orient yourself at the first-floor information kiosk.*

Nearby: George Washington Masonic National Memorial, the Lyceum, Gadsby's Tavern, Boyhood Home of Robert E. Lee, Fort Ward Musuem.

Directions: *From the Beltway, take Route 1 North to a right on King St. and a left on Union St.*

GLEN ECHO PARK
7300 MacArthur Boulevard (at Goldsboro Road), Glen Echo, Md.

HOURS: Daily dawn-dusk (see below for tour information). **COST:** Free, though there are fees for the carousels and various theaters. **PHONE:** 301/492-6282. **WEB:** www.nps.gov/glec. &

Once an outpost of the 19th Century Chautauqua movement (self-improvement through education), then an amusement park (self-improvement through bumper cars), Glen Echo's somewhat ramshackle buildings now house Adventure Theatre and Puppet Co. Playhouse (see Performing Arts), the Discovery Creek Children's Museum (see Nature and the Outdoors) and a carousel. It also has artists in studios creating such things as pottery, paintings, jewelry, and fused and stained glass. Some are in Mongolian-style yurts that look like something out of a fairy tale — picture sod-covered muffins. The problem is that artists are, well, artistic, and can't always be counted on to be creating when you stroll in. Your best chance of catching one at work is to visit on a weekend. Better still, call ahead: 301/492-6229. You can make a reservation to see a particular artist. Best bet of all: Take one of the 50-minute tours of Glen Echo at 2 on Sundays. You'll usually see five or six studios.

Words to the wise: *The carousel runs only from May through September, 12 to 6 on weekends, 10 to 2 on Wednesdays and Thursdays.*

NOTES: Wheelchair access is limited by the steps to many of the galleries. **Nearby:** Adventure Theatre, Puppet Co. Playhouse, Discovery Creek Children's Museum, Clara Barton House, C&O Canal.

Directions: *From the Beltway, take Clara Barton Parkway to MacArthur Boulevard and follow signs.*

MAKING YOUR OWN ART

HERE ARE a few places where children can exercise their own imaginations. They'll make crafts or works of art a cut above the construction-paper-and-crayon masterpieces that are right now cluttering your home.

KIDSHOP
6925 Willow Street NW, Washington

HOURS: Available only by advance registration (weekdays and weekends). Summer mini-camps available. Call for times. **RESERVATIONS:** Required. **COST:** $17-$28 and up, depending on project (prepayment required). **PHONE:** 202/726-0028. **METRO STOP:** Takoma.

This small shop in Old Town Takoma Park is the perfect place to introduce kids 4 and up to woodworking, without the trepidation and hassle of trying to go it alone. The shop's owner has selected tools that are easier for kids to handle — 7-ounce hammers, a kind of saw that cuts on the pull stroke only, special clamps and custom-made holders to assist with project-specific tasks. Children also work at kid-size workbenches with good lighting, a significant improvement over squatting in a dim garage or basement floor.

Choose a specific project your child is interested in: airplanes, Beanie Baby beds, birdhouses, step-stools, treasure chests, book shelves, collector's boxes, mazes and more. Older kids are permitted more freedom — some have been known to build stilts — and younger ones are supervised more closely. Kidshop makes for a great rainy-day activity; our 6-year-old came away deeply proud of the simple wooden airplane that he had cut, glued, sanded, nailed and pegged together — and, more important, pleased with his newfound familiarity with tools and wood. If your child comes away enthused, classes are available. Kidshop is also a wholesome and unusual birthday party alternative, one that permits guests to bring home a self-made party-favor (mini-tool goodie bags are available).

Words to the wise: *It's smart to call ahead to avoid birthday parties or classes, either of which can fill the shop.*

NATIONAL CATHEDRAL MEDIEVAL WORKSHOP
Massachusetts and Wisconsin avenues NW, Washington

HOURS: Sat 10-2; also extended weekday hours in July and August. **COST**: $3.
PHONE: 202/537-2934. **WEB**: www.cathedral.org/cathedral.

A visit to the cathedral's Medieval Workshop is basically an exploration of the arts and skills required to build something like the cathedral itself, from the stone archways to the decorative tapestries. Visitors can shape a gargoyle or grotesque out of modeling clay that will air dry to a little gray keepsake. They can build (or try to build) an arch out of wooden blocks. They can do brass rubbings, take a stab at needlepoint and create a bookmark by tracing the letters and figures of an illuminated manuscript. Some of these projects can be beyond the littlest "Hunchback" fans (the cathedral recommends that visitors be 5 and older), but the volunteers have such an endearing combination of patience and enthusiasm that you may be surprised by what your child creates — and learns.

Words to the wise: *The workshop is held in a cozy crypt. Like all crypts, it gets very uncomfortable when filled with bodies. Do your best to visit early.*

NOTES: There's no wheelchair access to the crypt, where the workshop is held.

PAINT-YOUR-OWN-POTTERY PLACES

THERE'S BEEN A BOOM recently in places that will let you buy a bisqueware bowl or plate and slop on the glaze. Come back a week later after it's fired, and you've got a real piece of pottery. The cost can be high: anywhere from $3 to $45 for the pottery item, $6 to $8 an hour to decorate it.

Unless you've got a young Da Vinci, encourage your child to start with a bold, simple pattern that uses few colors and doesn't take too long to complete. Weekends can be busy, so call for reservations. Birthday party packages are available at all locations.

MADE BY YOU

District of Columbia
- ❑ 3413 Connecticut Ave. NW. **Hours:** Sun-Tu 10-6, W-Sat 10-9. **Phone:** 202/363-9590.
- ❑ 1826 Wisconsin Ave. NW. **Hours:** Sun-Tu 11-6, W-Sat 10-9. **Phone:** 202/337-3180.

Maryland
- ❑ 4923 Elm St., Bethesda. **Hours:** Sat-Tu 10-6; W-F 10-9. **Phone:** 301/654-3206.
- ❑ Harbor Center, 2542 Solomons Island Rd., Annapolis. **Hours:** Sat-Tu 10-6, W-F 10-9. **Phone:** 410/571-0171.

Virginia

❏ 2319 Wilson Blvd., Arlington. **Hours:** Sun-Tu 11-6, W-F 10-9, Sat 10-6. **Phone:** 703/841-3533.

THE MUD FACTORY. Downstairs in The Village at Shirlington, 2772 S. Arlington Mill Dr., Arlington. **Hours:** Tu-Th 11-8, F-Sat 11-10, Sun 12-6, closed M. **Phone:** 703/998-6880.

PAINT YOUR OWN POTTERY. 10417 Main St., Fairfax. **Hours:** M-F 10-6, Sat 10-5, Sun 12-5; evening appointments for groups. **Phone:** 703/218-2881. Kids paint for half-price weekdays. Limited wheelchair access.

3

PLANES and TRAINS and BOATS...

KIDS ARE FASCINATED with the big metal machines that take us places. They spend so much of their time playing with mini-versions of cars and boats and trains and planes that the chance to experience the real thing is an almost guaranteed good time. You don't have to travel far to give your kids a chance to wrap their minds around — and get their hands on — a variety of vehicles in the region. Some even offer rides.

FLYING MACHINES

District of Columbia

NATIONAL AIR AND SPACE MUSEUM
7th Street and Independence Avenue SW

HOURS: Daily 10-5:30 (extended summer hours). Closed Christmas. **COST:** Free. Imax movies and planetarium shows: Adults (21-55) $3.50, older and younger $2.25, under 2 free. **PHONE:** 202/357-2700 (TDD: 202/357-1729). **METRO STOPS:** Smithsonian, L'Enfant Plaza. **WEB:** www.si.edu.　♿

With displays ranging from the Wright Brothers early craft to today's space suits, this museum easily can consume not just a day but a half a dozen visits. It has more than 26 exhibits. Many aircraft hang from the ceiling, and if your kids aren't easily embarrassed, encourage them to lie on their backs and soak up the view. The Imax Theater's screen is so enormous that kids under 3 may be overwhelmed by the sounds and images. Kids 8 and up may want to catch the sky show at the Einstein Planetarium. But if you have time for only one show, make it an Imax film. The guided tours, at 10:15 and 1, can be hard to follow, so only those serious about understanding aviation history and technology should bother. One of Washington's most memorable souvenirs is the sort-of-genuine NASA freeze-dried ice cream available at the gift shop. The shop's loaded with stuff to induce cravings, so make sure you discuss spending limits on your way in. The museum has good stroller access and changing facilities for babies.

Words to the wise: *Most years,this is the world's most visited museum; if you can help it, you want to avoid the place when it's busy (summer, fall and spring weekends). With pre-schoolers, go when school's in session: You'll encounter field-trip groups but few others. Otherwise, go*

Sunday and arrive by 9:30 for the 10 a.m. opening (another good option is evenings during extended summer hours). When you arrive in the morning, take a left (from Mall entrance) and line up at the Langley Theater for Imax tickets. Folks who wait often find early shows sold out.

NOTES: For **Food**, the glass-and-tubular-metal Flight Line Cafeteria, with inspiring Mall views, is open 10-5 daily (5:30 in summer). Avoid peak lunch hour, especially if you're visiting with kids who can't hold their own trays. If you want to make things easy, make reservations at the sit-down Wright Place restaurant above the cafeteria (202/371-8777; open 11:30-3). **Nearby:** U.S. Capitol, National Gallery of Art, other Smithsonian museums.

Maryland

COLLEGE PARK AVIATION MUSEUM
1985 Corporal Frank Scott Drive, College Park

HOURS: Daily 10-5. **COST:** adults $4, under 18, $2. **PHONE:** 301/864-6029 (TTD: 301/864-5844). **METRO STOP:** College Park. &

This 27,000-square-foot museum, opened in 1998, is at the world's oldest continuously operating airport. More importantly, it offers a wonderful way to introduce kids to aviation away from the crush of the Air and Space Museum. The exhibits are aimed mainly at kids. Highlights include an "animatronic" Wilbur Wright, who (when prompted by a ceiling sensor) explains what life was like at the tiny field in 1909, when he and brother Orville trained Army men to pilot the service's first two aircraft. The airport was the site of a number of aviation firsts, all chronicled here. The first airplane bomb drop was tested here in 1911. The first mile-high flight was achieved in 1912. The first U.S. Air Mail was dispatched in 1918. Other exhibits: a "wall of propellers," several vintage craft (including a 1918 Jenny and a rare 1924 Berliner helicopter), computerized flight simulators and a hands-on control panel from an old air mail plane. One station lets you listen in to real-time air traffic control dispatches from five local airports. You'll also enjoy watching private craft take off and land at the runway, just beyond the museum's huge picture window. And outdoors, the under-6 set can pedal small biplanes around a modest oval track.

Words to the wise: *No food or beverages are available or permitted in the museum, so you may want to eat lunch or an early dinner at the 94th Aerosquadron Restaurant (301/699-9400), along the runway. It's decked out in World War I era-decor: sandbags at the door, vintage uniforms, photos on the walls. The food's pricey and mediocre, but get a window seat, order burgers, and the kids will have a blast watching the takeoffs and landings.*

NOTES: Nearby: Calvert Road Park, which has a disc golf course, Herbert G. Wells Ice Skating Rink and Swimming Pool, Goddard Space Flight Center.

Directions: *From the Beltway, take Exit 23 (Kenilworth Ave.) south. Go right on Paint Branch Pkwy., right at Corporal Frank Scott Dr., and follow the signs to the parking area.*

BALTIMORE-WASHINGTON INTERNATIONAL AIRPORT OBSERVATION GALLERY

Baltimore-Washington International Airport, Linthicum

HOURS: Daily 9-9. **COST:** Free (but see parking below). **PHONE:** 410/859-7111, 800/435-9294 (TDD: 410/859-7227). **WEB:** www.bwiairport.com. &

Of the area's three major airports, BWI is by far the best for kids just to bask in contemporary aviation. The airport's gallery has multiple attractions. A first-floor area features plane- and truck-shaped play sculpture for toddlers. On the second floor you'll find a mini-museum with video, pictures and interactive exhibits, huge chunks of a Boeing 737 displayed for maximum impact (a cross-section of the first-class seating compartment, a 45-foot chunk of wing, an instrument-packed nose cone), a super flight gift shop run by the Smithsonian, and spectacular views of three runways and several acres of tarmac. Both levels have comfortable, well-placed seats. Although designed for families killing time at BWI, the mini-museum and observation facility are so well done and child-friendly that they are worth a special trip with kids of just about any age.

Words to the wise: *Parking, at $4 an hour, is the major cost here. But hourly satellite parking is only $1 (maximum $7 a day), and the kids may enjoy the shuttle ride to the main terminal. Once you arrive, go to the upper level and aim between Piers B and C.*

NOTES: For **Food**, BWI has a variety of concessions, ranging from soft pretzels, frozen yogurt and hot dogs to fast-food franchises and sit-down restaurants.

Directions: *From I-95, take I-195 and follow the signs.*

GODDARD SPACE FLIGHT CENTER

Soil Conservation Road, Greenbelt

HOURS: Daily 9-4. **COST:** Free. **PHONE:** 301/286-8981 (TDD: 301/286-8103). **WEB:** www.gsfc.nasa.gov. &

The Hubble Space Telescope is the most famous project at this NASA facility, whose mission is to monitor any space endeavor that doesn't involve humans or other planets. The small visitors center contains models of satellites, a space capsule kids can sit in, computer terminals where they can design their own rockets (and see whether they work or blow up on the launch pad), and information on the center's namesake, Robert Goddard, the father of American rocketry. Spread out below the visitors area are the places where the scientists toil; you can tour some of them Monday through Saturday at 11:30 and 2:30 and the first and third Sundays of each month at 11. Also on the first and third Sundays, at 1, a model rocket club performs launches.

Words to the wise: *Resist the temptation to take anyone below 4th grade on the tours, which will be over their heads.*

NOTES: Sign-language interpreters can be provided with one week's notice. Also, tours take visitors down a long sidewalk, so call ahead for any special needs. A gift shop sells NASA memorabilia. No food service is available.

Directions: *From the Beltway, take Exit 23 (Kenilworth Ave.) to Route 193 East. Pass Goddard's main entrance to Soil Conservation Rd. Turn left and follow signs.*

Virginia

GRAVELLY POINT PARK
Off the George Washington Memorial Parkway, Arlington

HOURS: Dawn-dusk. **COST:** Free. ♿

While it affords a lovely view of the Washington skyline, the main attraction of this little park, built on landfill just north of National Airport, is the airport's runway, just 400 feet away. Depending on wind direction, planes either take off or land here, sweeping by at 150 mph and as low as 100 feet overhead. Takeoffs are louder, while landings create a false sense of drama — the plane is coming in too low! — that won't be lost on kids. It's a fun diversion, but parents may not want to stay too long. During airplane rush hours (corresponding roughly with the automotive equivalent, plus Sunday afternoons), as many as 30 planes an hour land or take off — one every two minutes. At slower times, the action is every eight or nine minutes. There's a big lawn where you can play catch or just run around. When the Potomac is quiet, the planes' vibrations create an almost surreal crackling across the river's surface. Weather permitting, you can walk down the Mt. Vernon hiking/biking trail toward the gorgeous new National Airport terminal, which lacks a good observation facility but otherwise is a wonderful, art- and light-filled place to visit and grab something to eat. Or you can head north up the trail, where you'll find LBJ Memorial Grove, Lady Bird Johnson Park and a memorial to those who have died at sea. You also can bring bikes, park your car in the Gravelly Point lot and bike in either direction.

Words to the wise: *Don't let kids play on the rocky shore of Roaches Run, as rats like it there, too. You need to be heading north on the GW Parkway (i.e., into D.C. from Virginia) to reach it; no southbound access.*

THE FLYING CIRCUS AERODROME
Off Route 17, Bealeton

HOURS: May-Oct.: Sun 11-dusk; show: 2:30. **COST:** Adults $10, kids 3-12, $3. Rides before and after the show extra. **PHONE:** 540/439-8661. ♿

A visit to the aerodrome, with its World War I-style air show, is a nice way to highlight a Sunday family outing in the country. The vintage aircraft performing here include biplanes and open-cockpit fighters. The pilots do all kinds of stunts,

34

including dogfighting, barnstorming and even wing-walking. Before and after the show, the brave and flush can take open-cockpit rides over the countryside ($30 for regular rides, $60 for longer, more acrobatic ones).

Words to the wise: *Since admission's not cheap — it'll set a family of four back $24 — you may want to pack your own lunch. This is a great place to picnic.*

Directions: *From the Beltway, take Route 66 west to Route 28, the Dulles/Centreville exit. Follow Route 28 through Manassas to Route 17 at Bealeton.*

RAILROADS BIG and SMALL

LET'S FACE IT: Our rail passenger industry is in tough shape, with declining ridership, more than occasional derailments and competition from bargain airlines. Yet for kids it's hard to match the choo-choo for basic coolness. Maybe there'll be a massive renovation of Amtrak's crumbling infrastructure starting in 2020, when today's 6-year-olds, weaned on "Thomas the Tank Engine," begin rising to leadership roles in U.S. government and industry. Until then, youngsters can play on the railroad in various ways. They can visit such RR museums as Baltimore's B&O Railroad Museum and a smaller one in Ellicott City. They can take a ride on miniature trains at a half-dozen area parks. They can wander the soaring spaces of Union Station. Even sitting in the front car of a Metro train is a bit of a thrill for them.

District of Columbia

UNION STATION
50 Massachusetts Avenue NE

HOURS: Station open 24 hours; shops, food places daily 10-9, Sun 12-6 . **COST:** Free admission to buildings. **PHONE:** 202/371-9441. **METRO STOP:** Union Station. &

Beautifully renovated to its 1908 Beaux-Arts splendor, Union Station is a great place for kids fascinated by trains or simply by big, old beautiful places. You can tour the platforms where Amtrak's passenger trains depart, watch the action in the enormous train yard from the parking garage or walkway behind the station, or simply absorb the cosmopolitan rush of people departing, arriving or just waiting for trains. Train buffs will appreciate the Great Train Store in the shopping mall area. The Main Hall is a gorgeous public entrance, the East Hall has a collection of small vendors, and the shopping mall pulls up the rear. On the basement level is a multi-screen movie theater.

NOTES: Strollers are available from the information booth in the Main Hall, as are wheelchairs. **Food:** The basement level holds a shopping mall-style, multi-vendor eatery. On the main floor are several quick-service restaurants and carryouts plus sit-down establishments. **Parking:** The huge garage, accessible via North Capitol Street, is rarely full. **Nearby:** Capital Children's Museum, National Postal Museum, U.S. Capitol.

Maryland

B&O RAILROAD MUSEUM
901 W. Pratt Street, Baltimore

HOURS: Daily 10-5 except Christmas, Thanksgiving and Easter. **COST:** $6.50 adults, $5.50 seniors, $4 kids 3-12, under 2 free. **PHONE:** 410/752-2490. **WEB:** www.borail.org.

If your kids are excited by trains — or simply by big metal hulks and places that smell of oil and metallic parts — you have to go to the B&O, the biggest collection of railroad artifacts and hardware in the Western Hemisphere. The main attraction is the huge round-house, built in 1884 and now the showcase for 22 of the collection's most impressive locomotives and train cars. Kids can climb into some of the cabs and get an engineer's-eye view (but only on the cars so marked). Upstairs is a spectacular, 12-by-40-foot scale model railroad, built in 1956 and maintained by several of the museum's many old-timer volunteers, who love to pass along railroad lore to today's kids. There's also a historical exhibit section, one of the finest railroad-themed gift shops around and, outside, on the 37-acre site, plenty of other engines, cars and equipment to explore.

> **Words to the wise:** *Four rides on historic trains are offered only on weekends and holidays, so arrive early at those times to buy the first-come, first-served tickets ($2; kids 2 and under free).*

NOTES: The downstairs is wheelchair-accessible, but not the upstairs for the model railroad layout. Insides of cars are not accessible. **Food:** One of the old dining cars holds vending machines for soda and snacks. In summer, a cafe serves hot dogs, hamburgers and sodas. Picnic tables provided. **Nearby:** Little Italy, Inner Harbor attractions and restaurants.

Directions: *Take I-95 North to I-395 North (Exit 53) to Martin Luther King Jr. Blvd. and Lombard. Hang a left on Poppleton St. and a left again into the parking lot. Free on-site parking is plentiful.*

ELLICOTT CITY B&O RAILROAD STATION MUSEUM
Main Street and Maryland Avenue, Ellicott City

HOURS: F-M 11-5. **COST:** $3, under 12 and seniors $1, under 5 free. **PHONE:** 410/461-1945. **WEB:** www-rcf.usc.edu/~gkoma/bando.html. &

Housed in the nation's oldest railroad station, this facility is packed with maps, historic photos and artifacts documenting the history of the B&O. The working model railroad may be the highlight. Visitors can view parts of the 50-foot turn-table and walk through a 1927 caboose. A visit to this museum makes a good side trip when you want to go antiquing or browsing in Ellicott City and need a target for the kids.

> **Words to the wise:** *At last report, museum renovations were under way, so check whether prices or hours have changed.*

Nearby: Ellicott City's 50-some shops and restaurants.

MINIATURE TRAIN RIDES

ON A MINIATURE trade ride, where's the best place to sit? At the very back, you see the whole thing snaking out in front of you, its engine taking curves long before you get there. At the very front, you can watch how the iron horse (iron pony?) is tamed by the engineer (though "engineer" might be too grandiose a word for the gangly teenager who's usually at the helm). Lots of families debate this as children board. But whichever seat your child prefers, the following parks run tiny trains during warmer months. Rides last from 10 to 15 minutes, and the fare is about a dollar. Lines can be long on summer weekends.

Maryland

CABIN JOHN REGIONAL PARK. 7401 Tuckerman Lane, Rockville. **Hours:** Late Apr.-May: weekends 10-4:30, weekdays 10-3; June-Sept.: weekdays 10-4:30, weekends 10-5; Oct.: weekends 10-4. **Phone:** 301/469-7835, 301/299-0024. ♿

WATKINS REGIONAL PARK. 301 Watkins Park Dr., Upper Marlboro. **Hours:** Memorial Day-Labor Day: Tu-Sun 10-7; Labor Day-late Sept.: weekends 10-7. **Phone:** 301/249-9220. ♿

WHEATON REGIONAL PARK. 2000 Shorefield Rd., Wheaton. **Hours:** late Apr.-late June: weekdays 10-3, weekends 10-5; late May-early Sept.: weekdays 10-5, weekends 10-6; Sept.: weekends 10-5; closed on rainy days. **Phone:** 301/946-7033. ♿

Virginia

BURKE LAKE PARK. 7315 Ox Rd., Fairfax. **Hours:** May-Labor Day: daily 11-6; Sept.: weekends 11-6. closed Oct.-Apr. **Phone:** 703/323-6601. ♿

LAKE FAIRFAX PARK. 1400 Lake Fairfax Dr., Reston. **Hours:** late May-mid June: weekdays 1-8, weekends 10-8; late June-Labor Day: daily 10-8. **Phone:** 703/471-5415.

WALKERSVILLE SOUTHERN RAILROAD
34 West Pennsylvania Avenue, Walkersville

HOURS: May-Oct.: Weekends 11, 1 and 3 (also two weekends in December). **COST:** $7 adults, $3.50 kids 3-11. Santa Claus Special: Adults $7, children $5. Mystery Trains: $35 a person, including meal. **PHONE:** 301/898-0899. ♿

Weekends from May through October, two vintage railroad cars and a caboose are hooked up to an engine for a leisurely, hour-long chug through the Central Maryland countryside. The train moves at a slow, kid-friendly, 10 miles an hour, going past a restored lime kiln, over the Monocacy River via an old railroad bridge and through farmland.

There are also various theme outings during the season, including "Civil War Days," when Rebel re-enactors stage a raid on the train and hold it for ransom (don't worry, the ransom is always paid); the "Zoo Choo," where folks from the nearby

Catoctin Wildlife Preserve board to show off snakes, birds and reptiles; and "Circus Day," with clowns, juggling and face-painting. St. Nick boards the train two weekends each December for the "Santa Claus Special." Grown-ups may enjoy the "Mystery Train" excursions, on which actors play characters in a tale of crime and passengers participate in figuring out whodunnit.

Words to the wise: *You can't make reservations, and though they claim that they "hardly ever" sell out, be aware that the train can fill up on high-demand days, such as Mother's Day and Father's Day. If you get there early and find the first excursion sold out, you can purchase a ticket for a later departure.*

NOTES: The Catoctin Wildlife Preserve and Zoo is nearby in Thurmont.

Directions: *From the Beltway, take I-270 west to I-70 to Route 15 north. Turn right on Biggs Ford Rd. and proceed two miles to station.*

NATIONAL CAPITAL TROLLEY MUSEUM
1313 Bonifant Road, Wheaton

HOURS: Weekends 12-5, additional December and summer hours. **COST:** Free admission. Trolley rides: $2.50 adults, $2 kids 2-17. **PHONE:** 301/384-6088.

This modest museum and collection of vintage trolleys tells the story of the Washington area's trolley service, the public transportation system that preceded today's Metro. Visitors can climb into a well-preserved trolley car and take a short ride on a track that winds through the woods. Most children think that the highlight is a scale model of an operating trolley line.

Words to the wise: *The museum is tucked in a semi-isolated rural area, so few amenities (food, gas stations) are nearby.*

NOTES: There's no wheelchair access to the trolleys.

Directions: *From the Beltway, take New Hampshire Ave./Route 650 north to a left on Bonifant Rd. The museum is on the right.*

CHESAPEAKE BEACH RAILWAY MUSEUM
On Route 261, Chesapeake Beach, Md.

HOURS: May-Sept.: daily 1-4; Apr. and Oct.: weekends 1-4; other times by appointment. **COST:** Free. **PHONE:** 410/257-3892 (TDD: 410/535-6355 or 301/855-1862). &

Conceived in the late 19th Century as a resort to lure visitors from Washington and Baltimore to its carousel, band shell, dance pavilion and roller coaster, this Southern Maryland town was served by a railway line called the Honeysuckle Route. The Depression and the rise of the automobile killed the route, but the train station survives and is the setting for this museum exploring the resort's heyday, the rail line that served it and early 20th Century transportation. It mostly houses photographs of trains and the town, but there's a model train, a diorama of the resort and a surviving kangaroo from the carousel. The museum is a good stop on the way to or from Calvert Cliffs.

Words to the wise: *If you don't think this modest museum will hold kids' attention very long, try visiting on a Thursday morning from mid-June to mid-August, when children's programs are offered.*

NOTES: There's ample food in town.

MODEL TRAINS

YOU CAN'T RIDE on model trains, but you can see entire towns re-created down to the smallest detail. The best places to see model train sets are the B&O Railroad Museum and the Ellicott City B&O Railroad Station Museum (see p. 36), but other hobbyists open their doors from time to time. Call to confirm details; admission is free unless otherwise noted.

Maryland
NATIONAL RAILWAY HISTORICAL SOCIETY, POTOMAC CHAPTER. B&O Freight House, Old Town Gaithersburg at the corner of Diamond and Summit avenues. **Hours:** Most of the year: Th-Sat 10-2, June-Labor Day: 10-4, Sun 12-4. **Phone:** 301/258-6160. ♿

BALTIMORE SOCIETY OF MODEL ENGINEERS. 225 W. Saratoga St., Baltimore. Incredibly detailed scale layouts, along with assorted railroad memorabilia, can be found here. **Hours:** Sun in Jan. or Dec. **Phone:** 410/837-2763. **Web:** www.bcpl.lib.md.us/~jberg/bsme/.

Virginia
FAIRFAX STATION RAILROAD MUSEUM. 11200 Fairfax Station Rd., Fairfax. **Hours:** Members of Northern Virginia NTRAK set up their scale-model trains the third Sunday of every month, 1-4. **Cost** (suggested donation): $2 adults, $1 children. **Phone:** 703/425-9225. **Notes:** Trains are at adult waist level, so you may have to lift smaller children so they can see. ♿

VIENNA RAILROAD STATION. 231 Dominion Rd. NE, Vienna. **Hours:** From 1-5 on the second Saturday (usually) of every month except June and Aug., the Northern Virginia Model Railroaders host an open house in this 1880s train station, a remnant of the W&OD line. **Notes:** You need to go four steps up to the "visitors aisle." **Phone:** 703/938-5157.

RACING CARS and SUCH

MODELS ARE FINE, but the real thing is better — or certainly louder. You can see auto racing at the tracks below. Drag races are truly fast (they're over in about 8 seconds), but you can spend the time between races wandering the pits, where owners tinker. Most drag strips even allow you to race the family car. (That'll impress the kids at the bus stop.) Speedways or oval tracks are the closest thing we have to NASCAR racing: big American metal going around and around in circles. The only area European-style road-racing course in the region is Summit Point in West Virginia.

Admission to area tracks ranges from $7 to $15, depending on the level of racing. Children under 12 pay less and are often free. At some tracks a "pit pass" is extra.

Words to the wise: *Tracks are closed in winter months. In bad weather, call to see if races have been canceled. At a racetrack it can be — well, it is — loud. If engine whine and tire squeal bother you, bring earplugs.*

Maryland

MARYLAND INTERNATIONAL RACEWAY. Route 234, Budds Creek, St. Marys County. **Hours:** Drag racing generally Friday, Saturday and Sunday. **Phone:** 301/449-7223. ♿

CAPITOL RACEWAY. Route 3 South, Crofton. **Hours:** Drag racing every Saturday. **Phone:** 410/721-9664.

CECIL COUNTY DRAGWAY. 1575 Theodore Rd., Rising Sun. **Hours:** Drag racing every Sunday. **Phone:** 410/287-6280.

75/80 DRAGWAY. Intersection of Routes 75 and 80, Monrovia. **Hours:** Drag racing every Friday and Saturday and most Sundays. **Phone:** 301/865-5102. ♿

MASON-DIXON DRAGWAY. Route 40, Hagerstown. **Hours:** Drag racing every Sunday. **Phone:** 301/791-5193.

HAGERSTOWN SPEEDWAY. Route 40, Hagerstown. **Hours:** Oval track racing Sundays, depending on season. **Phone:** 301/582-0640. ♿

Virginia

OLD DOMINION SPEEDWAY. Route 234, Manassas. **Hours:** Drag racing every Friday. Oval racing on Saturdays. **Phone:** 703/361-7223. **Web:** www.olddominionspeedway.com. ♿

COLONIAL BEACH DRAGWAY. Route 205, Colonial Beach. **Hours:** Drag racing every Sunday and some holidays. **Phone:** 804/224-7455. ♿

SUMMERDUCK DRAGWAY. Route 17, Culpeper. **Hours:** Drag racing on Saturdays and Sundays. **Phone:** 540/439-8080.

SLOT CARS

THE TRACK
16806 Oakmont Avenue, Gaithersburg, Md.

HOURS: Typically weekdays 1-9, Sat 10-9, Sun noon-5. **COST:** Rental slot cars are $4.50 for 15 minutes. **PHONE:** 301/417-9630.

Remember slot cars, those teeny autos and sections of track you'd set up in the living room until the thing got clogged with carpet fuzz and stopped working? Vast improvements are on display at this hobbyists' mecca, a good place for youngsters about 7 to 13. The cars are larger than the home version (1/24th scale instead of 1/64th), and they run on a twisting, eight-lane, 156-foot-long track. Each "driver" has a little box to regulate the car's speed. Go too fast around a curve and it'll clatter off the track. Kids as young as 5 can handle the controllers, but they may not have the finesse to slow down for the hairpins or the height to reposition their errant vehicle. However, they may enjoy watching the hardcore racers. There's also remote-controlled racing at The Track on a 500-square-foot carpeted area. If you get bitten by the bug, car and controller prices start at $60.

Directions: *From the Beltway, take I-270 north to Exit 8E. Make a right on Shady Grove Rd. north to a left on Oakmont Ave.*

West Virginia
SUMMIT POINT
Route 13, Summit Point

HOURS: Races usually are held on weekends (but you should call for details). **COST:** $20-$25; under 12 free with paying adult. **PHONE:** 304/725-8444. **WEB:** www.summitpoint-raceway.com. ♿

Summit Point isn't a drag strip or an oval but a road course, meaning that its two miles twist and turn. It's more European and, to many, more interesting. "The Point," as its fans call it, features sports car racing, motorcycle racing, kart racing and vintage car racing. Public events are held from March through December. Since some events are spread out over a weekend, many hardcore fans camp at Summit Point (there's no charge to do so once you've bought your admission ticket). There's nothing quite like being awakened by the roar of engines and the squeal of tires as cars start their early morning practice laps. Bleachers are scattered throughout the track, and many visitors wander (or drive) from place to place, getting different vantage points on the action. As at a drag strip, a walk through the pits is fun.

Words to the wise: *It can get hot in summer. There's some shade, but bring a hat and sun block, and drink plenty of liquids.*

Directions: *From Maryland: Take I-270 north to Route 340 through Charles Town, W.Va., toward Route 51 west. Bear left at the three-way stop sign onto Summit Point Rd./Route 13, and drive eight miles to the entrance on left. From Northern Virginia: Take Route 7 west through Leesburg to a right onto Route 632 past Berryville. Follow Route 632 to a right onto Route 761. Turn right at the next intersection, and drive to the entrance on the right.*

BOATS

WATER, WATER . . . WELL, not quite everywhere, but in enough places so that getting your feet wet (figuratively, we hope) is a relatively easy prospect. Some boats noted here do nothing more than float, pretty much stuck in one place while you scramble over them. Others do move. Take your pick.

District of Columbia

U.S.S. BARRY
Washington Navy Yard, 9th and M streets SE

HOURS: Daily 10-5 in summer, 10-4 in winter (last tour begins a half hour before closing). **COST:** Free. **PHONE:** 202/433-3372.

This decommissioned Navy destroyer, which served between 1956 and 1982, is permanently docked at the Washington Navy Yard and represents the best opportunity between Baltimore and Norfolk to explore the inside of a big ship. Sailors lead a fascinating tour, good for kids 5 and up, that lets them see how the crew worked, slept, ate and carried out its missions. The ship's narrow passageways, steep ladders and low overheads will challenge the less-than-nimble, but kids love navigating their way through it all.

We think the Barry is the best kid magnet here, but there are several other attractions. The Navy Museum is an artifact-packed place to explore U.S. naval history (ask about the scavenger hunt booklet for kids if you want to spend serious time here). The Marine Corps Museum traces the history of this Navy unit from 1775 to today. There's also a Combat Art gallery and a rarely visited submarine museum tucked in the rear of Building 70. If you have time for only one attraction aside from the Barry, make it the Navy Museum. Out on the lawn, you'll also find a bunch of historic weaponry on display.

Words to the wise: *The Navy Yard is in a dicey neighborhood, so you'll probably want to stay within the Yard itself. Don't try the Barry until your kids are out of strollers, which are not permitted on board.*

NOTES: The Naval Yard has a McDonald's, a cafeteria and an officer's club restaurant.

Maryland

BALTIMORE MARITIME MUSEUM
Pier 3, Pratt Street

HOURS: Generally daily 10:30-6; winter F-Sun only. Closed major holidays.
COST: $5.50 adults, $3 kids 5-12, seniors $4.50, under 5 and active military free.
PHONE: 410/396-3453. **WEB:** www.livingclassrooms.org.

This "museum" is really a collection of three ships plus a lighthouse, all docked in Baltimore's Inner Harbor. Families can tour all four facilities for the price of one ticket, and each has something to recommend it. The Coast Guard cutter Roger B. Taney is the only ship still afloat that survived the attack on Pearl Harbor. The U.S.S. Torsk, a state-of-the-art submarine circa 1944, has the distinction of being the last ship to bring down an enemy craft in a hostile confrontation in World War II. While the Lightship Chesapeake lacks similar bragging rights, it's a gorgeous, 1930-vintage communications vessel with a polished wooden deck and brass wheel. Each ship and the lighthouse, which was moved to the Inner Harbor after years of service in the Chesapeake Bay, offers opportunities for kids to climb, explore, touch and learn. Kids love seeing the bunks stacked to within 24 inches of the ceiling in the Torsk and wiggling through its narrow passages to the torpedo room. They love the Lightship's awesome black anchor, the size of a Volvo. They love the mess halls and map rooms. You'll have to be vigilant, though, as there are plenty of places for kids (and grown-ups who forget to duck through low doorways) to get bumped and "stranded" in tight spaces.

> **Words to the wise:** *This is not for babies in backpacks or kids under 5, or anyone who is not spry and energetic. Also, go to Pier 3 to get tickets first; many people approach individual ships for a tour, only to learn they must go to the ticket booth.*

NOTES: Since access for the disabled is poor, those with wheelchairs or canes will have to pass on this one. **Food:** The Inner Harbor is packed with places to eat. **Parking:** Inner Harbor lots are $3 for the first hour, $7 for three hours and $10 for the day. You can try on-street parking in Little Italy, just east of the harbor, but finding a spot can be tough. You also can save a few bucks by parking in a lot a few blocks away. **Nearby:** Fort McHenry, Maryland Science Center and Baltimore Harbor Ferry as well as Little Italy.

CALVERT MARINE MUSEUM
14200 Solomons Island Road, Solomons

HOURS: Daily 10-4:30. **COST:** $5 adults, $2 kids 5-12, seniors $4, under 5 free (lighthouse tour free with museum admission). **PHONE:** 410/326-2042. **WEB:** www.co.cal.md.us .   ♿

At the tip of Calvert County, a good two hours' drive from many Washington-area locations, this fine museum is worth the haul and makes a terrific day trip that's full of activities and chances to learn. In the museum you'll find art and artifacts related to Chesapeake Bay maritime history and ecology (including prime examples of the miocene shark teeth and other fossils from nearby Calvert Cliffs). Outside is a basin where various boats are displayed, a restored boat-building shed, a live otter habitat, a recreated salt marsh and the Drum Point Lighthouse. Built in 1883, decommissioned in 1962 and moved from nearby Drum Point on the Patuxent River in 1975, this is one of three remaining examples of the screwpile lighthouses that used to guide sailors in the bay. Tours, which cover the lighting mechanism and the housekeeper's quarters, are given several times a day. Wednesday through Sunday, you also can board the Wm. B. Tennison, dating from 1899, for a cruise around the Solomons area (adults $5, kids $3, under 5 free; May-October at 2 only; additional 12:30 cruise on July-August weekends). Nearby is the J.C. Lore Oyster House, which preserves parts of the mid-century oyster trade (open daily 10-5 June-August; holidays and weekends May and September, 1:30-4:30; closed October-April).

NOTES: Disability access good, except to lighthouse.

Directions: *From the Beltway, take the exit for Route 4 south, toward Prince Frederick. Continue on Route 4/2 to Solomons; bear right just before the Thomas Johnson Bridge.*

WHITE'S FERRY
24801 White's Ferry Road, Dickerson

HOURS: Daily 5 am-11 pm. **COST:** $3 per car one way; $5 round trip. Picnic table use is $1.50, as is use of the ferry's boat launch for your private craft. **PHONE:** 301/349-5200.

Kids love the ferry's five-minute chug across the Potomac, during which the preposterously overnamed General Jubal A. Early ferry boat is tethered to a fat metal cable reaching from the Maryland to Virginia side of the river. While the trip lacks drama, kids appreciate the funky anachronism of the operation. It's a great way to get from upcounty Maryland to upcounty Virginia, and vice-versa, without getting drawn into Beltway hassles. Still, the ferry is best seen not as a destination in itself but as a memorable way to spice up a trip elsewhere — for Virginians visiting Maryland's Sugarloaf Mountain or Frederick, for instance, or Marylanders headed to Leesburg or Morven Park. If you like, however, you can treat the ferry as a day-trip itself. You can pick up the C & O Canal towpath from the Maryland side parking lot and hike or bike upstream or downstream. The small store on the Maryland side rents bikes and sells lunch and snacks. If you're interested in fishing, the store also rents boats and tackle; the area is said to be good for fishing, thanks to warm water just upstream coming from Dickerson.

Words to the wise: *The ferry is used daily by Virginia and Maryland commuters, so avoid weekday rush hours*

NOTES: The accompanying store/rental facility is open from mid-April through October, from 6 am to 7 pm (8 pm weekends). Disabled riders probably won't be able to get out of the car and move around the deck, as most passengers prefer to do. **Nearby:** Morven Park, Sugarloaf Mountain, Ball's Bluff Battlefield Park.

Directions: *From the Maryland side take the Beltway to 270 North, and exit at Route 28 West. Turn left on Route 107, White's Ferry Rd. On the Virginia side, the entrance is about two miles from Leesburg, off Route 15.*

FIGHTING FIRE WITH...

FIRE MUSEUM OF MARYLAND
1301 York Road, Lutherville

HOURS: May: Sat 11-4, Sun 1-5; June-Aug.: W-Sat 11-4, Sun 1-5; Sept.-Oct.: Sat 11-4, Sun 1-5. **COST:** $5, seniors $4, 4-15, $3, under 4 and firefighters free. **PHONE:** 410/321-7500. ♿

The amazing collection at this museum includes firefighting equipment that dates back to 1822, ranging from firefighters' axes and helmets to more than 40 gleaming fire trucks. Displays relate the history of putting out fires, from the bucket brigade to the hook and ladder. You can count on kids wanting to climb all over the shiny red machines, but there's only one they're allowed to scramble aboard, a 1957 Seagrave pumping engine. There also is a dress-up area where kids can try on real (and really heavy) firefighters' gear.

BOAT RIDES

THE FOLLOWING vessels range from a sedate mule-drawn barge to a neck-snapping speedboat. Call first, even if reservations aren't necessary, since bad weather may scuttle your plans.

District of Columbia

C&O CANAL NATIONAL HISTORICAL PARK. 1057 Thomas Jefferson St. NW. **Hours:** The Georgetown, a replica of a mule-drawn, 80-person canal boat, follows this schedule: Apr. to mid-June, W-F 11 & 2:30; mid-June-Nov. 1, W-F 11, 1 & 2:30; Sat & Sun Apr.-Nov. 1, 11,1, 2:30, 4. **Cost:** $4, children and seniors $3.50. **Phone:** 202/653-5190. Kids can bring fruits or carrots to feed the mules. In summer, free concerts take place on the canal, between Thomas Jefferson and 30th Street, at 4 every other Sunday. ♿

CAPITOL RIVER CRUISES. Washington Harbor, 3050 K St. NW, at the end of 31st Street. **Hours:** The Nightingale II, a 65-foot riverboat, departs on daily 50-minute Potomac cruises on the hour, M-Th noon-8, Sat noon-9 and Sun 11-8. **Cost:** $10 adults, $5 kids 3-12, under 3 free. **Phone:** 301/460-7447. The boat, with a 91-person capacity, has a snack bar, restrooms and tables suitable for picnics. The narrated tour highlights monuments and other sights along the cruise, which travels about three miles to National Airport.

DC DUCKS. Departs from Union Station, 50 Massachusetts Ave. NE. Guided 90-minute tours aboard these ungainly, World War II-era amphibious vehicles take visitors around city streets before splashing into the Potomac at Columbia Island Marina. The 28-person boat/truck travels by water to Gravelly Point near National Airport before returning to Union Station. The trip's expensive, but kids love it. Call at least a week in advance for times and reservations. **Cost:** $24 adults, $12 kids 4-12, under 4 free. **Phone:** 202/832-9800.

SHORE SHOT. Washington Harbor, 31st and K streets NW, Georgetown. This 53-foot speedboat breezes along at 40 mph on its 45-minute Potomac trips from Georgetown to Bolling Air Force Base. **Hours:** Narrated tours depart summer weekends at 7:30-9:30 pm; Sat 12:30-10:30 pm; Sun and holidays 12:30-8:30 pm. **Cost:** $10 adults, $8 seniors, $5 kids 4-12, under 4 free. **Phone:** 202/554-6500. A snack bar and restrooms are available on the boat, which seats up to 100 people.

SPIRIT CRUISES. Pier 4, Sixth and Water streets SW. **Hours:** The double-deck Potomac Spirit, which holds 350 passengers, embarks on a 90-minute Potomac excursion to Mount Vernon at 9 am Tu-Sun, Mar.-Oct. Passengers spend 2½ hours at Mount Vernon, returning to D.C. at 2:30. **Cost:** (including Mount Vernon admission) $25.50 adults, $24 seniors, $17 kids 6-11, under 5 free. **Phone:** 202/554-8000. The line also offers lunch and dinner cruises on the triple-deck, 600-person Spirit of Washington. ♿

Maryland

BLACK HILL REGIONAL PARK. 20930 Lake Ridge Dr., Boyds. **Hours:** Pontoon-boat rides on Little Seneca Lake given on the hour, noon-6, F-Sun, Memorial Day-Labor Day. **Cost:** Admission $2. **Phone:** 301/972-3476. A tour guide describes the lake's history and wild inhabitants, such as beavers, muskrats, otters and various birds. The pontoon boat also is used for special family programs such as "Storytime on the Lake" for kids 3 to 5 and their parents and "Family Beaver Patrol" for ages 6 and up. Call for details. ♿

GREAT FALLS TAVERN. C&O Canal National Historical Park, 11710 MacArthur Blvd., Potomac. **Hours:** The schedule for Canal Clipper departures: Apr.-mid-June, weekends at 11, 1, 2:30; mid-June-early Sept., W-F 11,1 and 2:30; mid-Sept.-Nov. 1,

W-F 2:30. Call to check for changes in schedule. **Cost:** $7.50 adults, $6 seniors, $4 kids 3-14. **Phone:** 301/299-2026. The 80-person boat, guided by mules Ida and Ellie or Rhody and Lil (with the latest addition, Ada, pitching in as well) takes passengers on a narrated, hour-long ride accented by lots of trees and occasional wildlife.Special reserved trips also are available for school groups and others. To make group arrangements, call 202/299-3613.

ROCK CREEK REGIONAL PARK. Lake Needwood, 15700 Needwood Lake Circle, Rockville. **Hours:** Excursions aboard the Needwood Queen, a 20-person pontoon boat, depart on the hour, noon-5 on weekends, Memorial Day-Labor Day. **Cost:** $1. **Phone:** 301/762-1888. The 20-minute tour focuses on the park's wildlife, including beavers, turtles, deer and several water birds. &

SENECA CREEK STATE PARK. 11950 Clopper Rd., Gaithersburg. The Blue Heron pontoon boat takes up to 24 people on naturalist-guided, one-hour tours on the 90-acre lake. **Hours:** Mid-May through Sept., weekends 1:30 & 3. **Cost:** $1. **Phone:** 301/924-2127. &

ANNAPOLIS. Maryland's capital was literally put on the map because of its lovely harbor. The best way to see it is, naturally, by boat. Chesapeake Marine Tours and Charters offer a bunch of different excursions, from under an hour to an entire day. Good bets for youngsters are the 40-minute harbor and Spa Creek tours. Catch them at the City Dock. **Hours:** Varied. **Cost:** $6 adults, $3 kids 11 and under. **Phone:** 410/268-7600 or 410/268-7601. **Web:** member.aol.com/boattours/cmt.html.

BALTIMORE. One of the nicest ways to take in Baltimore's Inner Harbor is to get out on the water. Either of the following services permits you to do that and, perhaps more important, to decompress after a visit to the Maryland Science Center, the Visionary Art Museum, National Aquarium or other Inner Harbor attraction. The cheapest and easiest is the Baltimore Water Taxi, which makes 15 stops around the harbor and lets you jump from, say, ships of the Maritime Museum to Fell's Point. While water taxis were intended chiefly to move tourists among harbor attractions, you can stay seated for the whole route and enjoy a cheap, slow-paced circumnavigation of the harbor. **Phone:** 410/563-3900. **Cost:** $3.50.

If you're feeling more ambitious, the best bet for a longer, more memorable family cruise is the Clipper City, a replica of an 1850s "tall ship" schooner (constructed in 1984 from original plans). It takes you on two-hour, narrated cruises to Fort McHenry and the commercial docks of the rarely seen "outer harbor." The dock is near the Maryland Science Center. **Phone:** 410/931-6777. **Hours:** Daily Apr.-Oct., noon-2, 3-5, 6-8. **Reservations:** Required. **Cost:** $12 adults, $2 kids 10 and under. &

Virginia

BURKE LAKE PARK. 7315 Ox Rd., Centreville. **Hours:** The Lady Burke pontoon boat leaves on the hour for a half-hour cruise around the 218-acre lake, Memorial Day-Labor Day: F-M 10-6; weekends only in Sept. **Cost:** $1.50. **Phone:** 703/323-6601. A guide describes wildlife at the park, including waterfowl that nest on an island refuge in the middle of the lake.

HARBOR RIVER CRUISES. 201 Mill St., Dock A, "Lady's Landing," P.O. Box 724, Occoquan. **Hours:** Forty-minute Potomac River cruises aboard the 32-passenger Harbor Lady leave at 11, 1 and 3 daily. Evening "Romancing the River" cruises depart at 7 and 9. **Cost:** $11 adults, $8 children with paying adults. **Reservations:** Required. **Phone:** 703/385-9433.

LAKE ACCOTINK PARK. 5660 Heming Ave., Springfield. **Hours:** Twenty-minute, guided, 23-person, pontoon-boat cruises on the 77-acre lake. May: weekends 11-7; Memorial Day-Labor Day: daily 11-7. **Cost:** $1. **Phone:** 703/569-0285. ♿

LAKE FAIRFAX PARK. 1400 Lake Fairfax Dr., Reston. Fifteen-minute, guided, pontoon-boat rides around the 20-acre lake. **Hours:** Memorial Day-June 12: weekends 10-9, weekdays 1-8, W 1-5; June 13-Aug. 16: daily 10-8; Aug. 17-Aug. 30: daily 10-7; Aug. 31-Sept. 7: weekdays 3-7, weekends 10-7; the 16- to 20-person boat runs according to demand rather than on a set schedule. **Cost:** 75 cents. **Phone:** 703/471-5414. ♿

POTOMAC RIVERBOAT COMPANY. Alexandria City Marina, King and Union streets, directly behind the Torpedo Factory Art Center. **Hours:** A 50-minute Mount Vernon cruise departs Tu-F at 11:30. Visitors tour Mount Vernon, then reboard the boat at 3 or 5:30. **Cost** (including admission to Mount Vernon): $22 adults, $20 seniors, $10 kids 6-11. **Phone:** 703/548-9000. ♿

A 90-minute "See Washington by Water" excursion travels past the monuments to Georgetown. **Hours:** Tu-F 11:30, 1:30, 3:30, 7:30 and 9:30; Sat also has a 5:30 departure; Sun 11:30, 1:30, 3:30 and 5:30. **Cost:** $14 adults, $13 seniors, $6 kids 2-12.

A 40-minute "See Alexandria by Water" tour along the waterfront offers narration about the city's history and landmarks. **Hours:** On the hour, Sat noon-6, 7-10; Sun noon-6. **Cost:** $7 adults, $6 seniors, $4 kids 2-12.

4

$\mathscr{S}\mathscr{C}\mathscr{I}\mathscr{E}\mathscr{N}\mathscr{C}\mathscr{E}$

GIVE ME A LEVER and I'll move the world." So said Archimedes. The modern equivalent might be, "Give me a touch-screen computer program and some hands-on experiments and I'll move an entire generation to be interested in science." At least that seems to be the case at attractions here.

Visiting even the best science museums with kids can be problematical. These places try not only to get kids to think but also to excite their senses with staggering dollops of interactivity. This usually is great fun, but there can be downsides. Touch-screens break. Long lines form for the cool movie. Kids ultimately may not share your wonder at the process by which blood is oxygenated. That means parents should approach these museums with patience. Try not to force younger kids to take too much in or to sit still while you read the text on every panel. They'll just want to push buttons, listen to a snippet from those recorded-information "wands," open doors and throw levers — in other words, play. There's plenty of value in this kind of exploration, even if it isn't precisely what the designers had in mind. When they're older, your kids will be well prepared for more in-depth lessons. And then, just maybe, they'll move the world.

District of Columbia

NATIONAL MUSEUM OF NATURAL HISTORY
Constitution Avenue and 10th Street NW

HOURS: Daily 10-5:30. **COST:** Free. **PHONE:** 202/357-2700 (TDD: 202/357-1729). **METRO:** Smithsonian, Federal Triangle. **WEB:** www.si.edu. &

Play your cards wrong and this may be the best museum you'll ever have a terrible time visiting. Crowds can drain the fun from this place, whose anachronistic design and presentations can't cope with the massive daily audiences the facility draws. Still, if you approach Natural History correctly, it can become one of the places you and your kids cherish most, a familiar spot where you can return repeatedly to dig more deeply and differently. The trick is never to try to take in the entire place at once. The most kid-friendly area is the O. Orkin Insect Zoo (see p. 9), which you should head for as early as possible to beat the crowds. (At this writing another kid treat, the Discovery Room, where children can handle bones, rocks, fossils and other scientific samples, was closed for renovation, with completion scheduled for spring 1999.) After the kids get their dose of bugs, you can noodle your way through the rest of the place. On the first floor you'll find the inevitable Dinosaur Room — which, frankly, is less infotaining than just about any other dino-show your kids are likely to see these days. The presentations are patient, even pedantic, and kids raised with "Jurassic Park" expectations can get impatient after the first few skeletons wear off. With enough prodding, though, some highlights may grab them. There's a glassed-in studio where scientists delicately scrape away at fossil remnants in chunks of stone, making clear just how tedious and exacting the practice of "real" paleontology can be. There also are vivid dioramas depicting extinct mammals, demonstrating that there's more to this evolution and extinction stuff than an-asteroid-wiped-out-the-dinosaurs-and-then-came-man.

Across the rotunda, on the opposite side of the 13-foot African bush elephant that dominates the space, a narrow hallway leads to a gallery featuring, first, taxidermied bird specimens and, eventually, taxidermied mammals. These presentations, while among the world's most exhaustive, are almost sweetly anachronistic, recalling a time when museums were simple repositories of "examples" of "natural life" in its many forms (in fact, many of the specimens were shot and made available to the Smithsonian by rough-rider Teddy Roosevelt in 1911 and 1912). Speaking of anachronism, the first floor also offers displays of Native Cultures, where mid-century dioramas depict life on these shores before Europeans arrived (with only occasional contemporary apologies and corrections added to assuage the more perceptive folk in the audience). Upstairs, the renovated Hall of Gems is full of startling examples of minerals. (Before you visit, you can prepare your kids to appreciate the magnitude of the 45.52-carat Hope Diamond, which rotates in a precious glass box, by showing them the half-carat and one-carat stones at a mall jewelry store. Oddly, in the context of all the exotic gems in the museum, the Hope can fail to make an impression.) And there are more time-machine galleries of dioramas depicting what early 20th Century scholars deemed "exotic cultures."

While the first floor marine ecosystems displays are of more recent vintage — and the 92-foot whale model hanging from the ceiling is quite compelling — both the Baltimore and Washington aquariums offer far better stuff, so feel free to skip this area during your early visits (though you'll want to check out the spectacularly icky giant-squid-in-a-gelatinous-block at the rear of that area). In the hallway outside the downstairs restaurant (also under renovation at this writing), you'll see a gallery of D.C. birds — a nice touch that serves to connect the museum to your hometown. And out in the yard, on the Ninth Street side of the building, on the border of a freeway ramp, is a new, multi-habitat butterfly garden, said to attract many of the 80 species of local butterflies.

> **Words to the wise:** *The recorded museum tours, while informative, don't serve families or groups very well. The live guided tours, good for kids 8 and up, are free. They start at the elephant at 10:30 and 1:30 daily, except for July and August.*

NOTES: Disability access is via Constitution Avenue. **Food:** While food service has been closed during the renovation, there are plenty of choices nearby at the National Museum of American History, the Old Post Office Pavilion and elsewhere. **Nearby:** National Gallery of Art, National Aquarium, Navy Memorial, Washington Monument, Freer Gallery, Sackler Gallery, National Museum of African Art, Smithsonian Castle, Arts and Industries Building, Hirshhorn Museum, National Air and Space Museum.

HANDS ON SCIENCE ROOM, NATIONAL MUSEUM OF AMERICAN HISTORY
On the Mall at 14ᵗʰ Street and Constitution Avenue NW

HOURS: Daily 10-5:30. **COST:** Free. **PHONE:** 202/357-2700. **METRO STOPS:** Federal Triangle, Smithsonian. **WEB:** www.si.edu. ♿

Most of the Smithsonian complex is devoted to static displays of artifacts; this compact center, on the first floor of the American history museum, is a welcome departure. It has tables full of intriguing puzzles, mini-experiments and even a laser you can aim at a picture of the moon across the room. But the best thing here is sitting at the laboratory-style tables and, with the assistance of patient, Socratic Smithsonian scientists, performing experiments designed to illustrate scientific concepts. During our visit, kids mixed dyes, observed color changes and learned something, maybe, about different elements' molecular structures. Other experiments involve DNA, light and food additives. We — and our kids — consider this one of the highlights of the Smithsonian's offerings for young people. This museum is one of the Smithsonian's best, with a wide array of exhibits, a great cafeteria and a massive gift shop (see p. 124).

> **Words to the wise:** *Try to get there right at the 10 a.m. opening. Admission to the hands-on area is controlled, and access to seats at the lab bench requires (free) tickets — which go quickly. If you're not among the first to arrive, you'll have to wait around for others to leave. As the day goes on, the crowds get grouchy and big. Kids 5 and up can get lab tickets, but the activities will go over many kids' heads until they're about 7.*

NOTES: For **Food**, as noted, this museum has an excellent cafeteria. **Nearby:** See preceding entry on the National Museum of Natural History.

NATIONAL GEOGRAPHIC EXPLORERS HALL
17ᵗʰ and M streets NW

HOURS: M-Sat 9-5, Sun 10-5. **PHONE:** 202/857-7588 (TDD: 202/857-7198). **METRO STOP:** Farragut North. **WEB:** www.nationalgeographic.com. **COST:** Free.

There's a whiff of the pop quiz about this place — you're forever being asked about average annual rainfall and the world's largest estuaries — but when you remember that lots of Americans can't find, well, America on a map, perhaps that's excusable. Brought to you by the folks behind the magazine, National Geographic Explorers Hall does a good job of laying out the geographic society's mandate ("Bringing the world to the world") and includes both static displays (What are fossils? How did humans evolve?) and interactive exhibits. Kids in third grade and up probably will get the most out of the place, though younger ones might enjoy the hustle, bustle, colors and touch screens of the exhibits. These range from a tiny tornado that swirls atop a fan to Earth Station One, a 72-seat amphitheater overlooking an 11-foot globe that spins around. The 15-minute Earth Station One presentation is a bit corny; it purports to take you on a flight 23,000 miles above Earth, ignoring the fact that astronauts don't see "North Atlantic" in letters hundreds of miles high floating atop the ocean. But the quiz is neat — there's an answer pad at each seat, and the audience's responses are tallied on monitors. As you would expect, the photography throughout is superb, especially in the introductory 7.5-minute film. Other features include a pint-sized planetarium, "your face on the cover of National Geographic" photo booths and a gift shop filled with maps, videos and educational toys.

Words to the wise: *While Geographica, the collection of permanent exhibits to the left of the main entrance, is the main draw, you might time your visit to include one of the rotating special exhibits frequently mounted. Recent shows have ranged from skulls found at the site of America's first colony to a tribute to the cat.*

NOTES: For **Food,** area restaurants are plentiful. **Nearby:** The Washington Post.

NATIONAL MUSEUM OF HEALTH AND MEDICINE
Building 54, 6825 16th Street NW (on Walter Reed Army base)

HOURS: Daily 10-5:30. COST: Free. PHONE: 202/782-2200. WEB: www.natmedmuse.afip.org

This Army-supported museum is devoted to exploring the human body — how it works and especially what happens when it doesn't, whether because of infection, parasite or, oh, a bullet in the head. It's graphic, but it's not sensational. Yes, there's a two-headed baby floating in a bottle. And a one-headed, two-bodied baby. And a one-eyed baby. But these serve to illustrate that while most babies are born fine, some aren't. They are displayed in an exhibit that shows quite clearly how babies move from inside the mother's body to outside. Younger kids may find this disturbing and thus shouldn't visit. But older kids — once they get past the inevitable "Oooh, gross!" reaction — actually may learn something: how bones go together (lotsa skeletons) or how various organs work (you can feel the inside of a stomach!). An exhibit on microscopes contains dozens of historic examples. An HIV exhibit is frank. One on Civil War medicine shows how far treatments have advanced since that conflict, in which government doctors were forced to learn a great deal. Weekends from 2 to 4, volunteers man "Discovery Carts" where visitors can look through a micro-scope or handle brains and other organs encased in plastic. Parents and teach-ers can request "Discovery Boxes" that contain little medical lessons. (Kids might enjoy looking at an X-ray of a girl who swallowed an earring.)

Words to the wise: *Resist any urge to take anyone under 10, and be prepared for pre-adolescent reactions.*

NOTES: For **Food,** the hospital cafe is a short walk away. It's open for lunch from 11 to 2 and has a variety of dishes at unbeatable, government-subsidized prices.

Directions: *Everyone presumably knows how to drive up or down 16th St., but that entrance is closed weekends. Use the Georgia Ave. entrance then, near Elder St.*

Maryland

MARYLAND SCIENCE CENTER
601 Light Street, Baltimore

HOURS: Weekdays 10-5 (F-Sun until 8 in summer), weekends 10-6; closed major holidays. **COST:** $9.75 adults, $8 ages 13-18 (and seniors), $7 kids 4-12. **PHONE:** 410/685-2370; recording: 410/685-5225. **WEB:** www.mdsci.org ♿

Now don't get us wrong: We love the Smithsonian. It's just that that esteemed institution sometimes has its priorities a little too straight, erring on the side of preserving and main-taining rather than, say, giving kids a good time. Maryland's Science Center is part of the newer generation of museums that invites interaction and works constantly to engage visitors. Recent exhibits have included a race car simulation backed with a "science of speed" tutorial and a Visible Human exhibition with leading-edge imaging technology revealing mysteries of the human body. Permanent exhibits include a crackling Van de Graaff electrostatic generator, a display on Chesapeake Bay ecology and a science arcade full of hands-on demos on light, mechanics, sound and whatnot. There's the inevitable Imax theater (usually with movies very different from those at Air and Space; we recently saw a thrilling "Everest"), and the Davis Planetarium, whose show is aimed at audiences 10 and up (though even toddlers are amused and hushed just to see the rendering of the sky). If you've got the 3-to-7 crowd in tow, don't miss the K.I.D.S. room, a see-touch-do bonanza. And watch for the "curiosity carts," which wheel mobile, hands-on experiments around during down times.

Words to the wise: *Do the math: A family of four won't get out of here for less than $30. Call ahead to see what special exhibits are on tap; it can be worth planning a trip around them.*

NOTES: Certain Imax and Davis shows are interpreted for the hearing impaired. **Food:** A Friendly's restaurant is in the building, but there are plenty of other snack and meal offerings around the Inner Harbor and Little Italy. **Nearby:** Baltimore Maritime Mu-seum, Baltimore Public Works Museum, Baltimore National Aquarium.

Directions: *Take I-95 north to the Inner Harbor exit and turn right on Light St.*

DR. SAMUEL D. HARRIS
NATIONAL MUSEUM OF DENTISTRY
31 S. Green Street, Baltimore (on University of Maryland campus)

HOURS: W-Sat 10-4, Sun 1-4; closed holidays. **COST:** $4.50 adults, $2.50 ages 7-18, students and seniors, under 6 free. **PHONE:** 410/706-0600. **WEB:** www.dentalmuseum.umaryland.edu. &

This place is a hoot, much more fun than it has any right to be. From the opening display — a life-size model of an inverted, sequined circus performer grasping a weight with her teeth — to the exhibit that once and for all debunks the story of George Washington's "wooden" teeth (they had ivory, among other materials), this dental museum strikes the tone you'd hope your favorite dentist would have: friendly, fun, a little corny perhaps but very competent. It may not be worth a special trip — except for the most dental-philic (or -phobic) — but it's a nice stop before an Orioles game or during a day of "Balmer" sightseeing.

The organizers seem aware of the reputation most dentists have, especially among children, and so have eschewed the scary, rotting tooth visuals of years past. Instead, there's lots of advertising memorabilia, historic instruments and such odd pop-cultural items as Sugar Ray Leonard's mouthpiece and Mrs. Tom Thumb's dentures. One TV screen shows dentist-related Charlie Chaplin and Little Rascals shorts. Another, surrounded by the cutest little plastic molar-shaped stools you've ever seen, shows old public service announcements. (The video on a little girl's first trip to the dentist is fairly disappointing, though.) The gift shop has everything from tooth-covered boxer shorts to a whole range of tooth fairy accessories (earrings, necklace, little box for collecting baby teeth).

Words to the wise: *Visit on a Sunday and you'll have this place to yourself — unless there's a dentists' convention in town.*

NOTES: For **Food,** choices are limited nearby, but the museum is just a five-minute drive from the amenity-rich Inner Harbor.

Directions: *Take I-95 north to Martin Luther King Jr. Blvd. make a right on Baltimore St. and a right again on Greene St.; the museum is at the corner of Greene and Lombard. Metered street parking is scarce, but there are metered lots at the intersection of Paca and Pratt, near Oriole Park.*

BALTIMORE PUBLIC WORKS MUSEUM
751 Eastern Avenue, Baltimore

HOURS: Tu-Sun 10-4. **COST:** $2.50 adults, $1.50 kids 6-17, $2 seniors, under 6 free. **PHONE:** 410/396-5565. &

It's a good thing this place was not named the Infrastructure Museum, but that's basically what it is — an institution dedicated to preserving and under-standing all the largely invisible systems that sustain our contemporary environments: water treatment, sewage, natural gas, electricity, dams, bridges, storm drainage and so on. There's a 15-minute video, some good exhibits (explaining, for instance, how water treatment has progressed since the 19th Century and what's going on underground when you see those workers in yellow suits descending beneath the streets) and a play area. But the real highlight, and most memorable lesson, is outside: a two-story, full-sized cutaway of a city street and the web of wiring, pipes, tubes, sewers and other tunnel work below. If your kids pay attention, they'll have a much better understanding of what all those manhole covers and anachronistic valves sticking out of the sidewalk are about. They may even go on to become more appreciative taxpayers.

Words to the wise: *If you're walking from another Inner Harbor attraction, the stroll is pleasant but demanding for very small kids.*

NOTES: You can walk from the museum to Little Italy, where a number of restaurants serve excellent, inexpensive Italian food. **Nearby:** Little Italy, Baltimore National Aquarium, other Inner Harbor attractions.

Directions: *Take I-95 north to the Inner Harbor; turn right onto Pratt St. Pass the Inner Harbor attractions and take a right on President St. Museum is two blocks on the right. Parking is available in several public lots ($4 to $6), or, if you're feeling lucky, try street parking in nearby Little Italy.*

SMITHSONIAN NATURALIST CENTER
741 Miller Drive SE, Leesburg

HOURS: Tu-Sat 10:30-4; closed federal holidays and two weeks before Labor Day. **COST:** Free. **PHONE:** 703/779-9712 or 800/729-7725. **WEB:** www.si.edu. &

For kids age 10 and up inspired by the assortment of artifacts at the National Museum of Natural History, a trip out to Leesburg might be in order, especially if they want to look *and* touch. Natural History's Naturalist Center houses a collection of preserved specimens, along with books and scientific equipment. Nearly all of it is hands-on, meaning a young naturalist can pull open a drawer filled with tiny, carefully-arranged rodent bodies or handle an eagle wing or canine skull, examining it from all angles. It's like stepping behind a door marked "Museum Staffers Only." Special programs include "Draw-Ins," where professional scientific illustrators help young artists sketch objects from the center or from their own collections; and "Identi-Days," where visitors bring in fossils, plants, seashells, bones and the like and get help determining exactly what the heck they are. This is the perfect place to fan the embers of a burgeoning interest in natural science.

Directions: *From the Beltway, take the Dulles Toll Rd. to the Toll Rd. Extension (the Greenway) to Exit 1B (Route 15). Make the first right (Sycolin Rd.), then the second right (Miller Dr.). The center is the first building on the left, next to the Leesburg Air Park. There's plenty of parking.*

Virginia

U.S. PATENT AND TRADEMARK MUSEUM
2121 Crystal Drive, Suite 0100, Crystal City

HOURS: Weekdays 8:30-5:30. **COST:** Free. **PHONE:** 703/305-8341. ♿

This modest museum in the canyons of Crystal City might not appeal to little kids, but it may well strike a chord with older ones inspired by the stories of Thomas Edison and Alexander Graham Bell. While the museum does the expected trumpet blowing about the importance of a strong patent, trademark and copyright operation, it also has cases filled with neat stuff. Until 1880 inventors submitted models of their contraptions along with their applications, and some of these tiny, well-crafted creations are on display, from a little washing machine to an itty-bitty stove. You'll also find a model of the only invention patented by a U.S. president: a bellows system for raising riverboats off of sandbars dreamed up by Abe Lincoln. On the trademark end of things are some of the branded names and shapes we encounter, from the Nike swoosh to Alfred E. Newman's gap-toothed mug, a Reggie Jackson candy bar and a Roy Rogers lunchbox. Five Coca-Cola bottles illustrate how even a shape can be trademarked. Changing exhibits have explored bicycle design and the development of the camera. For two bucks you can get your kid's face on 16 tiny little stickers courtesy of a "NeoPrint" machine.

Words to the wise: *Parking is tough, so take the Metro. You can walk from the Crystal City station without ever being outside, courtesy of underground and overhead walkways that kids might find to be a kick. Follow signs to Crystal Park Two.*

NOTES: For **Food,** Crystal City's rabbit warren of underground malls has plenty of dining options.

U.S. GEOLOGICAL SURVEY
12201 Sunrise Valley Drive, Reston

HOURS: Visitors center, weekdays, 8-4:30; closed weekends and holidays. **COST:** Free. **PHONE:** 703/648-4748. **WEB:** www.usgs.gov. ♿

This federal agency devoted to earth science is open to visitors only on weekdays; a shame, because it's a full of stuff that will fascinate kids (and adults). For instance, two seismographs right next to each other monitor, respectively, the ground directly in front of the machine and a chunk of remote terrain in New Mexico. Kids love to jump and dance to make the needle that picks up "local" vibrations shimmy across the scrolling paper. Of course, the right needle trembles only to the rhythms of the distant southwestern desert. Kids can stand on a mold of a dinosaur footprint that was discovered right nearby, in Culpeper. In a hands-on room, kids can play with all sorts of earth-science tools, from microscopes to water flumes. The agency has some astonishing videos of floods, volcanoes, tornadoes and other examples of nature's extreme behaviors. And the Geological Survey shop is full of bargains and a stunning array of maps. You can pick up an official agency map of, say, the "quadrant" that includes your neighborhood, school or favorite vacation area for a mere $4. The store also peddles some beautiful and fascinating posters and related publications, most under $10 (our kids' favorite: a to-scale presentation of our solar system's planets and their various moons). Some educational pamphlets, like those on rock collecting and dinosaur fossils, are free. The interiors are modern and handsome, the campus is lovely, and a modest network of asphalt trails, featuring huge rock specimens, leads to a well and through a grove of identified trees.

Words to the wise: *Call ahead to arrange a guided tour. Families may be grouped with others for the tour, which usually involves an introductory video, some supervised time in the hands-on room, opportunity to view the exhibits and observe computer mapping in action and a visit to the agency's loud map-printing plant.*

NOTES: On the **Food** front, this is an excellent place for a picnic, but if you prefer there's a cafeteria on the first floor. Or, if you're feeling flush, you're close to Reston City Center, where you'll find plenty of restaurants, an ice cream place, a book store and so on. Parking there is free.

Directions: *From the Beltway take Exit 12B and follow the signs to Route 267 West, the Dulles Toll Rd. Take the toll road to Exit 12, Reston Pkwy. (you'll have to stop twice to pay tolls, totaling 75 cents each way as of this writing). Turn left onto Reston Pkwy. (Route 602), heading south. Go half a mile and turn right onto South Lakes Dr. The agency is a half mile on the right. Parking is free.*

EYES on the SKIES

LIGHT POLLUTION and plain-old pollution mean that the heavens around Washington aren't quite as dramatic as, say, those in Montana. Maybe that's why we have more than our fair share of planetariums, those curious theaters of the night sky where stars and planets, constellations and galaxies are projected on the ceiling. And when you want to see the real thing, visit an observatory, where you can clothe the naked eye with a telescope.

The District

ALBERT EINSTEIN PLANETARIUM. National Air and Space Museum, between Fourth and Seventh streets on Independence Avenue SW. **Hours:** Daily 10 to 5:30. **Cost:** $3.75 a person. Tickets can be purchased at the planetarium box office or the Langley Theatre box office. **Phone:** 202/357-1686 or 357-2000. **Metro Stops:** L'Enfant Plaza, Smithsonian. **Web:** www.si.edu. "The Stars Tonight," a 30-minute lecture on the current night sky, is presented daily at 3. "Sky Quest," a 30-minute children's program, is shown daily at 11 and 1. "The New Solar System," a 30-minute multimedia presentation on the planets, is shown every 40 minutes throughout the day (except at 11 and 1), beginning at 11:40. ♿

ROCK CREEK NATURE CENTER. 5200 Glover Rd. NW. **Hours:** Planetarium shows weekends at 1 (ages 4 and up) and 4 (7 and up). "The Night Sky," at 1, focuses on the current star map (children under 4 not admitted). Various theme-related astronomy programs are presented weekends at 4 (children under 7 not admitted). A night sky presentation focusing on Native American star legends is offered Wednesdays at 4. **Cost:** Free. Pick up tickets at the Nature Center a half hour before show time; groups of eight or more must make reservations at least two weeks in advance. **Phone:** 202/426-6829.   ♿

U.S. NAVAL OBSERVATORY. Massachusetts Avenue at 34th Street NW. **Cost:** Free. **Phone:** 202/762-1467. **Web:** www.usno.navy.mil. Observatory tours, which last 90 minutes, are given Mondays at 8:30 p.m. The tour has three parts: a 20-minute video on the history of the observatory, a viewing of the master clock and, weather permitting, a look through the 12-inch telescope. **Notes:** Disabled access is limited. Tours are not recommended for those in wheelchairs, and note the late starting time.

Maryland

DAVIS PLANETARIUM. Maryland Science Center, 601 Light St. (next to the Inner Harbor), Baltimore. **Hours:** M-Th 10-6; F-Sun 10-8. Films shown daily at 15 and 45 minutes past the hour, beginning at 11:15. **Cost:** Free with Science Center admission ($9.75 adults, $7 kids 4-12, $8 ages 13-18 and seniors). **Phone:** 410/685-5225.

HOWARD B. OWENS SCIENCE CENTER. 9601 Greenbelt Rd., Lanham. **Hours:** Open only during school year. Planetarium shows: F 7:30. **Cost:** $4 adults, $2 students, under 12 and seniors. **Phone:** 301/918-8750.   ♿

UNIVERSITY OF MARYLAND-ASTRONOMY DEPARTMENT. Metzerott Rd., between Adelphi Rd. and University Blvd., College Park. **Hours:** Open house at 9 p.m. on the 5th and 20th of each month, including a lecture, slide show and telescopic viewing (weather permitting). **Cost:** Free. **Phone:** 301/405-0355.

Virginia

ARLINGTON PLANETARIUM. 1426 N. Quincy St., Arlington. "The Stars Tonight," a lecture on the current night sky, runs the first Monday of each month at 7 p.m. Special seasonal shows offered. **Cost:** $2.50 adults, $1.50 children under 12 and seniors. **Phone:** 703/228-6070. ♿

WEATHER or NOT

TWO NEARBY PLACES explore the science of weather prediction. One is rather static, the other somewhat technical. Neither is a good place to bring young children or anyone who hasn't expressed an interest in meteorology.

NATIONAL WEATHER SERVICE
SCIENCE AND HISTORY CENTER
1325 East West Highway, Silver Spring, Md.

HOURS: Weekdays 8:30-5. **COST:** Free. **PHONE:** 301/713-0622. **METRO STOP:** Silver Spring.   ♿

Near the lobby of the National Oceanic and Atmospheric Administration headquarters is this odd little one-room exhibit. Monitors display satellite images of Earth while TV screens scroll regional and national weather forecasts. There's a re-creation of a typical weather bureau regional office of the 1890s and a sad model of a weather satellite, with bits of it peeling off at last sighting. An exhibit on a storm warning system called "Weather Radio" relates the quixotic hope that the system will one day be as common as the smoke detector.

NATIONAL WEATHER SERVICE
Route 606, Sterling, Va.

TOURS HOURS: M noon (ages 10 and up). **COST:** Free. **RESERVATIONS:** Required. **PHONE:** 703/260-0107, Ext. 225.

Turn on the radio or open the newspaper and you'll probably find the results of the work done here, at the weather service's Baltimore-Washington Forecast Office. Real meteorologists (not the blow-dried TV type) employ an arsenal of technology to predict the weather. On the hour-long tour for fifth graders and up, kids will see the banks of computers on which satellite images are displayed and millions of calculations take place. But some of this place's work is refreshingly low tech. How else to measure snowfall than to plunge a ruler into a snowbank? And while you can't deploy a weather balloon yourself, they'll show you the instrument-laden hydrogen balloons they release twice a day.

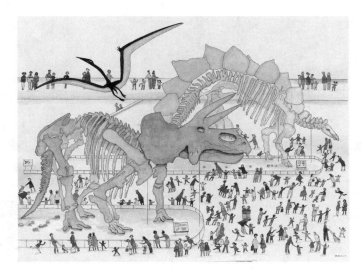

5

ROOTING for the HOME TEAM

OUTINGS WITH CHILDREN to pro football, basketball, baseball, hockey or soccer games can be filled with memorable moments — the excitement of the crowd, the whole family pulling for the home team, the sense of the entire community coming together. The games also offer lessons for kids, from mastering the math of scoring and the strategies of coaching to understanding that hard work pays off and that heroes and heroines come in all colors and nationalities. Not least, kids may learn that loyalty means sticking with your team even in the worst of times (some Washington-area teams have seemed devoted in recent years to instilling that principle).

Thanks to intense competition for family leisure dollars, nearly every pro sport also has pumped up the "entertainment factor" of games. With improved food service, pre-, mid- and post-game contests, endless mascot hijinks and prize giveaways, thumping music, cheerleader performances and video screens that kick out great shows unto themselves, most pro sports games have been transformed into far more complete entertainment experiences. While purists may look back wistfully on the days when people just rooted for their team and filled out scorecards, few families with kids will feel that way.

The problem with most pro games, however, is expense or, with the Redskins, the inability to get tickets at all. Excluding perhaps some astronomically priced seats, Redskins games have long been sold out before the season begins. At Camden Yards, on the other hand, a family of four with mid-priced seats for Baltimore Orioles baseball is likely to drop $100 to $120 or more by the time admission, food, parking, transportation and incidental costs are all tallied. Nor are visits to the MCI Center for Wizards games or Washington Capitals hockey face-offs exactly inexpensive.

That's one reason why the arrival of new pro teams with cheaper tickets — DC United of pro soccer and the Washington Mystics of women's basketball — has been such a boon. It's also one reason why the region's minor league teams are so alluring.

Since most people know lots about our area's Big Four sports franchises, we have provided only brief information about their games and costs (for all pro games, tickets also are available, with a service charge, from TicketMaster, 202/432-7328, 703/573-7328, 410/481-7328). Some franchises, though, offer things other than games, and we have included their museums and a special stadium tour that are likely to intrigue kids. At the end of the chapter, we examine the minor league teams. A nice way to introduce kids to sports is by starting with one of these inexpensive alternatives. Take a picnic to a minor league game, ride the carousel that many parks have and enjoy.

THE BIG FOUR PRO TEAMS

AT JACK KENT COOKE STADIUM
Raljon, Md.
Phone: 703/589-1994.
Online Stadium Views: www.ascticket.com/cooke.html. &

WASHINGTON REDSKINS. Ticket Office: 301/276-6060. **Web:** www.nfl.com/redskins/index.html. Washington's (well, Raljon's,) NFL team plays four pre-season games in August before starting the 16-game season in September. You already know about tickets: Unless you already have one, you can't get one. If you must go to an NFL game, try pre-season or look in *The Washington Post* classified ad section for ticket brokers or scalpers (or try the Baltimore Ravens; see p. 65). You can watch the Redskins prepare for the season during their three-week training camp (including practices and scrimmage games), starting in mid-July at Frostburg State University in Frostburg, Md.

AT THE MCI CENTER
601 F Street NW, Washington
Phone: 202/661-5050
Metro Stop: Gallery Place/Chinatown
Online Arena Views: www.mcicenter.com. &

❑ **WASHINGTON WIZARDS. Web:** www.nba.com/wizards/. **Cost:** $19-$85. The National Basketball Association team's season goes from early October to late April.

❑ **WASHINGTON CAPITALS. Web:** www.washingtoncaps.com. **Cost:** $19 to $60. The regular season of Washington's National Hockey League franchise runs from early October to late April. The alcohol-free and less rowdy family sections are numbers 422 and 423.

MCI NATIONAL SPORTS GALLERY
HOURS: Daily 10-6; extended hours with evening events. **COST:** $4, under 5 free. **PHONE:** 202/661-5133. Admission includes four credits for games; extra credits available for $1 each or as low as 50 cents each if purchased in volume. Most games require 1-2 credits per play. &

The MCI National Sports Gallery, on the third floor of the MCI Center, presents an unusual mix of historic sports memorabilia and high-tech sports simulation games. Visitors enter a multimedia exhibit called "A Nation of Sports Lovers" featuring film and sound clips and artifacts. Elsewhere, collectors and memorabiliasts will find the most impressive collection of stuff outside a sports halls of fame or an All-Star Cafe. There's a 1909 Honus Wagner baseball card, said to be worth more than $500,000; Negro League baseball memorabilia; a jersey worn by Cleveland Brown fullback Jim Brown; a driver used by golf legend Arnold Palmer, and a robe worn by Rocky Marciano in his penultimate fight. You can reach through a glass case to touch a bat used by Babe Ruth. On the floor above the museum is the American Sportscasters Association Hall of Fame, which has sound-and-image tributes to some of sports' greatest voices: Red Barber, Jim McKay, Harry Caray and Howard Cosell (one Cosell highlight is a soundclip of his announcing, on Monday Night Football, the death of Beatle John Lennon). The high-tech games are mostly pro sports simulations: You can toss footballs to on-screen receivers, try to blast shots past goaltenders in hockey or soccer, pitch or hit against on-screen major leaguers. Most of the games are considerably more dramatic and "realistic" than their more common arcade-machine predecessors. The youngest guests are best served by the basketball simulation, which has a "Junior" version

Words to the wise: *Before you buy a lot of game credits, check which machines are operating (this can fluctuate maddeningly). Also, beware of crowds. When the place is packed, you can suffer lines of Disneyesque dimensions: 20 minutes to play a two-minute game. If your child is under 6, don't bother with many credits, as most games are aimed at teens and adults.*

NOTES: Food: There are plenty of restaurants in the area, which includes Chinatown. **Nearby:** Discovery Center, National Portrait Gallery, National Museum of American Art.

AT ORIOLE PARK AT CAMDEN YARDS
333 W. Camden Street, Baltimore
Phone: 410/685-9100
Online Stadium Views: www.ascticket.com/camden.html &

❏ **BALTIMORE ORIOLES. Ticket office:**410/685-9800. **Web:** www.theorioles.com. **Cost:** Ranges from $7 for standing room to $9 for bleacher seats to $35 for club box seats, with other prices in between. Baltimore's American League team plays from April through September.

ORIOLE PARK TOUR
HOURS: In season, weekdays every half-hour from 11-2; Sat every half-hour starting 10:30, Sun 12:30, 1, 2 and 3. Tours less frequent in the off-season. (Call in advance, as tour schedules vary during some Orioles home stands.) **COST:** $5 adults, $4 ages 12 and under and seniors. **PHONE:** 410/547-6234. **WEB:** www.theorioles.com. &

We admit that we were skeptical about the value of touring a dormant Camden Yards. But both we and our kids loved our off-season visit to this beautiful ballpark.

Tour guides start by pointing out the ball-size plaques marking the massive home runs that have been hit onto the Eutaw Street plaza; astonished visitors look back at home plate and imagine the incredible arcs required to carry the balls there. Guides also point out the colored seats that mark where special batted balls have landed. You'll visit the press box (look for the holes in the wall where particularly vicious foul balls have left their marks), the training room and the network of tunnels normally closed to the public. You may be impressed by the ultra-sophisticated drainage system that keeps the field nearly dry, even in a steady rain, and you'll learn that every aisle seat bears an Orioles logo from 1890. But the highlight is sitting on the Orioles team bench and taking in the view from the dugout. Neither you nor your kids will ever view a baseball stadium the same way again.

Words to the wise: *During the off-season, you'll have more relaxed access. In-season movement is more restricted, though you can observe more behind-the-scenes action then. There's a big Oriole gift shop; establish spending limits en route.*

NOTES: Tours, held rain or shine, take 1 to 1.5 hours. You can buy tickets starting at 9 at the main box office. **Food:** In season, ballpark restaurants, including Boog's Bar-B-Q, are open. Otherwise, downtown Baltimore and the Inner Harbor offer assorted eateries. **Directions:** *Take I-95 north, get off at Exit 52 and follow the signs to Camden Yards. Parking is easy, except, of course, on game days.*

BABE RUTH BIRTHPLACE AND OFFICIAL ORIOLES MUSEUM
216 Emory Street, Baltimore

HOURS: Apr.-Oct. daily 10-5, (until 7 pm on Orioles home game days, until 4 pm in winter). **COST:** $6 adults, $3 ages 5-16, $4 seniors. **PHONE:** 410/727-1539 or 800/435-2223. **WEB:** www.baberuthmuseum.com. ♿

Located "a long fly ball" from Oriole Park at Camden Yards, the house where the Bambino was born in 1895 (along with three adjacent rowhouses) has been preserved as a shrine. It serves as a tribute both to baseball's greatest slugger (whose father was a saloonkeeper near what is now center field at Camden Yards) and to the Orioles (for whom the Babe played in 1914, when the team was a minor league franchise).

The museum houses some interesting Babe artifacts: Ruth's boyhood bat, a hymnal bearing the inscription, "George H. Ruth, world's worse singer, world's best pitcher," and the official score book from Babe's first professional game with the 1914 Orioles. There's a frank presentation of the Babe's lousy childhood, bad behavior and unhappy life, a useful warning to any aspiring athlete who thinks that physical accomplishment is all that matters. The rest of the museum is dedicated to Orioleania, including an exhibit about Cal Ripkin's heroic pursuit of Lou Gehrig's "unassailable" record of playing in 2,131 straight games.

NOTES: Wheelchair access is to the first floor only. The museum plans a major expansion, scheduled for completion in 2000, into the Camden Station railroad terminal adjacent to Camden Yards. **Directions:** *From the Beltway, take I-95 north, exit at I-395 (Downtown) and follow signs for Martin Luther King Jr. Blvd. On MLK, turn right at second light onto Pratt St. Pass one light (Penn), and take the first right at Emory St. The parking lot is on Pratt.*

THE RECENT PRO ADDITIONS

DC UNITED
RFK Stadium, 22nd and East Capitol streets, Washington

COST: $12 to $32. **PHONE:** 703/478-6600. **WEB:** www.dcunited.com. **METRO STOP:** Stadium/Armory. ♿

Washington's most successful pro sports team is its Major League Soccer franchise. (They were the MSL champs in 1996 and 1997.) With so many kids playing soccer in leagues and in school these days, DC United games provide a great chance for young players to observe top professionals in action. The regular season runs from mid-March to late November. While DC United has developed a loyal and international following, cavernous RFK stadium offers plenty of seats for everyone — even for high-stakes game tickets bought the day of the event.

WASHINGTON MYSTICS
MCI Center, 601 F Street NW, Washington

COST: $8-$20. **PHONE:** 301/622-3865. **WEB:** www.wnba.com/mystics/. **VIRTUAL VIEW:** www.mcicenter.com. **METRO STOP:** Gallery Place/Chinatown. ♿

The Washington Mystics, the area's franchise in the still-developing Women's National Basketball Association, offers a similarly accessible, affordable and entertaining venue for pro basketball. Mystics games may be especially attractive to families with girls, who are not overwhelmed with role models among pro sports teams, but they are fun for everyone. The season runs from mid-June to late August.

BALTIMORE RAVENS
Ravens Stadium, 1101 Russell Street, Baltimore

COST: $20 to $60. **PHONE:** General information: 410/654-6200; ticket information: 410/261-7283 **WEB:** www.nfl.com/ravens/index.html. ♿

Balmer's NFL team plays four preseason games in August before starting the 16-game season in September. Preseason training camp is at Western Maryland College in Westminster. Home games are in the new 68,400-seat Ravens Stadium. While the Redskins have been sold out forever, Ravens tickets are easier to get.

MINOR LEAGUE BASEBALL

LOCAL BASEBALL FARM teams go the extra mile to entice families. Bowie, Frederick and Salisbury all have relatively new stadiums that include carousels, playgrounds and other kid-friendly features. Alcohol-free family sections keep rowdy fans at a safe distance. Tickets are cheap (as little as $3 and not more than $12), and kids under 5 get in free. So do kids 6 to 12 at Bowie, Frederick and Salisbury if they're wearing uniforms from an organized athletic league.

Maryland

BOWIE BAYSOX. Web: www.theorioles.com/baysox.htm. **Phone:** 301/805-6000. This Baltimore Orioles' AA farm team plays at Prince George's County Stadium. **Directions:** *From the Beltway, take Route 50 east to Route 301 south, then left into the stadium.* ♿

FREDERICK KEYS. Web: www.frederickkeys.com. **Phone:** 301/662-0013. Baltimore's Class A farm team plays at Harry Grove Stadium. **Directions:** *Take I-270 north to Market Street (Exit 31A) and proceed for two miles. The stadium is on the left.* ♿

HAGERSTOWN SUNS. Web: www.hagerstownsuns.com. **Phone:** 301/791-6266. Toronto's Class A team plays in Municipal Stadium. **Directions:** *Take I-270 to I-70 west to Exit 32B, and make a left on Eastern Blvd.*

DELMARVA SHOREBIRDS. Web: www.co.wicomico.md.us/sbirds.html. **Phone:** 410/219-3112. While this Eastern Shore team plays its home games 120 miles from Washington in Salisbury, its stadium is on the way to the Delmarva beaches. **Directions:** *The Arthur W. Perdue Stadium is on Hobbs Rd. off Route 50 and the Route 13 bypass.* ♿

Virginia

PRINCE WILLIAM CANNONS. **Phone:** 703/590-2311. **Web:** www.pwcannons.com. This Class A St. Louis Cardinals team plays in G. Richard Pfitzner Stadium. **Directions:** *From I-95 south, take the Prince William Parkway/Manassas (Exit 158B) and take a right into County Complex Court.* ♿

MINOR LEAGUE HOCKEY

CHESAPEAKE ICEBREAKERS. **Phone:** 888/ICE-HOCKEY. **Web:** www.icebreakershockey.com. The Icebreakers play home games at the Show Place Arena, 14900 Pennsylvania Ave., Upper Marlboro, Md. The skaters may be a tad slower than those in the National Hockey League, but they're just as quick to settle things with fists if their sticks seem inadequate. One neat feature: On selected nights youngsters can skate on the ice after the game is over. Call to check for dates, and bring your skates. ♿

6

PERFORMING ARTS

CHILDREN spend an inordinate amount of time pretending and hamming it up. So do some adults. Do your children a favor and expose them to those who do it best — actors, musicians, puppeteers and others. Our area has all manner of performing companies catering to youngsters. For live plays, places like the Kennedy Center Theater Lab and the Smithsonian Discovery Theatre generally get national companies cut from relatively professional cloth. Local troupes sometimes have more enthusiasm than polish, but this isn't always the case, and so what if Cinderella can't quite hit all the high notes? Kids still will be entranced, just as they will be by the mimes and magicians and dancers and other performers in our area. Some advice before the show begins:

❑ Don't overestimate a child's attention span. Most kids' shows are in the 30- to 40-minute range. Even that may be too long for a squirmy 3-year-old. Take toddlers to shows for preschoolers or with audience participation. Puppet shows are especially good introductions to theater.

❑ Describe what's going to happen — not just the plot of a play (though if it's a familiar story you can go over it beforehand), but what happens at a theater: that others will be in the audience, that it often gets dark.

❑ Little ones sometimes get frightened. While they should learn not to talk at shows, let your child know ahead of time that it's okay to tell you if he or she is scared. If the child gets really upset, you should leave.

❑ If you can, sit on the aisle, especially with a first-timer.

THEATER
District of Columbia

DISCOVERY THEATRE
Smithsonian Arts and Industries Building, 900 Jefferson Drive SW

HOURS: Weekdays 10 & 11:30, some Sat 11:30 & 1. **COST:** $5. **RESERVATIONS:** Suggested. **PHONE:** 202/357-1500. **METRO:** Smithsonian. **WEB:** www.si.edu. ♿

The Smithsonian Associates sponsors this performance series, which runs every month except August in the 220-seat Discovery Theatre. The offerings are in the puppet show/children-and-youth theater/storytelling mold, with most performing groups visiting from out of town. The Smithsonian, of course, can cherry-pick the country's best talent. The performances run the gamut in age appropriateness, from preschool all the way up to 12th grade, so check *The Washington Post* or www.washingtonpost.com for what's scheduled.

Words to the wise: *Arrive early if you want a good seat.*

NOTES: You'll find **Food** in the Air and Space Museum and across the Mall in the National Gallery. **Nearby:** Hirshhorn Museum, Smithsonian Castle, National Air and Space Museum, Sackler Gallery of Art, National Museum of African Art, National Gallery of Art, Washington Monument.

NATIONAL THEATRE
1321 Pennsylvania Avenue NW

HOURS: Sept.-April: Sat 9:30 & 11. **COST:** Free. **PHONE:** 202/783-3370. **METRO STOP:** Metro Center. **WEB:** www.nationaltheatre.org. &

Bless the National Theatre. Who else would sponsor (with the help of the Marriott Foundation) free children's entertainment every Saturday for five months of the year? As it turns out, nobody else. The offerings are all over the map: clowns, magicians, puppet shows, mimes, storytellers. Shows are in the Helen Hayes Gallery, an open, mezzanine-level lobby area. Kids sit on the floor, grown-ups in chairs at the edges of the action. Seating is on a first-come basis.

Words to the wise: *Go for the 9:30 show. It's easier to find parking and, if all tickets are gone, you can get some for the 11 o'clock performance. Use the extra time to visit a nearby attraction.*

NOTES: You'll find food around the corner at the Shops at National Place. **Nearby:** Pershing Park Ice Rink, National Aquarium, White House, Old Post Office Pavilion, Shops at National Place, National Museum of American History.

KENNEDY CENTER: Performances for Young People and Families
New Hampshire Avenue and F Street NW

HOURS: Typically in the fall on F 7 pm; Sat at 11 & 1, Sun 1. **COST:** Usually $10. **PHONE:** 202/467-4600 or 202/416-8000. **METRO STOP:** Foggy Bottom (free shuttle bus every 15 minutes). **WEB:** http://kennedy-center.org. &

No matter your age, a trip to the Kennedy Center is an event. Young children seem dressed up: white tights and Mary Janes on the girls, clip-on bow ties on the boys. Most performances — classics from touring companies or original Kennedy Center productions — are presented in the Theater Lab or Terrace Theater. This usually is some of the best children's theater in Washington, and kids tend to be awed by the luxurious surroundings.

Words to the wise: *Performances often sell out, so reserve early. And remember those naps for younger kids before evening performances.*

NOTES: For **Food**, there's a cafeteria on the top level of the Kennedy Center, but it's a little pricey. If you're attending a weekend performance and the weather outside is good, you might want to consider bringing a lunch and sitting on the terrace overlooking the Potomac.

Maryland

ADVENTURE THEATRE
Glen Echo Park, 7300 MacArthur Boulevard, Glen Echo

HOURS: Sat & Sun 1:30 & 3:30. **RESERVATIONS:** Suggested. **COST:** $5. **PHONE:** 301/320-5331. **WEB:** www.nps.gov/glec.

Sturdy and dependable, Adventure Theatre probably has introduced more little ones to the world of drama than any other local group. It's the area's oldest theater troupe — it was founded in 1950 — and the people there know what they're doing. They present classic stories and fairy tales in a theater that seats about 200 on carpeted risers. It's perfect for children as young as 4 or 5. After performances, the cast members wait in the lobby, obligingly signing programs for the kids. Who knows whether that au pair playing Mary Poppins will one day be famous?

> **Words to the wise:** *Seating is general admission. If you believe that your child might be disappointed with seats that are far back, be sure to get in line early.*

PUPPET COMPANY PLAYHOUSE
Glen Echo Park, 7300 MacArthur Boulevard, Glen Echo

HOURS: W-F 10 & 11:30, Sat & Sun 11:30 & 1. **RESERVATIONS:** Suggested. **COST:** $5 (free under 2). **PHONE:** 301/320-6668. **WEB:** www.thepuppetco.org.

The folks at the Puppet Company, which has been around since 1983, also know their stuff. They focus principally on kid-lit staples, from "Jack and the Beanstalk" to Beatrix Potter tales. Shows are the perfect length for fidget-prone youngsters — about 40 minutes. Children sit on a comfy carpeted floor, with grown-ups to each side, so sight lines aren't blocked. The productions resist the urge to hip it up — there are few double entendres or gags pitched at parents. Instead, the Puppet Company presents the classics dependably. For youngsters who might be frightened by the occasionally scary marionette, puppeteers meet the children at the end of each show.

> **Words to the wise:** *Reward good behavior with a promise of a post-show ride on the Glen Echo carousel.*

NOTES: There's no food in Glen Echo Park. **Nearby:** Adventure Theatre and Clara Barton House as well as the carousel.

BETHESDA ACADEMY OF PERFORMING ARTS: IMAGINATION STAGE
White Flint Mall, 2nd level, 11301 Rockville Pike, North Bethesda

HOURS: T & Th 11, Sat 3, Sun 1 & 3. **RESERVATIONS:** Suggested. **COST:** $5.50.
PHONE: 301/881-5106. **WEB:** www.bapaarts.org. ♿

This company had the bright idea of setting up shop in a mall, where the families are. BAPA has a year-round season of simply but imaginatively staged classics ("Beauty and the Beast," "The Velveteen Rabbit"), along with more multicultural offerings ("Anansi the Spider"). As with most such groups, the audience sits close to the action. When you walk in, the stage is right *there*. It's not so much a stage as an open area in the center of the room. Kids sit either on the floor or in chairs on risers. BAPA also has a Deaf Access Company composed of both deaf and hearing teenagers who put on a sign-interpreted show once a year.

Words to the wise: *Park on the 2nd level near Bloomingdale's and enter there or through the mall food court, both of which are close to the theater. Then you won't have to schlep the kids across the mall.*

NOTES: Food: There's plenty in the mall. **Nearby:** Discovery Zone, Dave & Busters.

DIRECTIONS: *Take the Beltway to Route 355 north to the mall on the right.*

NOW THIS!
Blair Mansion Inn, 7711 Eastern Avenue, Silver Spring

HOURS: Sat 1:30. **RESERVATIONS:** Suggested. **COST:** $14, including lunch.
PHONE: 202/364-8292. ♿

A piano, a few costume elements, some imagination and a suggestive audience — these are the ingredients for this interactive musical theater group. Basically, kids shout out various scenarios, and the performers attempt to integrate them into the story as it rambles along. Songs and scenes grind along like bad "Saturday Night Live" skits, but to paraphrase Dr. Johnson: It is not necessarily done well, but it is surprising that it is done at all. And occasionally the troupers click, with satisfying results.

Words to the wise: *This is for kids old enough not to be confused by freeform zaniness but not so old as to cast a jaundiced eye on corny skits.*

Virginia

THE CHILDREN'S THEATRE, INC.
Thomas Jefferson Community Center, 3501 2nd Street, Arlington (most shows)

HOURS: Nov., Dec., March, June & Aug.: usually 3 & 7:30 or 2:30 & 8. **COST:** $8 adults, $6 students. **PHONE:** 703/548-1154.

The Children's Theatre isn't just *for* children — it's *by* children. Youngsters aged 9 to 21 are involved in all aspects of producing shows of this non-profit group, from casting to directing to acting. The young actors have taken the group's many classes. (Don't worry: A team of skilled professionals helps give substance to the kids' imaginings.) The Children's Theatre's season includes recognizable classics, such as "The Jungle Book," "Winnie the Pooh" and "Charlotte's Web." The company produces about five shows a year, with a half-dozen or so performances of each.

Words to the wise: *Remind your children that just because the actors are kids, that doesn't mean they can rush up on stage.*

CLASSIKA THEATER FOR YOUTH
Rosslyn Spectrum, 1601 N. Kent Street, Arlington (most performances)

HOURS: Typically Th-Sat 7, Sun 2 & 6. **COST:** $8 to $12. **PHONE:** 703/908-4870. **METRO STOP:** Rosslyn. ♿

What a concept! Russian émigrés start a kid's company based on theater traditions from the motherland. Will kids and Chekov mix, at least for those who are not offspring of Russian émigrés? While this is not the place to introduce most kids to theater, it should be considered as a horizon-widener. It has resulted in shows with a refreshingly non-American look ("The White Crane," "The Snow Queen," "Zolushka, the Russian Cinderella Story"). Wisely, Classika doesn't aim all productions at the broad 4- to 12-year-old segment. Some are appropriate for preschoolers and slightly older, others for preteens and young teens.

Words to the wise: *Some shows are longer than other kids' offerings (from 50 minutes to two hours). It's good value for the money, but this is another reason why Classika may not be for little ones.*

WOLF TRAP
1551 Trap Road, Vienna
PHONE: 703/255-1892. **WEB:** www.wolf-trap.org.

Wolf Trap is the only U.S. national park dedicated to the performing arts. Set on hundreds of acres of Virginia countryside, the park is a good place to explore, and well-behaved children may enjoy "adult" performances on the lawn of a Filene Center show. Wolf Trap also offers special programming for children:

A. CHILDREN'S THEATRE-IN-THE-WOODS   ♿
This outdoor venue's program features free family entertainment in July and August (call for current dates). Clowns, mimes, dancers, puppets and plays are some typical offerings, and workshops for ages 4 and up give tykes a chance to work closely with the performers. Reservations can be made starting in June, and the series usually is filled by the time the shows begin.

NOTES: You need to call ahead for wheelchair access (703/255-1827).

B. INTERNATIONAL CHILDREN'S FESTIVAL   ♿

At least once, every family should try to visit the International Children's Festival, held in mid-September (again, you'll need to call for current dates). Using the Filene Stage, it gathers acts from around the world, from Chinese tumblers to Scandinavian dancers. Best of all, they're *young* Chinese tumblers and Scandinavian dancers. Wolf Trap brings in some very talented children, and grown-up Americans perform, too. (Bob McGrath from "Sesame Street" has been coming for years.) Out in a meadow are tents filled with arts and crafts projects, storytellers and face painters. The face painters, restricted to painting the flags of countries being celebrated, are a tad disappointing, but kids seem to like everything else, especially rolling like runaway logs down a gently sloping hill. Costs for the festival: $10 for adults, $8 for kids 3-12 and seniors.

NOTES: For this, too, you need to call ahead for wheelchair access (703/255-1800).

Directions: *From the Beltway, take the Dulles Toll Rd. exit (have change for the toll) to Trap Rd. and the park.*

MUSIC

KENNEDY CENTER
New Hampshire Avenue and F Street NW

PHONE: 202/467-4600. **METRO STOP:** Foggy Bottom (free shuttle bus every 15 minutes). **WEB:** www.kennedy-center.org/nso.

Something melodic is almost always going on at the Kennedy Center, from opera to classical music. Not all of it is family-appropriate or family-affordable. Here are a few children-specific options:

A. MILLENNIUM STAGE   ♿

The Millennium Stage's free music concerts start every evening at 6 at one end of the Kennedy Center's massive, red-carpeted lobby. Offerings range from gospel to classical, with a fair amount of family fare. Given the freeform nature of the performances, they're perfect for introducing kids of all ages to different types of music.

B. KINDERCONZERTS   ♿

If you have a son or daughter who is grudgingly slogging through piano, clarinet or violin lessons, take them to a Kinderconzert — hour-long presentations aimed at children as young as 4 (though, frankly, 4-year-olds may fidget). Members of the National Symphony Orchestra demonstrate how they play their instruments and ably convey such simple concepts as melody and rhythm. They also answer questions from the children. The performances are given once a month on varying dates during the school year (call for current times) and generally cost $7.50 to $12.50.

C. NSO FAMILY CONCERTS ♿

You also should consider one of the National Symphony Orchestra's Family Concerts, for ages 5 and up. In an age of cheesy, recorded music, it's remarkable the effect on children of a professional coaxing beautiful sounds out of an oboe or harp. Some children can't seem to believe it's real. **Words to the wise:** Arrive in time for the "instrument petting zoo." Children can spend the 45 minutes before the performance getting a close-up look at various instruments, even if they can't "pet" the $12,000 sterling silver flute.

WASHINGTON CHAMBER SYMPHONY
At the Kennedy Center, New Hampshire Avenue and F Street NW

HOURS: Nov.-May: Sat or Sun 2:30. **COST:** $9-$32.50 (holiday performances); $22.50 (other performances). **PHONE:** 202/452-1321.

This local orchestra has a well-deserved reputation for introducing kids to serious music in a way that's anything but. Workbooks, sing-alongs, narration, onstage visits — anything is fair game. There are two Family Series concerts a year, appropriate for kids as young as 4. The symphony's eight annual Concerts for Young People are for 6 and up. Conductor Stephen Simon educates as well as entertains. He has composed works based on "Casey at the Bat" and "Mike Mulligan and the Steam Shovel," and even has put together an orchestra composed entirely of girls under 18 (a re-creation of something Vivaldi did).

Words to the wise: *Like anything that mixes the seemingly high brow with the invitingly accessible, the concerts tend to sell out fast.*

GETTING IN on the ACT

SUPERSTAR STUDIOS
7766 Woodmont Ave., Bethesda, Md

HOURS: Weekdays 10-6; weekends by appointment. **COST:** A music video for one person singing one song is $20.95; $2.50 for each additional person. Duplicate tapes are $5 each. Birthday parties (recommended for age 8 and up) are $10 a person, $125 minimum. **PHONE:** 301/913-0203. ♿

SuperStar, great for natural-born hams, might best be described as video karaoke. Kids pick a song, choose a few props (maracas, tambourine, microphone), don funky sunglasses and then smile for the camera. Young "singers" lip-synch to songs while staff in the control room punch in various backgrounds and special effects. You leave with a finished music video and, perhaps, a desire to make the leap to MTV. Need we note that this is a great place for parties?

Words to the wise: *Don't have the kids wear blue or purple or they'll fade into the blue-screen backdrop.*

DINNER THEATERS

NOT LONG AGO, local dinner theaters cottoned to the idea of using their stages on normally dark Saturday mornings or early afternoons. The plays they present tend to be the child equivalent of their grown-up fare: familiar workhorses. Food isn't included in the ticket price, which may be just as well. If you've ever eaten at a dinner theater, you know why. Here's one in Virginia, another in Maryland:

WEST END DINNER THEATRE. 4615 Duke St., Alexandria, Va. **Hours:** Sat at 2. **Reservations:** Recommended. **Cost:** $6. **Phone:** 703/370-2500. ♿

WAY OFF BROADWAY DINNER THEATER. 5 Willowdale Dr., Willowtree Plaza off Route 40, Frederick, Md. **Hours:** Sat at 12:30. **Reservations:** Recommended. **Cost:** $8.50. **Phone:** 301/662-6600. ♿

7

☆N the FARM

IF YOU HAD BEEN BORN 150 years ago, you probably would have been intimately familiar with the business end of a dairy cow, the dietary peculiarities of hogs and other aspects of farming. Today you're more likely to be abducted by aliens than to, say, slaughter a chicken. And your children? They seem to think that McNuggets grow on trees, right next to babbling brooks filled with chocolate milk. That's why a visit to a farm can be such an eye-opener.

Many area parks departments operate farms. These invariably are referred to as "working farms," despite the fact that a working farm of the late 20th Century probably is owned by a multinational conglomerate. That makes most of the farms here lessons in history as well as in animal husbandry: They recount farm life from the 18th or 19th centuries. Children will get a taste of the hardships of rural life and even may be thankful that a chore for them is emptying the dishwasher or taking out the garbage, not plowing the back 40. But any sense of perspective probably will be overwhelmed by the moos of cows, the quacks of ducks and the baaas of sheep. Animals are what kids find most appealing about farms, and these places are filled with them. Remember to dress appropriately: old jeans, boots if you have them. And that smell? That's a farm, kid.

Maryland

NATIONAL COLONIAL FARM
3400 Bryan Point Road, Accokeek

HOURS: Daily, dawn to dusk. Visitors center: Tu-Sun 10-4. **COST:** $2 adults, 50 cents under 12; $5 maximum per family. **PHONE:** 301/283-2113.

This is the best-funded and most impressive local "history" farm. Operated as a typical family farm of the 18th Century, its fields are tended with reproduction tools, the animals and plants are raised by 1700s methods, and the farm buildings have been impressively restored. It's useful for kids to think of the farm as a vivid example of the hardscrabble existence "the other half" carved out while George Washington lived in neo-regal splendor right across the Potomac at Mount Vernon. Highlights include the one-room house with sleeping loft that could hold a family of eight, plus the chance for your kids to grind corn kernels into flour, work the butter churn or check out the few simple implements the family used. Docents in period garb are enthusiastic and well informed. Elsewhere there's a spooky tobacco barn, several excellent period gardens and animals either let loose or penned with the simple twig-and-stick fences of the time. Head toward the river and the beautiful view of Mount Vernon and the Potomac nearly rocks you back on your heels. There are several excellent hiking and birding trails on this and adjacent properties, one leading to the wonderful Ecosystem Farm.

Words to the wise: *Don't go Monday, when the visitors center, which has lovely Colonial-era toys and Native American items, is closed.*

NOTES: Wheelchair access to the visitors center is good, but trails may be difficult to negotiate when the grounds are wet.

OLD MARYLAND FARM
Watkins Regional Park, 301 Watkins Park Drive (Enterprise Road/Route 193), Upper Marlboro

HOURS: Tu-F 10-2:30, weekends 11:30-4:30. **COST:** Free. Birthday package: $60 for 12 children, $5 per extra child (includes farm tour, nature craft, hayride and use of meeting room). **PHONE:** 301/249-7077 (TDD: 301/699-2544).   ♿

While not quite as ambitious as larger living-history farms in the area, Old Maryland Farm still delivers where it counts: with some 70-odd animals, including goats, sheep, chickens, rabbits, peafowl, turkeys, a hog, a donkey, a cow and a pony, all in an easily negotiated semicircular arrangement of pens. Produce and herb gardens round out the agricultural attractions. The staff is energetic and welcoming and the farm offers a relatively inexpensive birthday party package. Watkins Regional Park also features a miniature train, a miniature golf course and a (full-size) carousel and nature center.

Words to the wise: *"Livestock Lunchtime" is the best time to be here. Visitors can assist in feeding the animals Tuesday through Sunday at noon.*

Nearby: Adventure World.

Directions: *Take the Beltway to Central Ave./Route 214 East to a right at Enterprise Rd./Route 193.*

OXON COVE PARK
6411 Oxon Hill Road, Oxon Hill

HOURS: Daily 9-4:30. **COST:** Free admission. **PHONE:** 301/839-1176 (TDD: 301/839-1783).   ♿

This demonstration farm recreates an area family farm of the early 1900s, many years later than the farm life depicted at nearby National Colonial Farm.

Here the fascination derives less from the history lesson than from observing and, yes, interacting with farm animals. Kids can milk cows, feed chickens and gather eggs as well as pet the sheep and calves. The Cove (formerly known as Oxon Hill Farm) has a great family hiking trail with spectacular Potomac views and signage explaining how folks of yore lived off the land. On weekdays, make reservations to milk cows; on weekends it's first-come, first-served.

Words to the wise: *Oxon Cove is better for small kids, while National Colonial Farm probably will be more interesting to the 8-and-up crowd. Don't try to do both in a day; you'll be farmed out.*

NOTES: There's no food here, though you can picnic. Visitors with mobility problems may have some difficulty. **Nearby:** Fort Washington, National Colonial Farm.

Directions: *From the Beltway, take Exit 3A (Indian Head Hwy./Route 210) south and make an immediate right onto Oxon Hill Rd.*

CARROLL COUNTY FARM MUSEUM
500 S. Center Street, Westminster
HOURS: May-Oct.: weekends noon-5; July-Aug.: weekdays 10-4; closed M. **COST:** $3 adults, $2 kids 7-18 and seniors, under 7 free. **PHONE:** 410/876-2667 or 800/654-4645. ♿

Another county, another farm museum. This one showcases farm life in the late 1800s, with various exhibits in different buildings, including a farmhouse, a wagon shed, a carriage- and tool-filled barn and a one-room schoolhouse. Tour guides are in attire appropriate to the era, and volunteer artisans demonstrate such waning skills as blacksmithing, quilting, spinning, broom making and cooking over an open hearth. Oh, yes, there are animals too: sheep, pigs, goats, rabbits, ducks, turkeys and peacocks. The animal inhabitants, however, are strictly for observation. The buildings are surrounded by lots of green lawn that kids enjoy tearing across.

Words to the wise: *There are demonstrations every weekend, but they're all different. Call ahead to find out what's on the schedule.*

Directions: *Take I-270 to I-70 northwest to Route 97 north. Then turn left on Route 32 north and take that to Center St. and the farm.*

BELTSVILLE AGRICULTURAL RESEARCH CENTER
Agricultural Research Service National Visitor Center, Building 302, Log Lodge (on Powder Mill Road/Route 212), Beltsville
TOUR HOURS: Weekdays 10 and 1. **RESERVATIONS:** Recommended. **COST:** Free. **PHONE:** 301/504-8438.

This massive (7,000 acres) research facility near Route 1 and the Beltway is the agricultural equivalent of the National Institutes of Health. While scientists at NIH toil against diseases, scientists in Beltsville work on creating better foods, ones that are easier to grow and more healthful. You could easily make a meal with the breakthroughs developed here, including the dwarf apple tree, the disease-resistant potato and the low-fat hog. After seeing a short introductory film, visitors on this two-hour guided tour get on and off a bus as it stops at various sites. You'll see cows (including some sporting portholes so researchers can watch digestion in action), but you won't be able to touch any.

Words to the wise: *Kids below 4th grade probably won't enjoy this tour, which is best for older children interested in the science side of agriculture.*

Nearby: College Park Aviation Museum.

Virginia

CLAUDE MOORE COLONIAL FARM
6310 Georgetown Pike, McLean

HOURS: W-Sun 10-4:30; closed Jan.-Mar. and rainy days. COST: $2 adults, $1 kids 3-12 and seniors. PHONE: 703/442-7557.

Of the area's several Colonial-era farms, this is the most modest and least developed, and that's the source of its charm. No fancy paving or elaborate signage here; footpaths lead to pastures, a small barn, a single-room house and an orchard. A huge turkey lives in an enclosure of sticks. The farm is worked, by hand, by volunteers in period clothing, making clear the difficulties of working land with nothing but simple hand tools. Our kids were at first confused, but ultimately amused, by the wonderfully poker-faced child volunteers who earnestly played the role of 18th Century farm kids. If you're looking for production value demonstrations, it's best to wait for special events, which include musical performances and special demonstrations; call for a schedule.

Words to the wise: *This place will be difficult for the disabled, or for kids in that awkward age between backpack-riding and full mobility.*

Directions: *From the Beltway, take Georgetown Pike/Route 193 east. The park is on the left.*

KIDWELL FARM
Frying Pan Park, 2709 West Ox Road, Herndon

HOURS: Daily 10-6. COST: Free (though there is a charge for some special events). PHONE: 703/437-9101. &

This 100-acre working farm in Fairfax County recreates agricultural life from the 1930s, when family farms were first starting to experience the introduction of technology. The tractors, grain binder and other equipment on display — and in use — captivate kids, but just as appealing are the non-mechanical fixtures: horses, cows, pigs, ducks, chickens, goats, rabbits, sheep and peacocks. There's even a celebrity: The ceremonial presidential turkey, presented to and then pardoned by the chief executive, lives out its days at Kidwell Farm.

Words to the wise: *Domestic wildfowl not enough for your kids? Check out the adjacent equestrian center. Most weekends it's the setting for horse, livestock and dog shows. Call for information.*

NOTES: Bring your own food.

Directions: *From the Beltway, take I-66 west to Route 50 west. Turn right on Fairfax County Pkwy., then left on West Ox Rd. The farm is 1.5 miles on the right.*

HOOFING IT

THE LAND OF LITTLE HORSES
125 Glenwood Drive, Gettysburg, Pa.

HOURS: April-Labor Day: daily 10-5; Labor Day-Oct.: weekends 10-5. **COST:** $6.50 adults, $4.50 2-12. Carousel rides: 50 cents; carriage and train rides: $1; saddle rides: $2. **PHONE:** 717/334-7259. ♿

TALK ABOUT your pocket ponies. Horses at this Pennsylvania farm have been bred to grow no taller than about three feet high. The mini mares and puny ponies are entrancing, if more than a little odd. Be prepared for cries of, "Oh, Daddy, can I have one? I'll keep it in my room and feed it table scraps." There's also a carousel (featuring regular-size horses) and hayrides.

PICK-YOUR-OWN FARMS

WHAT MIGHT BE condemned as unfair child labor is instead celebrated every spring, as fruit bushes ripen all over rural Maryland and Virginia and families spread out across pick-your-own strawberry fields. Depending on the weather, strawberry picking starts around mid-May. Then come blueberries and raspberries, generally ripening in mid-June, with blackberries and peaches following in July, grapes in August and apples in September. Many farms listed here also have salad greens and other vegetables, but it's hard to imagine kids having much fun picking *that*.

Prices vary from season to season, but strawberries — the most popular produce for kid-picking —generally cost about $1 a pound. Most places will give or sell you baskets, but it's best to be prepared with your own containers.

Since these are small, family operations whose hours and supplies can change daily, and since some are not easy to find without detailed directions, always call before you visit.

Wear old clothes and keep an eye on children to make sure they're not destroying as much as they're picking (or that *too* much isn't going from plant to mouth rather than plant to bag — though some sampling is to be expected). Be especially watchful for bees, who like the sweet scent of ripening fruit.

Produce picking is hard work: You'll be dirty, dusty and dog-tired. And be mindful that the urge to pick "just one more" will be replaced when you get home with: "Where will I put all these dang things?"

Maryland

Baltimore County
HUBER'S FARM. Strawberries and an array of vegetables, pumpkins and other produce. 12208 Old Philadelphia Rd., Bradshaw. 410/679-4018 or 410/679-1941.

MOORE'S ORCHARD. Peaches, apples. 5242 E. Joppa Rd., Perry Hall. 410/256-5982.

WEBER'S CIDER MILL FARM. Apples. 2526 Proctor Lane, Parkville. 410/668-4488.

Calvert County
SEIDEL FARM. Thornless blackberries, grapes. 2790 Plum Point Rd. (Route 263), Huntingtown. 410/535-2128.

Carroll County
BAUGHER'S ORCHARD. Strawberries, sweet and sour cherries, black raspberries, peas, green beans. 1236 Baugher Rd., about three miles west of Westminster on Route 140. 410/857-0111 or 410/848-5541.

SEWELL'S FARM. Strawberries. 3400 Harney Rd., Taneytown. 410/756-4397.

Charles County
ROSE HILL FARM. Strawberries. On Route 6 in Port Tobacco, about three miles west of La Plata. 301/934-4006.

Frederick County
CATOCTIN MOUNTAIN ORCHARD. Strawberries, blackberries, black raspberries, blueberries, sweet and sour cherries. On U.S. 15, north of Thurmont. 301/271-2737.

GLADE-LINK FARMS. Strawberries, blueberries, red raspberries, vegetables. Route 194, New Midway. 301/898-7131.

MAYNES FARM. Strawberries. 3420 Buckeystown Pike, Buckeystown. 301/662-4320.

PRYOR'S ORCHARD. Blueberries, sweet and sour cherries. 13841-B Pryor Rd., Thurmont. 301/271-2693.

Howard County

LARRILAND FARM. Strawberries, blackberries, black and red raspberries, peaches, sour cherries, blueberries, apples, vegetables. 2415 Woodbine Rd. (Route 94), three miles south of I-70 Exit 73, near Lisbon. 301/854-6110 or 410/442-2605.

SHARP'S FARM. Strawberries. 4003 Jennings Chapel Rd., Brookeville. 301/854-6275.

Montgomery County

BECRAFT'S FARM. Strawberries, blueberries, vegetables. 14722 New Hampshire Ave., Silver Spring. 301/236-4545.

BUTLER'S ORCHARD. Strawberries, blueberries, red raspberries, vegetables. 22200 Davis Mill Rd., Germantown. 301/972-3299.

HOMESTEAD FARM. Strawberries, blackberries, black and red raspberries, apples, vegetables. 15600 Sugarland Rd., Poolesville. 301/977-3761.

ROCK HILL ORCHARD. Strawberries, sour cherries, blackberries, red raspberries, apples, vegetables. 28600 Ridge Rd., Mount Airy. 301/831-7427.

Prince George's County

CHERRY HILL FARM. Strawberries, red raspberries, blackberries, peaches, nectarines, apples. 12300 Gallahan Rd., Clinton. 301/292-1928 or 301/292-4642.

JOHNSON'S BERRY FARM. Strawberries, thornless blackberries, black and red raspberries, blueberries, sour cherries. 17000 Swanson Rd., Upper Marlboro. 301/627-8316.

MILLER FARMS. Strawberries, vegetables. 10140 Piscataway Rd., Clinton. 301/297-9370.

St. Mary's County

OWEN'S BERRY FARM. Blackberries. Route 235, two miles south of Lexington Park. 301/862-3427.

Virginia

Fairfax County

POTOMAC VEGETABLE FARMS. Raspberries, blackberries. 9627 Leesburg Pike, four miles west of Tysons Corner. 703/759-2119.

Fauquier County

HARTLAND ORCHARD. Sour cherries, peaches, apples. In Markham; from I-66 Exit 18, north on Leeds Manor Rd. (Route 688), west on Belle Meade Rd. (F-284), follow signs one mile to orchard. 540/364-2316.

LINDEN VINEYARDS. Blueberries, apples. In Linden; from I-66 Exit 13, east on Route 55, south on Route 638 two miles to signs. 540/364-1997.

STRIBLING ORCHARD. Peaches, grapes, apples. On Route 688 off I-66 Exit 18 in Markham. 540/364-3040.

WILLOW OAKS BLUEBERRY FARM. Blueberries. At Midland Rd. (Route 610) and Bristersburg Rd. (Route 616), Somerville. 540/788-1086.

King George County
RICK & VAN'S. Strawberries, vegetables. On Route 3, 12 miles east of Fredericksburg. 540/775-7890.

Loudoun County
CROOKED RUN ORCHARD. Strawberries, blackberries, apples. On Business Route 7 at Route 287, between Purcellville and Hamilton. 540/338-6642.

Orange County
DOUBLE B FARMS. Strawberries, thornless blackberries. In Rhoadesville; from Fredericksburg, Route 3 west 11 miles to Route 20, south nine miles to signs. 540/854-4277.

MOORMONT ORCHARDS. Pears, plums, cherries, peaches, summer and fall apples, grapes. 6530 Moormont Rd. (Route 697), Rapidan. 540/672-2730.

Rappahannock County
MUSKRAT HAVEN. Strawberries, blueberries, thornless blackberries, red raspberries, peaches, nectarines, apples, vegetables. On Route 211, four miles west of Amissville. 540/937-5892.

Spotsylvania County
BELVEDERE PLANTATION. Strawberries, blueberries, raspberries, vegetables. 1601 Belvedere Dr. On Route 17 seven miles southeast of Fredericksburg. 540/371-8494.

FINNEGAN'S BERRY FARM. Blackberries, raspberries and blueberries. 5701 Partlow Rd., Spotsylvania. 540/582-5668.

SNEAD'S ASPARAGUS FARM. Strawberries. About 12 miles southeast of Fredericksburg on Route 17. 540/371-9328.

FARM FRESH

THESE TWO privately run farms open their barn doors to young visitors. Hours are sometimes sporadic, so call before you visit.

CEDARVALE FARM
2915 Coale Lane, Churchville, Md.
HOURS: Sun 1-5. **COST:** Free. **PHONE:** 410/734-7467.

This farm north of Baltimore probably is too far away for a casual visit, but it's the place to go if your offspring are interested in its main claim to fame: a small herd of bison. Paul and Emily Hines maintain the 20-head herd to show how Native Americans once used the versatile beasts. You can see the bison through a fence even if the farmers aren't there. Bring apples and stale bread to feed them through the fence (the buffalo, not the farmers).

NOTES: Nothing is paved, so wheelchair access is limited.
Directions: *From I-95, take Exit 80 (Route 543) toward Churchville. Turn right on Route 136. The farm is three miles up on the right.*

CIDER MILL FARM
5012 Landing Road, Elkridge, Md.
HOURS: Apr.-June: daily 9-3; Sept.-Thanksgiving: daily 10-6; closed Dec.-Mar. Guided tours on weekdays. **COST:** Petting farm $1.50 for kids 12 months and up, hayrides $1.25, pony rides $2. **PHONE:** 410/788-9595.

This Howard County farm features a well-equipped petting zoo (chickens, ducks, goats, sheep, cows, rabbits, etc.), but its main distinction is its functioning cider mill. If you've ever wondered how apples make the transition from solid to liquid, this is the place to visit. Special activities (hayrides, pony rides, music and dance) are offered often. There's room to picnic.

Directions: *From the Beltway, take Colesville Rd. (Route 29) north past Columbia to Route 100 east. Go right on Montgomery Rd. (Route 103). Then turn left on Ilchester Rd. and right on Landing Rd. to the second driveway on the right.*

8

NATURE and the OUTDOORS

AH, WILDERNESS! (Or at least a reasonable facsimile thereof.) Some times you've just got to get outside. So here we explore family-friendly outdoor attractions, most close to the metropolitan area. Many are nature centers, fiendishly inviting places for kids. They're filled with neat stuff: animal skins, turtles in fish tanks, plaster casts of animal footprints and the like. Most of the area's larger parks have some sort of nature center, and we've provided thumbnail sketches of what they offer. The centers all have special programs for kids. Call for specific information or to get on mailing lists.

We go into more detail on a few notable places that operate outside the traditional nature center universe. Some have visitors centers, others don't. We've also included a few outdoor trails, paved or level, that are perfect destinations for kids in strollers or people with mobility problems. Finally, you'll find sections here on beautiful gardens and nearby commercial caverns. The caverns technically aren't "outside," but they're natural, which was good enough for us. Though we've included several places outside this book's general 40-mile radius, we've had to leave out a lot of other popular spots beyond that range, lest this chapter became a book unto itself. For information on more distant attractions, including those in West Virginia and Pennsylvania, see The Washington Post's WEEKEND and TRAVEL sections, its Wednesday ESCAPES page, its ESCAPE PLANS getaways book and its WASHINGTON POST GARDEN BOOK, or check the OUTDOORS AND RECREATION section of www.washingtonpost.com.

Maryland

DISCOVERY CREEK CHILDREN'S MUSEUM
7300 MacArthur Boulevard, Glen Echo

HOURS: Weekends. **COST:** From $8 for regular sessions to $15 for more elaborate "Outdoor Adventures." **PHONE:** 202/364-3111. **WEB:** www.discoverycreek.org.

Several years ago, Discovery Creek set up shop in Washington's sole remaining one-room school house, organizing a continuing series of truly fun and insinuatingly educational programs. Now they've upped the ante and moved to a new facility at a site destined to give them more visibility: Glen Echo Park. They've turned the park's stable into an exhibition and classroom space, planted a children's garden in the former paddock area and are offering programs on everything from fossil collecting to ant behavior to aquatic animals. Activities are by reservation, typically on Saturdays (but call for details), and usually include instruction, live animal demonstrations, crafts and a hike down to nearby Minehaha Creek. The real stars are the teachers, who involve and inspire their young charges, whether it's getting them to pretend to be a fish or having them turn over a rock to see what lives underneath. Discovery Creek still has facilities on MacArthur Boulevard in Washington, but that location is mainly for school groups. Depending on the success of its new Glen Echo site, the museum eventually may offer programs in both places.

Words to the Wise: *Reservations are a must.*

Nearby: Glen Echo Park and Carousel, Adventure Theatre, Puppet Company, Clara Barton House.

AUDUBON NATURALIST SOCIETY
8940 Jones Mill Road, Chevy Chase

HOURS: Grounds daily dawn-dusk; bookshop weekdays 10-6 (Th 10-8), Sat 9-5, Sun 12-5. Woodend house: weekdays 9-5. **COST**: Free. **PHONE**: 301/652-5964; 301/652-3606 (Woodend store); 301/652-1088 (recorded bird sighting information). **WEB**: www.audubonnaturalist.org.

This 40-acre nature preserve is wedged between the Capital Beltway, Connecticut Avenue and East West Highway, but its grounds are serene and loaded with small animal life. A hilly path winds around the property. While the self-guided hiking paths cover plenty of ground, they're also accommodating places for the sort of very young hikers who may poop out within half a mile. Woodend, the property's impressive Georgian-style estate designed by National Gallery and Jefferson Memorial architect John Russell Pope, serves as headquarters for the society, which is dedicated to preserving habitat for birds and other creatures. During the week there, you can see a collection of nearly 600 bird species. The society offers numerous educational programs for all ages.

Words to the wise: *The house is rented for events such as weddings, so you may find it overrun on a weekend and its bathroom inaccessible.*

NOTES: There's neither food nor picnicking here.

Directions: *From the Beltway, take Connecticut Ave. south. Turn left on Manor Rd., right on Jones Bridge Rd. and left on Jones Mill Rd. The society is on the left.*

NATIONAL WILDLIFE VISITORS CENTER
10901 Scarlet Tanager Loop, Laurel

HOURS: Daily 10-5:30. **COST**: Free; tram tours: $2 adults, $1 kids 12 and under and seniors. **PHONE**: 301/497-5760. **WEB**: www.pwrc.nbs.gov. ♿

This inviting facility on the grounds of the Patuxent Wildlife Research Center combines the best of several worlds. It's a wildlife refuge crawling with critters. It's a large, airy building filled with exhibits on the environment. Best of all, it isn't swarmed with tourists. Inside the visitors center building itself are relatively standard-issue exhibits on such ecosystems as those of the Chesapeake Bay and America's prairies. There's lots of wall text to read, knobs to turn and answers to reveal; a child's involvement will depend on age and interest level. Oddly compelling is a collection of stuffed animals depicted in naturalistic settings, half-hidden behind frosted glass. Outside, the hiking trails are short and manageable (none is longer than 1.4 miles, and the shortest is less than a quarter mile, perfect for easily tired legs). But the best thing is the 40-person electric tram that takes a loop through the compound. The 30-minute tour's unhurried pace and concise narration make it a pleasant centerpiece to a visit. Other amenities: A small gift shop stocks plush animals, nature books and artwork. Nature films are shown on a regular basis. Fishing is allowed in Cash Lake (catch and release only).

Words to the wise: *The tram runs weekends March through November but does not always run on weekdays. Call ahead for information.*

NOTES: There's no food, and picnicking is not allowed. **Disability Access:** The tram is accessible for the wheelchair-bound, and the 0.3-mile Loop Trail is paved and excellent for strollers or wheelchairs.

Directions: *From the Beltway, take the Baltimore-Washington Pkwy. north to Powder Mill Rd. east. The center is on the right.*

BATTLE CREEK CYPRESS SWAMP SANCTUARY
South of Prince Frederick, Calvert County

HOURS: April-Oct. daily 10-5 (Nov.-March until 4:30). COST: Free. PHONE: 410/535-5327.

This is an interesting nature stop to make while on a journey to Southern Maryland. Massive cypress trees — some as much as six feet in diameter — stand tall in this swamp, their knobby "knees" jutting up from tea-colored water. Squirrels and birds dart among the cypress, and dragonflies buzz all about. A boardwalk leads through the swamp (operated by the Nature Conservancy, it's the only one of its kind in Maryland). While the oddly shaped trees themselves are the star attraction, the sanctuary's nature center displays other interesting residents — from snakes to opossum, salamanders to turtles — and features a typical hands-on area.

Words to the wise: *Put non-walkers in a backpack, not a stroller, to negotiate the boardwalk. Wear long socks, and bring insect repellent during the summer.*

Directions: *From the Beltway, take Route 4 southeast through the town of Prince Frederick. Hang a right on Route 506 and a left onto Gray's Rd. to the sanctuary.*

PATUXENT RIVER PARK/JUG BAY NATURAL AREA
16000 Croom Airport Road, Upper Marlboro

HOURS: Daily 8-dusk. **COST:** $5 per car for Prince George's and Montgomery County residents, $7 for nonresidents. **PHONE:** 301/627-6074 (TDD: 301/699-2544). **WEB:** www.smart.net/~parksrec. &

Patuxent River Park is a collection of natural and man-made attractions scattered across 2,000 acres hugging the banks of the Patuxent. Nature trails lead off from the parking lot, none too rigorous. Planked walkways take you over a marshy area heavy with cattails and lilies. It's not unusual to spot turtles, herons, even a bald eagle. Kayaks and canoes can be rented (call for reservations), and larger groups can arrange for a guided trip on a pontoon boat. Among the other attractions is Patuxent Village, an assortment of log buildings — a house, a tobacco-packing barn, a smokehouse — showing how life was lived along the river in the 19th Century. The log cabin has a sleeping loft that kids enjoy climbing up to, and if the whole thing looks a little dirty and cobwebby, well, that's what rural houses were like in the days before linoleum. The **DUVALL TOOL MUSEUM** (open 1-4 Sun, Apr.-Oct.) displays hundreds of antique tools, including a foot-operated dentist drill and sturdy-looking implements that once cut, drilled, compressed, chiseled, squeezed and shaped everything from wood to butter.

Adjacent to Jug Bay is the **MERKLE WILDLIFE SANCTUARY** (301/888-1410; TDD: 410/974-3683; $2-per-vehicle fee &), 2,000 acres of marsh, woods and ponds. Sundays between 10 and 3, you can go on a driving tour of the sanctuary. At about the drive's halfway point is an observation tower children might enjoy tackling, and at the end is a nice visitors center (open daily 10 to 4). It features live animals (snakes, turtles), objects for kids to handle, crafts for them to do and, best of all, big picture windows overlooking a field that is invariably filled with geese. Bring binoculars if you want to do some bird watching.

> **Words to the wise:** *If you doubt your ability to engage your offspring at this subtle natural site, it might be better to check when a special kid program is going on. These include storytelling and guided hikes.*

Directions: *From the Beltway, take Route 4 southeast to Route 301 south. Then make three lefts: on Croom Station Rd., Croom Rd. and Croom Airport Rd.*

CATOCTIN MOUNTAIN/CUNNINGHAM FALLS PARKS

Both the U.S. and Maryland governments manage chunks of this 10,000-acre mountain wilderness and recreation area, but we'll consider them a single destination. About 60 miles from Washington, the parks are the closest substantial chunk of wild mountain land to the metropolitan area. If you're headed this way, you can visit either or both and feel confident that you'll have a refreshing outdoor getaway.

NOTES: For **Food,** Cunningham's concession area is very modest, and it operates only in-season, so bring snacks and water or be prepared to buy them in Thurmont, which has a couple of country-style family restaurants. **Nearby:** The private Catoctin Mountain Zoo (see Chapter 1 on zoos). To make a two- or three-day visit of it, both areas have camping (cabins in Catoctin, camp sites in Cunningham Falls), and Thurmont has a couple of inexpensive family-style hotels.

Directions: *Take I-495 to I-270 North to Frederick. Pick up Route 15 north to Route 77 west and follow signs to either park. Catoctin Mountain Park lies to the north of Route 77, Cunningham Falls to the south.*

CATOCTIN MOUNTAIN PARK
Off Route 77/6602 Foxville Road, Thurmont

HOURS: Trails daily, daylight to dark; visitors center weekends 8:30-5, weekdays 10-4:30. **COST:** Free. **PHONE:** 301/663-9388. Cabin reservations: 301/271-3140 (bathhouses at cabins not wheelchair accessible). **WEB:** www.nps.gov/cato.

Among other things, the park offers hiking trails that lead to interesting and challenging geologic structures, plus in-season ranger talks about the Whiskey Still Trail, providing a peek into the world of mountain bootlegging during Prohibition. The park also is home to the President's mountain retreat, Camp David (closed to the public, of course). You can get a guide to the park at the visitor's center off Route 77. Four trails are worth noting for family day trips: Spicebush Nature Trail, an asphalt path that's good for both strollers and wheelchairs (park at the Chestnut Picnic area); Hog Rock Nature Trail (a modest 1.5-mile loop); Wolf Rock, a tough climb ending at a high rock with superb overlooks and riven with deep crevices (not for toddlers, but the 8-and-up set will love this hike); and Falls Trail, which leads to the falls over on the state side of the park. Rustic cabins in the Misty Mount area are available from April through October.

NOTES: Disability access to the visitors center is good.

CUNNINGHAM FALLS STATE PARK
14039 Catoctin Hollow Road, Thurmont

HOURS: Daily 8-sunset (Nov.-Apr. 10-sunset). **COST:** Memorial Day-Labor Day weekends $3, weekdays $2 (various lower off-season fees), children in car seats and seniors free. **PHONE:** 301/271-7574. **WEB:** www.fred.net/fredrick/CunninghamFalls.html.

Cunningham offers, among other things, swimming, boating and fishing at the park's 43-acre lake and hikes to the 79-foot-falls. There are two major areas to the park: the Manor area, accessed off Route 15, and the William Houck area, off Route 77 west. Start at the Manor, where you'll find a big parking lot, the 43-acre Hunting Creek Lake and several well-blazed trails that lead to Cunningham Falls. In season, you can rent boats and aqua-cycles for the lake. There's a bathhouse and beaches, so bring bathing suits or shorts. In the spring, maple syrup demonstrations are given. Once you make it to Cunningham Falls, agile kids 8 and up can climb the rocks along the falls, perhaps all the way to the top. For camping, you need to make reservations up to a year in advance.

Notes: The small parking lot beside Route 77 opens to a wheelchair-accessible path, part boardwalk and part hard-packed gravel, to the base of Cunningham Falls. If you have toddlers, seniors or strollers, this is the way to approach the falls.

CALVERT CLIFFS STATE PARK
765 Middleham Chapel Road and Route 765, Prince Frederick

HOURS: Daily dawn-dusk. PHONE: 301/888-1410; 301/872-5688. COST: Suggested donation $2 per car.

Located in Calvert County, this park is a long haul from practically anywhere in the Washington area, but it's worth it. A two-mile hike through a piney forest and cypress swamp leads to a spectacular mile-long span of cliffs and a bracing view of the Chesapeake Bay. Better yet, the cliffs are filled with Miocene-era marine fossils, allegedly 600 varieties, free for the taking on the beach. Our kids could not believe their good fortune to discover, embedded within big gray chunks of sandy stone, fossilized creatures between 8 and 15 million years old. Fossil shark teeth are easy finds. Near the parking lot there's a big play area; save it for when you return from your four-mile round-trip.

Words to the wise: *Because the cliffs are soft and constantly eroding, they aren't safe to climb or explore. Limit fossil hunting to the beach area. This is a serious warning: Not long ago a 12-year-old girl was killed when a part of the cliff collapsed on her and her father. It's also a long haul to the cliffs and back (45 minutes each way). Bring a pack loaded with water, snacks, tissues, binoculars, a small hammer, a plastic container and Ziploc bags for your finds. In spring and fall, dress everybody in layers; the winds off the bay can be powerful and chilling.*

Directions: *From the Beltway, take Route 4 southeast to Upper Marlboro. Pass Upper Marlboro, Prince Frederick, Port Republic; along the way, Route 4 becomes Route 2 and 4. Fourteen miles south of Prince Frederick, look for the sign and turn left into the park.*

SUGARLOAF MOUNTAIN
7901 Comus Road, Dickerson

HOURS: 8 to an hour before sunset. COST: Free. PHONE: 301/874-2024; 301/869-7846. WEB: patc.simplenet.com/sug_loaf.html.

Sugarloaf, which protrudes from the farmlands of Frederick County like a misplaced Western mesa, is one of the area's finest places to take a family hike. It's privately owned and maintained by the Stronghold Foundation, established by the property's owner to permit people to enjoy the pristine little mountain stub

Continued on p. 92

"HIKING" TRAILS for STROLLERS

PUSHING A STROLLER along a hiking trail usually is an exercise in futility. The wheels get stuck in ruts, and the tiny passenger gets shaken up a lot. Paved bike paths are better — as long as you don't mind the constant chorus of "Passing on your left," "Passing on your right" and "Look out! I'm about to hit you!" Luckily, there's a handful of modest paved or planked trails perfect for pushing the Graco or Aprica. They're also ideal for children or grown-ups in wheelchairs or others with mobility problems. The following are in addition to those noted in the entries for the National Wildlife Visitors Center in Laurel, the Huntley Meadows Visitors Center in Alexandria and the Spicebush Nature Trail in Catoctin Mountain Park in Thurmont.

Maryland

CLEARWATER NATURE CENTER. Cosca Regional Park, 11000 Thrift Rd., Clinton, Md. **Phone:** 301/297-4575. A half-mile paved trail loops through some woods, taking hikers past such caged raptors as a great horned owl, a merlin falcon and a red-tailed hawk. ♿

LAKE ARTEMESIA. 55th Ave. and Berwyn Rd., College Park, Md. **Phone:** 301/927-2163. A short, 0.3-mile trail goes around the edge of this man-made lake. ♿

NATURE AND SENSORY TRAIL. Opportunity Park at Allen Pond Park, 3330 Northview Dr., Bowie, Md. **Phone:** 301/262-6200. Seven interactive stations along this short trail through the woods include bark samples, footprints of native animals and recorded bird sounds. The trail is an outgrowth of the totally accessible Opportunity Park. Visitors to Allen Pond Park can also walk on the longer paved trail that encircles the pond. ♿

Virginia

MOUNTAIN LAUREL TRAIL. National Wildlife Federation's Laurel Ridge Conservation Education Center, 8925 Leesburg Pike, Vienna, Va. **Phone:** 703/790-4437. This half-mile asphalt trail sets out from an office center parking lot before entering an open field and then a shady wood. There are 10 interpretive stops along the way, with signs placed in easy-to-see locations. ♿

PRINCE WILLIAM FOREST PARK. Off Route 619, Triangle, Va.. **Phone:** 703/221-7181.This woodland park features a quarter-mile paved route with audio description along the way, perfect for strollers or persons with disabilities. ♿

RIVERBEND NATURE CENTER. Riverbend Regional Park, 8814 Jeffery Rd., Great Falls, Va. **Phone:** 703/759-9018. This paved third-of-a-mile trail winds through upland forest hard by the Potomac River. ♿

(elevation: 1,282 feet) in perpetuity. Consequently, it's visited mainly by locals who happen to know about it and is rarely as crowded as many national and state parks. Park your car in the highest (West View) lot the first time you visit; a network of well-blazed trails leads to the top. The green-blazed trail from this lot is probably the easiest; the orange-blazed trail is steep. Either way, it's a challenging but safe climb that robust kids 4 and up love to make. (Older kids and energetic parents will enjoy parking at the bottom and climbing the entire mountain, which takes more than an hour.)

The payoff for the hike is spectacular: a broad vista of nearly pristine farmland as far as the eye can see. (Okay, an incinerator smokestack is clearly visible, and you can make out a cluster of Gaithersburg office buildings in the distance, but it's still pretty impressive.) The peak is covered by gigantic chunks of quartzite, and any weekend you're sure to see other parents watching their kids climb around and fighting the urge to bark commands to "be careful!" On a good day, you'll see impressive birds — one time we saw a gorgeous hawk — hanging motionless in the air near the peak, riding the funky air stream that often flutters across this odd bit of geology.

Words to the wise: *This is a largely amenity-free park, so bring snacks and a water bottle or two. You'll find a few picnic tables, but fires aren't permitted. Though the park draws only a couple of hundred visitors on beautiful days, the "go early" rule still applies if your heading for the parking lots near the top, which are small and can fill up quickly.*

NOTES: Nearby are Whites Ferry and Seneca Creek State Park.

Directions: *From the Beltway, take I-270 north to Exit 22. Turn right on Route109; go 2.5 miles and take a right at Comus Rd. Continue for a bit more than 4 miles until you see the entrance on the right.*

Virginia

HUNTLEY MEADOWS PARK
3701 Lockheed Boulevard, Alexandria

HOURS: Daily sunrise-sunset, visitors center M & W-F 9-5, weekends noon-5; closed Jan.-Feb. **COST:** Free. **PHONE:** 703/768-2525. **WEB:** www.fairfaxcounty.resource-management.com. ♿

This place is cool. There's no other word for it. An actual wetland plunked incongruously in the middle of busy Fairfax County, Huntley Meadows is so picturesque that it seems more like a Hollywood re-creation than an actual wetland. You start by ambling down a finely graveled trail (level and hard-packed enough for strollers and wheelchairs) that leads from the visitors center through the woods. Hardcore birders, already finishing their morning's work, are likely to pass you on their way back to the parking lot, toting serious hardware: massive spotting scopes and heavy-duty tripods. Hmm, you think, must be something good up there. Suddenly — boom! — the vista opens and you're on a network of boardwalks that seem to float atop the water. This almost primordial wetland scene is abuzz with life. There's the noisy splash of geese coming in for a landing or powering up for a takeoff. Ducks nest just a few feet from you, their heads twisted back under their wings. Red-winged blackbirds flit from cattail to cattail. Lazily pyramidal beaver lodges dot the waterscape, their nocturnal inhabitants asleep inside. You can spend your time on the boardwalks, head over to an observation tower or continue your hike back into the woods. The urban world will seem very far away.

Words to the wise: *No running on those boardwalks, kids! And don't lean too far over, either. (Parents: There's an entrance to Huntley Meadows off South Kings Hwy., but you don't want that one. You can get to the visitors center only from the Lockheed Blvd. entrance.)*

NOTES: Neither food nor picnicking is available at the park.

Directions: *From the Beltway, take Route 1 south, to a right on Lockheed Blvd. The park is three-quarters of a mile up on the right.*

MASON NECK STATE PARK
7301 High Point Road, Lorton
HOURS: Daily 8-dusk, visitors center 10-6. **COST:** weekends $2 per car, weekdays $1, W free. **PHONE:** 703/550-0362, 703/550-0960.

Mason Neck is a perfect place for birdwatchers-in-training. Its claim to fame is the bald eagle, which has made a comeback here, where the Occoquan River feeds into the Potomac in a series of bays. More than 60 of the national birds live here year round, and nine nesting pairs help assure a steady supply of eaglets.

Start your visit at the visitors center (a typical well-equipped nature center, with live animals, dead animals, crafts and displays on Native Americans). The friendly staff can give you eagle-watching tips, even if they can't guarantee you a sighting. Kayakers often push off from a small beach at the foot of the center, paddling into Belmont Bay. Interconnected trails, none longer than a mile and none requiring too much strenuous activity, pass along the bay or head through the woods.

As you drive to the park, you'll first pass the **MASON NECK NATIONAL WILDLIFE REFUGE** (703/690-1297). Its three-mile Woodmarsh Trail may be too long for littlest hikers to do in its entirety, and its most interesting feature (a trail that skirts Great Marsh) is about halfway in. Still, its clear brochure and interpretive stops do a good job of explaining the various natural phenomena you'll encounter. Though the path is graveled, with boardwalks over wet areas, kids seem to get a kick out of looking for the next orange-blazed tree that originally marked the trail: It's the nature-walk equivalent of Hansel and Gretel's trail of pebbles.

Less than a mile from Mason Neck is **POHICK BAY REGIONAL PARK** (703/339-6100), a less nature-intensive area with picnic shelters, boat ramps, paddleboat rentals and miniature and disc golf courses. If bald eagles don't do it for your kids, stop for a round of mini golf.

Words to the wise: *Bring binoculars if you have them.*

NOTES: Access by wheelchair to the vistors center only. There's no food, but there are picnic tables and grills if you've brought your own. Also, note that I-95 gets maddeningly backed up on Sunday afternoons. You may want to use Route 1 if you're trying to escape from Mason Neck.

Directions: *From the Beltway, take I-95 south to the Lorton Rd. east. Make a right on Armistead, another right on Route 1 and a left on Gunston Rd. Signs will lead you to the park.*

THEODORE ROOSEVELT ISLAND
Accessible via George Washington Memorial Parkway, Arlington
HOURS: Daily 7-dusk. **COST**: Free. **PHONE**: 703/285-1925.

Smack in the middle of the Potomac River between the Kennedy Center and the George Washington Parkway is this memorial to our 26th president. It's an island for kids who aren't up for more than a nice bite-sized piece of nature. Big slabs of stone in a circle with a heroic statue of Teddy form the monument and are fun to ramble over. But the real lure is the manageable network of trails that loops around the teardrop-shaped island. They cut through woods, swamp and marsh. If you don't spot a beaver, you may spot his handiwork: tree stumps, pointed as if they'd been run through a pencil sharpener.

Words to the wise: *Hiking paths, though broad and fairly level, are not paved. When it rains they get muddy, and the low-lying (and interesting) Swamp Trail is closed completely. Also, bugs can be a problem in summer.*

NOTES: There are restrooms and water fountains but no food here.

Directions: *Accessible only from the northbound lanes of the GW Pkwy.*

NATURE CENTERS

IT'S SAFE TO ASSUME that nearly all nature centers in this section have "touch tables," "discovery rooms" and a contingent of formerly wild animals. You also can assume that they are staffed with rangers and volunteers who are knowledgeable about their particular area's ecosystem. Call for information on special kid-specific programs or to add your name to the mailing list of centers near your home.

District of Columbia

ROCK CREEK NATURE CENTER. In Rock Creek Park, 5200 Glover Rd. NW. **Hours:** W-Sun 9-5. **Phone:** 202/426-6829. Two box turtles and a corn snake call the center home, as does a colony of bees. Exhibits explore the flora and fauna found in Washington's lovely urban wilderness, from the flood plain to the woodland. There's also a planetarium, offering shows Wednesdays at 4 and weekends at 1 for ages 4 and up and weekends at 4 for ages 7 and up. Outside, there's a lake that attracts deer and two trails leading through the woods around the center. You can explore on your own or take a ranger-led weekend tour. ♿

Maryland

BLACK HILL REGIONAL PARK. 20926 Lake Ridge Dr., Boyds. **Hours:** Memorial Day-Labor Day: daily 11-6; weekends only and until 5 the rest of the year. **Phone:** 301/972-3476. More visitors center than nature center, this beautiful building does have some exhibits, books for kids to read and a nature video they can watch. A garden out front is planted to attract hummingbirds and butterflies. ♿

BROOKSIDE NATURE CENTER. Wheaton Regional Park, 1400 Glenallen Ave., Wheaton. **Hours:** Tu-Sat 9-5, Sun 1-5. **Phone:** 301/946-9071. There are the standard tank-dwelling snakes, salamanders, turtles and fish and stuffed wildlife (both taxidermied and plush), along with a demonstration butterfly and hummingbird garden. A short hike through wooded trails takes you next door to beautiful Brookside Gardens (see p.102). ♿

CLEARWATER NATURE CENTER. Louise Cosca Regional Park, 11000 Thrift Rd., Clinton. **Hours:** M-Sat 8:30-5, Sun & holidays 11-4. **Phone:** 301/297-4575. Highlights of the lava-rock building include an indoor pond with fish and turtles, an exhibit on "The Natural Treasures of Prince George's County" and a nearby lake, greenhouse and gardens, one featuring insectivorous plants. ♿

LOCUST GROVE NATURE CENTER. Cabin John Regional Park, 7777 Democracy Blvd., Bethesda. **Hours:** Tu-Sat 9-5. **Phone:** 301/299-1990. This is a small facility whose main exhibit, "Life in a Tree," is an interactive look at squirrels, birds, worms and other branch- and bough-dwelling critters. ♿

MEADOWSIDE NATURE CENTER. Rock Creek Regional Park, 5100 Meadowside Lane, Rockville. **Hours:** Tu-Sat 9-5. **Phone:** 301/924-4141. Who cares if it's raining? Meadowside has an indoor forest peopled (animaled?) with little stuffed critters, a working waterfall and stream, and an artificial cave. Children can dress up like pioneers in a replica of a 19th Century cabin. They might also enjoy the manageable hike around a pond to a goat pen. Lake Frank is a short drive away. ♿

MOUNT RANIER NATURE AND RECREATION CENTER. 4701 31st Pl., Mount Rainier. **Hours:** Tu-F 11-5, Sat 9-5. **Phone:** 301/927-2163. Reptiles, amphibians and mammals call this relatively new nature center home. There's a children's art area for coloring and scribbling. Outside is a butterfly and herb garden. ♿

WATKINS NATURE CENTER. Robert Watkins Regional Park, 301 Watkins Park Dr., Upper Marlboro. **Hours:** M-Sat 8:30-5, Sun 11-4. **Phone:** 301/249-6202. You'll find standard nature center fare, highlighted by an indoor pond filled with turtles and catfish. Outside are ponds with massive bullfrogs and caged raptors. ♿

Virginia

BUDDIE FORD NATURE CENTER. Dora Kelly Nature Park, 5700 Sanger Ave., Alexandria. **Hours:** Tu-Sat 10-5. **Phone:** 703/838-4829. The typical snakes/rabbits/birds, plus after-school programs and a nature trail. 🚻

ELLANOR C. LAWRENCE PARK. 5040 Walney Rd., Chantilly. **Hours:** M & W-F 9-5, weekends noon-5. **Phone:** 703/631-0013. Technically a visitors center rather than a nature center, this facility still has the requisite reptiles and amphibians and touchable stuff. Most displays recount the history of the 400-acre park, once a working farm. At the south end, a pond with a boardwalk is popular with families. 🚻

GULF BRANCH NATURE CENTER. 3608 N. Military Rd., Arlington. **Hours:** Tu-Sat 10-5, Sun 1-5. **Phone:** 703/228-3403. This former private home sits in a 47-acre wooded, stream-valley park leading to the Potomac. Kids can try on a variety of animal costumes in the upstairs Discovery Room. There's also an enclosed bee colony.

HIDDEN OAKS NATURE CENTER. Annandale Community Park, 7701 Royce St., Annandale. **Hours:** M & W-F 9-5, weekends noon-5. **Phone:** 703/941-1065. You'll again find snakes, toads, turtles and fish, plus hands-on stuff. Parents can get an "activity bag" filled with items to supplement a walk on nearby trails. Nature films often are shown at 3 on weekends. For the less naturally inclined, there's a playground outside. 🚻

HIDDEN POND NATURE CENTER. Hidden Pond Park, 8511 Greeley Blvd., Springfield. **Hours:** M & W-F 9-5, weekends noon-5; Jan.-Feb.: daily noon-5; closed Tu. **Phone:** 703/451-9588. The center overlooks the two-acre Hidden Pond and concentrates on the reptiles, amphibians and other aquatic animals that call it home. There's not as much as some in the way of touch tables, but you can hike a self-guided nature trail down the Pohick Stream Valley, and there's a recently built playground (donated by the Saturn car company). 🚻

HUNTLEY MEADOWS VISITORS CENTER. 3701 Lockheed Blvd., Alexandria. **Phone:** 703/768-2525. **Hours:** Daily sunrise-sunset, visitors center generally M & W-F 9-5, weekends noon-5. The visitors center concentrates more on setting the stage for a visit to this wetland park, a birder's dream, than on being a destination in itself, though there are the requisite discovery boxes. 🚻

LONG BRANCH NATURE CENTER. 625 S. Carlin Springs Rd., Arlington. **Phone:** 703/228-6535. **Hours:** Tu-Sat 10-5, Sun 1-5. Good array of live reptiles and amphibians inside, while outside are theme gardens and trails that lead to two ponds, a stream and a wetland. Biking families take note: The center has direct access to the W&OD Trail. 🚻

POTOMAC OVERLOOK NATURE CENTER. Potomac Overlook Regional Park, 2845 N. Marcey Rd., Arlington. **Hours:** Tu-Sat 10-5, Sun 1-5. **Phone:** 703/528-5406. This one's a little different: Besides the expected animals, there are displays on an unexpected one — humans. Exhibits explore the impact of humans on the land and include artifacts dug up from a nearby Native American village. 🚻

PRINCE WILLIAM FOREST PARK VISITORS CENTER. 18100 Park Headquarters Rd., Triangle (off Route 619). **Hours:** Daily 8:30-5. **Cost:** $4 per car. **Phone:** 703/221-7181. Here's a rarity: This nature center has no corn snake sitting under a heat lamp! Instead, the visitors center in this second-growth forest has such inanimate objects as bones, snake skins and "beaver chews" (pieces of wood chewed on by beavers). There's a quarter-mile paved route with audio description along the way, perfect for strollers or persons with disabilities. &

RIVERBEND PARK. 8814 Jeffery Rd., Great Falls. **Hours:** M, W-F 9-5, weekends noon-5; later in summer. **Phone:** 703/759-9018. The nature center is open only during programs at this 409-acre multi-use park, so the visitors center is where you'll find the cheetahs and gazelles (just kidding: amphibians and reptiles). There's always a themed "Nature Escape" program going on, wherein kids can do word games, coloring and crafts. You can hike a paved quarter-mile trail from the nature center; it's a half-mile from the visitors center, so you may want to drive.

GARDENS

District of Columbia

DUMBARTON OAKS
31st and R streets NW (museum entrance on 32nd Street)

HOURS: 2-5 daily except M and federal holidays; until 6 Apr.-Oct. **COST:** $4 adults, $3 under 12 and seniors, Nov.-March free. **PHONE:** 202/339-6401 (or 202/339-6400). Adjacent Pre-Columbian and Byzantine art collections: weekdays 2-5. Suggested donation: $1.

The sign by the entrance of Dumbarton Oaks — the most storied private garden in Washington and one of the most richly diverse examples of European-style formal landscape design in the United States — says it all regarding its welcome to children: "This is not a public park . . . children must be supervised by adults, and must not play games . . ." As if to emphasize the point, the first sign beyond the entrance — "Please keep off the grass" — is posted alongside a stone path inaccessible to strollers. We'll be even plainer: Don't take kids here until they're 6 or older (10 if you're taking several) and ready to absorb a place without doing anything to it. Dumbarton Oaks, an astonishingly elaborate garden now operated by Harvard University, is not "interactive" in any way.

But if and when your child is ready, you're both in for a treat. The garden consists of numerous distinct areas, or "rooms," each with a different purpose and prospect. There's a Fountain Terrace with a pair of playful lead sculptures; Lover's Lane Pool, a 50-seat miniature Roman-style amphitheater; a meticulous pebble garden, revealing a subtle pattern made of fist-sized rocks of different natural hues and on and on over 10 sloping, multi-terraced acres. The views and the ambition are equally stunning, especially in spring and fall. Much of the brickwork is old and fragile, and some paths are difficult for the less mobile to negotiate. It's easy to spend a pleasant hour or more here taking the self-guided tour. If you're looking for just one knockout item, check out the spreading Katsura tree right near the entrance booth on R Street. It's one of the oldest trees on the property, and its branches spread nearly horizontally into a gorgeous, ground-level canopy. But, you guessed it: No climbing.

Words to the wise: *Kids too rambunctious for the refined gardens? Just to the east of the garden entrance, down the steep and unmarked road called Lover's Lane, is Dumbarton Oaks Park, a mostly natural area that once was part of the garden property. There are several hiking/walking trails here and a few old outbuildings and waterways. But the path to and from it is too steep for the stroller and toddler crowd. If you're packing tots, check out adjacent Montrose Park (see P. 147), another worthy green space with playgrounds, picnic areas and open space that's ideal for those who are not yet ready for the Oaks.*

NOTES: While this generally isn't a good choice for the disabled, you can call to make special arrangements, and wheelchair tours are available. **Food:** Restaurants (and shops) are plentiful along Georgetown's Wisconsin Avenue and M Street. **Parking:** With Metro access poor, you'll need to drive. On-street parking (two-hour limit) often is available within a block or two. **Nearby:** C&O Canal, Old Stone House.

KENILWORTH AQUATIC GARDENS
1900 Anacostia Avenue at Douglas Street SE

HOURS: Daily 6:30-4; visitors center daily 8-4. **COST:** Free. **PHONE:** 202/426-6905. **WEB:** www.nps.gov/nace.

Unless your young companions have an unusual interest in water lilies and lotuses, they're likely to see these delightful water gardens mostly as a great place to spot frogs, turtles, fish and an occasional snake in something resembling their natural habitats. But that's saying a lot. The 12-acre site consists of more than 40 ponds planted with thousands of water-based plants, some huge, colorful, fragrant and of considerable horticultural significance. The African water lily, for instance, has a leaf span of six feet.

If your children really want to see the exotic flora, go early in the morning (some plants pull themselves closed in the midday heat) between May and September, preferably in June or July. A 1.4-mile river trail sends you on a pleasant walk alongside the natural wetlands of the Anacostia River, where you are likely to spot herons and other unusual birds. Bring binoculars if you have them. A small visitors center tells the park's story and has a gift shop and rest rooms. Guided garden walks, suitable for ages 8 and up, are offered Tuesday through Sunday at 10, 11 and 1 (reservations recommended). The National Park Service staffers, happy to greet visitors to this largely under-attended park, enjoy taking time with kids on weekdays and slow weekends.

Words to the wise: *While maps make Kenilworth Gardens and the National Arboretum appear next to each other, they are in fact separated* *by the Anacostia. Going from one to the other is trickier than you might expect. If you plan to start at Kenilworth and end at the arboretum — actually a great idea — get detailed directions from Park Service personnel (and take notes).*

NOTES: For **Food,** there are restaurants on Kenilworth Ave.

Directions: *From the Beltway, take Route 50 south to Kenilworth Ave. and follow signs.*

NATIONAL ARBORETUM
3501 New York Avenue NE

HOURS: Daily 8-5, bonsai collection 10-3:30. Educational displays in administration building: weekdays 8-4:30, weekends 9-5. **COST**: Free. **PHONE:** 202/245-2726. **WEB:** www.ars-grin.gov/ars/Beltsville/na.　♿

Tell kids that you're going to a giant garden and chances are you'll get mixed reactions, some excited by the prospect, others not exactly jumping for joy. Encourage any doubters to think of the National Arboretum as a vast backyard (444 acres) perfect for running around in, one with plants that are inevitably more interesting than your own. Spring and summer days, when the trees and flowers are in bloom, are obvious times to visit. But even on cold and forbidding fall and winter days, an expedition to the National Arboretum can be a good antidote to cabin fever. Some suggestions for visiting with children:

Small kids may get a kick out of the collections of little bonsai plants: A perfectly scaled stand of cypress could fit in the trunk of your car. Meticulously pruned trees, some hundreds of years old, look majestic in their little trays. Have your kids see if they can find this contradiction in terms: the biggest bonsai. From the very small go to the very big: It's a bracing walk through an herb garden and up a grassy slope to an arrangement of towering sandstone columns that once graced the U.S. Capitol. They look like an ancient ruin, their ornate capitals stark against the sky. From there you can walk directly across a grassy field to the Lee azalea gardens, a riot of color in April and May.

Children who don't tire easily also may enjoy the Asian-style garden; get a map of the arboretum's grounds and drive there. Pathways crisscross terraced plantings that are highlighted with a bright red pagoda. You can walk all the way down to the Anacostia River, your descent punctuated, perhaps, by the repetitive *thonk* of a woodpecker's beak. (There's lots of upping and downing, so don't try it with a stroller.) If you think your kids can sit still for 40 minutes, take a narrated, open-air tram ride past the arboretum's highlights. The tram operates on spring and summer weekends at 11:30, 1, 2, 3 and 4; tickets are $3 for adults, $2 for children 4-6 and for seniors, under 4 free.

Words to the wise: *Though the National Arboretum setting is bucolic, remember that you're still in the city, so don't let the children wander off too far from you.*

NOTES: There are restrooms and vending machines but no restaurant. You can picnic at tables if you bring your own food. **Nearby:** Kenilworth Aquatic Gardens.

Directions: *From the Beltway, take the Baltimore-Washington Pkwy. south to New York Ave. and follow signs to the arboretum on your left.*

Virginia

GREEN SPRING GARDENS PARK
4603 Green Spring Road, Alexandria

HOURS: Grounds: dawn-dusk. Horticulture Center: M-Sat, 9-4:30 (until 7 in summer), Sun noon-4 (until 7 in summer). Manor House: W-Sun, noon-4. **COST:** Free. **PHONE:** 703/642-5173. ♿

This 27-acre park, snuggled on a parcel of farmland hard by a cluster of huge retail stores and light manufacturing facilities, is worthy of an outing with any child who indicates an interest in gardens. The new horticulture center has a smart but easily digested exhibition on conservation, and it tells the tale of how this once private farm was delivered into public protection. It also has a big and productive greenhouse, a horticulture library, a small gift shop and plenty of information for visitors and gardeners. The pathway around the central lawn takes in a 20-station demonstration garden that's instructive to both parents and kids: There's a water-wise garden, a swale garden, even three knockout "townhouse" gardens that illustrate how even a modest chunk of turf can be made beautiful and natural. There's a fruit orchard (no picking — pesticides at work), an herb garden, a hearty vegetable garden and more. One of the embedded messages at Green Spring is that gardens can bloom and produce year round. Unlike public "show" gardens that say, "Look at me, aren't I beautiful?" Green Spring says, "Hey, you could actually do this." A path in the woods leads to an undeveloped area featuring two ponds swarming with geese and other waterfowl. While signs make much of the fact that the Manor House's ornamental garden was designed by Beatrix Farrand of Dumbarton Oaks fame, little remains of her handiwork; the semicircular border garden behind the house has been replanted many times.

Words to the wise: *The farmhouse (circa 1780) looks compelling from the outside, but it has little to offer small children. Its interior has been renovated nearly beyond recognition, and the house functions mostly as a fussy art and gift shop. If your charges are 10 years old and under, there's more to lose than gain by going inside. Older kids interested in crafts and nature probably will enjoy it.*

NOTES: If you and your family are thrifters, there's a huge, well-stocked Salvation Army store at the corner of Green Spring and Little River. **Food:** You'll find restaurants on Little River Turnpike. **Disabled Access:** While there's excellent wheelchair access to the Horticulture Center and many display gardens, the manor house, ponds and stream-valley trail are not accessible.

Directions: *From the Beltway, take Little River Tpk. (Route 236) and choose the Annandale exit ramp. Stay on Little River Tpk. for 3.5 miles; turn left on Green Spring Rd. and follow it to the end.*

MEADOWLARK GARDENS REGIONAL PARK
9750 Meadowlark Gardens Court, Vienna

HOURS: Daily 10-7:30 (5 when sun sets earlier). Closed major holidays. **COST:** $3 adults, $1 ages 7-17, under 7 and seniors free. Nov.-March: free. **PHONE:** 703/255-3631.

Less than five miles outside the concrete cauldron of Tysons Corner, this 97-acre horticultural park has been handsomely installed on former farmland donated by the improbably named economist Gardiner Means. It is one of the region's best spots to take kids in strollers or toddlers just getting their legs (although you'll need to clarify the strict no-picking policy along the way). It's also one of those true "win-win" family destinations. Kids enjoy being outside, following the many paths and checking out the wildlife along the three lakes; parents can get ideas for home plantings, as this is one of the best-labeled public gardens you'll find. Kids are sure to love the "spiral" garden (which winds around a small hill like a tiny interstate surrounding a mountain), the ruins of the spring house where water was fetched, the skipping-stone path across the lake and the several mulched pathways leading through the woods. Be sure to get a brochure when you enter the visitors center: The map is easy to read, and kids may enjoy "navigating" around the park. A recently installed highlight, certain to be an eye-opener for every family member: the so-called Cancer Garden, displaying live plants from which cancer treatment medicines are derived. The park also has a modest picnic area and a visitors center gift shop, restrooms and soda and juice machines.

Words to the wise: *Rules barring such recreational uses of the park as skating, ball-playing or fishing keep it pleasantly uncrowded, but the Atrium building and adjacent gazebos often are reserved on weekends for weddings and special events. You may want to call ahead to avoid crowds at those times.*

NOTES: While some trails here are steep, a good portion of this property is easily accessible for those with wheelchairs and strollers; a marked path indicates the most accessible routes. Neither food nor picnicking is permitted in the park proper.

Directions: *From the Beltway, take Route 7 west. In about five miles, turn left at Beulah Rd. The park is about 1.5 miles on the right.*

Maryland

BROOKSIDE GARDENS
1500 Glenallan Avenue, Wheaton

HOURS: Daily sunrise-sunset. Conservatories: daily 10-5. Visitors center: daily 9-5. **COST:** Free. **PHONE:** 301/949-8230. **WEB:** www.clark.net/pub/mncppc/montgom/parks/facility.htm. &

A visit to these wonderfully cultivated gardens never fails to improve the mood of our children. Even if the artful arrangements of flowers and trees and stones is beyond them, they appreciate the opportunity to get out and romp in a continually evolving landscape (while you're getting ideas for your backyard from the masterful and well-labeled plantings). There's usually a storybook garden created with children in mind, but there's much else besides. Two conservatories are like massive terrariums, bursting with color (and, for two months each summer, filled with butterflies). Geese and ducks frolic in a tiny lake crowned by a Japanese teahouse. The grounds are dotted with gazebos and fountains. A recently built visitors center hosts free children's programs in the spring and fall.

Words to the wise: *You may hear the whistle of the miniature train at Wheaton Regional Park. While Brookside is connected to the park, it's quite a hike to get there. You're better off driving.*

NOTES: You can't picnic at the garden, but there are tables at the nearby Brookside Nature Center and Wheaton Regional Park. Also **Nearby:** Wheaton Ice Rink.

Directions: *From the Beltway, take Exit 31A north to Georgia Ave. Make a right on Randolph Rd. and a right again on Glenallen Rd. The gardens are on the right.*

TWO REALLY GREAT FALLS

NATURAL SCENIC WONDER, hiking and biking trail, gentle canoeing route, picnic area, birding zone, presidential history site, nature center, serious outdoor sports observation area, living history exhibit — the Great Falls of the Potomac River offers all of this, making it one of the most potent family day-trip magnets in the area. At this spot in the river, the Potomac cuts through a rocky gorge and descends 70 feet from the piedmont plateau to sea level, creating a spectacular display of natural power and beauty. Kayakers tool around at the base of the falls, and rock climbers work the nearly vertical walls of the gorge. But such sport is not for amateurs: An average of seven people die each year by challenging or falling into the waters near Great Falls. It's wise to remind kids of the peril whenever you visit.

The facilities available on the two riverbanks, on the Virginia and Maryland shores, are very different. Each can sustain dozens of visits and different activities over the years. We used to love the Maryland side for its smooth path when the kids were in strollers and the Virginia side for the visceral power of the falls, to which even our babies seemed to respond. As the children have grown older, we've taken to more ambitious hikes on the Maryland side, and the kids are intrigued by the history and drama on the Virginia side.

MARYLAND SIDE
11710 MacArthur Boulevard, Potomac

HOURS: Daily 9-4:30; closed Christmas and New Year. **COST:** $4 per vehicle, $2 per hiker/bicyclist. **PHONE:** 301/299-3613.

The Maryland-side Great Falls park, operated by the National Park Service as part of its C&O Canal National Historical Park, provides some access to the falls and a variety of other attractions. Highlights include the Great Falls Tavern and Museum (dating from 1828, it has modest displays on the history of the C&O canal); mule-drawn, 90-minute canal boat rides ($7.50 adults, $4 children, $6 seniors, featuring guides in period garb, available from mid-April until Nov. 1; 301/299-2026); access to the C&O Canal towpath (perfect for easygoing family hikes and accommodating to bikes, strollers and wheelchairs); several challenging wooded trails (including the well-known Billy Goat Trail, a three-hour round trip that yields an awesome river overlook, and the obscure but wonderful Gold Mine Trail, which terminates at the wreck of an abandoned gold mine). A boardwalk across a fragile ecosystem ends at two spectator decks overlooking the falls. Pick up the boardwalk (which is accessible to strollers and wheelchairs) between Locks 17 and 18. The still canal waters are teeming with frogs, turtles, lizards and other aquatic life, and kids can be intrigued for hours. (Be wary, however, as they navigate the high walls of the canal lock.) You can rent canoes, bikes and boats at Swain's Lock, a few miles to the north (301/299-9006); the boats and canoes may be used only on the canal, not the river. Fishing is permitted, under D.C. and Maryland regulations.

NOTES: For **Food:** From April to October, a snack bar is open, and there are picnic tables near the tavern. There's wheelchair access to the Georgetown boat only, though there is full access to the museum.

Directions: *Take I-495 to Exit 41/Clara Barton Pkwy. Then take a left on MacArthur Blvd. and follow signs to the park entrance.*

VIRGINIA SIDE
9200 Old Dominion Drive, Great Falls

HOURS: Daily 7 am-dusk; closed Christmas. **PHONE:** 703/285-2966. **COST:** $4 per vehicle.

The 800-acre park on the Virginia side of Great Falls offers better and easier views of the falls themselves. If you're interested in simple observation and awesome photo backgrounds, this is the side to be on. Other features include a nature and interpretive center that tells the story of George Washington's ill-fated attempt to build the Patowmack Canal to circumvent the falls on the Virginia side, and a snack bar that's open March through November. The park's major trail takes you alongside the ruins of the canal, and some of them are spectacular. Our kids loved seeing the sheer walls that angle down toward the river, still bearing scars from hand-drill and dynamite. The high-water marker signpost, showing where floods have peaked in various years, is a real stunner. There are some daring, secluded overlooks along the path, and as long as your 5-and-up kids will respond to your stern I'm-not-kidding-you-need-to-be-care-ful-here warnings, all will be fine. There are over 15 miles of well-marked paths throughout the park, and the trail is fully accessible up to Lock 1. Picnic tables and informal sites abound.

Words to the wise: *Less parking is available here than on the Maryland side, so make sure that you don't arrive too late to get a spot, especially on beautiful weekends.*

NOTES: For **Food,** picnic tables and informal sites abound. **Disability Access:** Wheelchair access is limited to some paths, the visitors center and the picnic area.

Directions: *Take the Beltway to Exit 13 (Georgetown Pike/Route 193). Go west four miles and turn right on Old Dominion Dr. (Route 738). It's a mile to the park.*

THE CAVE PEOPLE

THE REGION'S HANDFUL of show (i.e., tourist) caves make great places to take the family — spooky, fascinating, beautiful chambers where the kids can learn some earth science from the inside out and gather experiences they'll long remember. Our kids love it when, during nearly every cave tour, the guide — offering plenty of opportunity for everybody to grab someone's hand — kills the lights and pitches the place into blackness. For older kids, cave visits can provide entry into the world of spelunking — more serious and ambitious cave exploration that ought not to be undertaken by an unguided, unequipped family of day-trippers (though guides at all sites here have information about area spelunking opportunities). Show caves are good bad-weather activities (the temperature hovers in the high 50s in most caves), and they make excellent day-end "rewards" for countryside day trips that the kids may find less thrilling (we speak, of course, of such things as antiquing).

Note the prices, however: A family of four may wind up paying more than $30 to tour any of the caverns listed below. All are open daily all year, but call before you go, as hours and frequency of tours fluctuate seasonally. To include caves in this book, we've again had to reach beyond our 40-miles-outside-the-Beltway range.

But caves, we think, are kid-friendly enough to merit the 1.5-hour to 2.5-hour rides required. Most Marylanders will be able to get to Crystal Grottoes within an hour, and any of the three Virginia caverns can easily be worked into a fall auto tour of Skyline Drive.

Maryland

CRYSTAL GROTTOES CAVERNS
19821 Shepherdstown Pike, Boonsboro

HOURS: Apr.-Oct. daily 10-5, Nov.-Mar. weekends 11-4. **COST:** $8.50, $4.50 under 12. **PHONE:** 301/432-6336. **WEB:** www.goodearth.com/showcave/md/crystal.html.

This is hardly the area's most spectacular cavern, but it's the closest cave for Marylanders and may make a good entry-level descent for families with small kids (but no strollers or backpacks). The 40-minute tour usually is small and quite informative, but you'll find fewer elaborately named and spectacularly lit formations than in, say, Luray. Still, it's a close-in place to learn about the basics of limestone caverns.

NOTES: Nearby are Antietam National Battlefield, Washington Monument State Park and, 18 miles away, Harper's Ferry, W.Va.

Directions: *Take the Beltway to I-270 north to I-70 west. Exit at Alternate 40. Continue on Alternate 40, passing Route 67; take a left at Route 34, toward Sharpsburg. The caverns are on the left.*

Virginia

ENDLESS CAVERNS
Road 793, New Market

HOURS: Sept.-mid-Nov. 9-5; mid-Nov.-mid-March 9-4; mid-March-mid-June 9-5; mid-June-Labor Day 9-5. **COST:** $11 adults; $5.50 ages 3-12. **PHONE:** 540/896-2283 or 800/544-CAVE.

Located in the quaint Civil War town of New Market, this is a "pure" cave that adds little razzle-dazzle beyond that which nature offers — which is plenty. Simple white lights illuminate all of the limestone formations, and the 45-minute tour is the most informative we've encountered. The owners claim that the end of the caverns has never been found (hence the name), though five miles of underground trails have been mapped since 1920. There's a gift shop (unique feature: Endless Caverns Spring Water) and a campground that accommodates RVs and tents.

NOTES: For **Food,** New Market has plenty of fast-food and family restaurants.

Directions: *Take I-66 west to I-81 south to Exit 264, and follow the signs.*

LURAY CAVERNS
970 U.S. Highway 211 West, Luray

HOURS: Opens daily at 9, closes between 4 and 7, depending on season. **COST**: $13 adults; $6 kids 7-13; under 7 free. **PHONE**: 540-743-6551. **WEB**: www.luraycaverns.com. ♿

This is the area's biggest show cave, with the highest production values and "wow" factor. It's also the most crowded and expensive. The hour-long tour takes you on a figure-eight loop past some memorable sights that have been assigned goofily dramatic names: Pluto's Chasm (a huge vault with big columns); Titania's Veil and Saracen's Tent (both elaborate drapery formations); the Giant's Hall (a big chamber the equivalent of 17 stories below ground-level); the oddly vivid "fried eggs" (leftovers from broken stalagmites), and what's described as the world's only "Stalacpipe Organ," which is said to use 37 stalactites to produce its "music." There's no extra charge to tour the appended Historic Car and Carriage Caravan Museum, a modest collection that includes an old Rolls-Royce.

NOTES: There is a 350-pound weight limit (including chair and person) on wheelchairs in the caverns. **Food:** Restaurants are plentiful in Luray. **Nearby:** The Luray Reptile Center and Dinosaur Park (540/743-4113).

Directions: *Take I-66 west to Front Royal. Pick up Route 340 south, which will bring you to Route 211. Go west on 211 three miles to Luray. Alternatively, take I-81 south to Exit 264 and follow the signs.*

SHENANDOAH CAVERNS
261 Caverns Road, Shenandoah Caverns

HOURS: Daily 9-7 (last tour: 6); closed Christmas. **COST**: $12 adults, $5.50 for kids 5-14. **PHONE**: 540/477-3115. ♿

This modest cavern, located just north of New Market, offers Bacon Hall (once featured in National Geographic), Rainbow Lake, Grotto of the Gods and other underground staples. An added attraction, called American Celebration on Parade, features relics from old department-store window displays and parade floats; an animated Cinderella scene features 15 animated figures and a line of model soldiers passing endlessly down a miniature historic Pennsylvania Avenue. The effect is a weird mix of defunct American commercialism, early 20th Century patriotism and Chuck E. Cheese without the pizza. Among area caves, Shenandoah, equipped with elevators that take you to a tour requiring no steps, offers the best access for seniors and people in wheelchairs, so it might be a good grandparents outing. The tour takes about an hour.

Words to the wise: *Note that American Celebration requires its own set of admission fees. Bring a sweater or jacket because the caverns are 54 degrees year round.*

NOTES: An elevator takes you into the caverns, but the passageways are covered in gravel. **Food:** There's an on-site coffee shop, open seasonally.

Directions: *Take I-81 south to Exit 269.*

SKYLINE CAVERNS
10334 Stonewall Jackson Highway, Front Royal

HOURS: Daily 9-6:30 (winter: 9-4). **COST:** $10 adults, $5 ages 7-13, under 6 free. **PHONE:** 540/635-4545, 800/296-4545. **WEB:** www.skylinecaverns.com.

Near the entrance to Skyline Drive, Skyline Caverns is the closest show cave to the Washington metropolitan area and the least expensive. While not as spectacular as Luray, it has three underground streams, a 37-foot waterfall and rare and delicate spiky formations called anthodites. The hour-long tour is high on content (though one part — when a booming narrator dares visitors to tremble before the handiwork of Almighty God — may trouble parents who prefer not to impart religious explanations of natural phenomena). In addition to a gift shop, a 10-minute miniature railroad ride is available for an extra $2 (weather permitting), and a dilapidated fiberglass brontosaurus is ripe for photo opportunities.

NOTES: For **Food,** restaurants are plentiful around Front Royal. There also are on-site picnic tables and a nearby country store if you want to buy some picnic items.

Directions: *Take the Beltway to I-66 West to Exit 13. Turn left under the bridge and right onto Route 55 west. Follow that for about five miles to Route 340 south, and take 340 one mile. The entrance is on the left.*

9

MILITARY MATTERS

SOME OF OUR region's most compelling attractions honor those who fought and died for our nation: Arlington National Cemetery, the Vietnam Veterans Memorial, Fort McHenry, the battlefields at Gettysburg and Manassas and others. While the intricacies of military history aren't likely to enthrall little kids, you'll be surprised by how intrigued many of them are by the lives of those involved, from presidents to generals to foot soldiers, or by the scarier aspects of military fortifications. Such matters not only fascinate the young but also can have a lasting effect on them. For children a bit older, military sites can breathe life into textbook tales of American history, attaching faces and places to the glories and tragedies, giving names to the many who paid so terrible a price for the rest of us. This chapter focuses on selected sites that we've found best suited for visits with children, including not only forts and battlefields and memorials but also the Naval Academy and museums, with a touch of the military bands thrown in for good measure.

FORTS

Maryland

FORT WASHINGTON
13551 Fort Washington Road, Fort Washington

HOURS: Daily 9-5, Nov.-Mar. until 4:30. **COST:** $4 per car. **PHONE:** 301/763-4600. ♿

If you put only one historic fort on your family's to-do list, make it Fort Washington. It occupies a prime piece of hilly shoreline overlooking the Potomac, with the view alone worth the price of admission. Built to provide coastal protection for the new nation's capital, the fort was in operation from 1808 to 1922. Its features illustrate the evolution of military strategies and defenses. The barracks date from 1821, while an officer's room is done up circa 1865 and some cannon are from the 1900s. Kids enjoy exploring the vast grounds and buildings, taking in the view, rolling down the spectacular hills and observing such details as the fort's historic drawbridge, the remnants of its dry moat and the dank munitions storage and prison areas (which a 6-year-old of our acquaintance proclaimed "the land of the dead").

A one-page, self-guided tour is available at the visitors center, along with the most accessible restrooms and a gift shop. Parts of the complex, including defunct gun batteries, are structurally unsafe and closed to the public. There's a small lighthouse by the river, and if your family likes to fish, this is a super spot. The Swan Creek Trail affords an excellent family hike along the river. Call ahead for special torchlight tours, a spooky delight.

Words to the wise: *There are plenty of ways for kids to get hurt here — steep stairways, high walls, dark passages — so be vigilant and require attentive behavior.*

NOTES: While there's good disability access to the visitors center, access to the fort (where the wheelchair ramp is long and steep) is limited. **Food:** You can go to restaurants on Indian Head Highway, but bring a water bottle and consider a picnic on the super grounds. **Nearby:** National Colonial Farm, Piscataway Park.

Directions: *Take the Beltway to Exit 3A (Indian Head Hwy./Route 210). Go 4.5 miles and turn right at Fort Washington Rd.*

FORT McHENRY
End of East Fort Avenue, Baltimore

HOURS: Daily 8-4:45, summer till 7:45. Closed major holidays. **COST:** $5, under 16 free. **PHONE:** 410/962-4290. **WEB:** www.nps.gov/fomc. &

While it lacks the sprawling, anachronistic funk of Fort Washington, Fort McHenry packs the most narrative punch of any nearby fort. During the War of 1812 — September 13 to 14, 1814 — a group of British ships bombarded Fort McHenry for 25 hours in an attempt to take Baltimore. But the defenders held. When 35-year-old lawyer Francis Scott Key saw the flag flying the next day, he penned "The Star-Spangled Banner" to the tune of an English drinking song; in 1931 it became our national anthem. Kids love walking the ramparts of the star-shaped fort (it's easy to imagine the British fleet in the Patapsco River), and a good, 16-minute (captioned) movie in the visitors center recounts the fort's history (in the Civil War, for instance, it turned its guns at Baltimore, to menace the city's many Southern sympathizers). Kids also get a bang out of an electrical light-up map illustrating the bombardment. In summer, costumed interpreters add to the festive air. As for that flag, the huge original is kept in the Smithsonian's National Museum of American History (see p. 124). The fort today usually flies a smaller but still remarkable version, measuring 25 by 17 feet.

Words to the wise: *Don't expect to walk to or from the Inner Harbor. It's three miles away.*

Directions: *From I-95, take Exit 55 to Key Hwy. Turn left on Lawrence St. and left again on Fort Ave.; the park is a mile ahead. From Baltimore's Inner Harbor, take Light St. south to Fort Ave.*

Virginia

FORT WARD MUSUEM
4301 West Braddock Road, Alexandria

HOURS: Daily 9-sunset. Museum: Tu-Sat 9-5, Sun noon-5. Closed major holidays. **COST:** Free. **PHONE:** 703/838-4848. ♿

After the Stonewall Jackson Museum listed below, Fort Ward is the local military site that most invites kids to imagine themselves living amid a war. The most completely restored of the 162 forts and earthworks that sprung up around Washington after the outbreak of the Civil War, Fort Ward provides an excellent view into both defenses and daily fort life. The 45-minute self-guided tour begins at the restored ceremonial gate and proceeds along the fort's earthen walls. The payoff: the restored Northwest Bastion, one of the fort's five originals and featuring gun emplacements. Exhibits in the museum tend to focus on human-scale issues: battle music, children during the war, medical care. These are far more likely to engage kids than the usual array of weaponry.

NOTES: Museum and some parts of the fort are wheelchair accessible. **Food:** You can drive a bit to Alexandria proper for restaurants.

Directions: *From the Beltway, take I-395 north to Seminary Rd. exit. Make a right onto Seminary and follow it to the fourth traffic light at Alexandria Hospital. Turn left on North Howard St. and right on West Braddock Rd. Park entrance is on left. You also can take King St. (Route 7) west to T.C. Williams High School; turn right on Kenwood St. and take the next left onto West Braddock Rd. Follow West Braddock for three-quarters of a mile. Park entrance is on right.*

𝔅𝔞𝔱𝔱𝔩𝔢𝔣𝔦𝔢𝔩𝔡𝔰

Pennsylvania

GETTYSBURG NATIONAL MILITARY PARK
97 Taneytown Road (State Route 134), Gettysburg

HOURS: Daily 6-10, visitors center 8-5 (till 6 in summer). **COST:** Free parking and access to visitors center, cemeteries, hiking and auto tour routes and battlefields. Charges for other attractions. **PHONE:** 717/334-1124 (for non-National Park Service attractions, 717/334-6274). **WEB:** www.nps.gov/gett. ♿

Site of the major Civil War conflict and of Abraham Lincoln's much-memorized 272-word address, Gettysburg is the most richly presented and thought-provoking Civil War site in the region, making it well worth a day trip and additional visits as the kids grow. You can start with the free or low-cost attractions operated by the National Park Service. The visitors center offers an engaging museum. Kids may be particularly intrigued by the encampments downstairs, showing artifacts of soldiers' daily life, including playing cards, hardtack biscuits and eating utensils. The huge selection of weaponry, from derringers to cannon, is similarly compelling. There's also a 30-minute Electric Map presentation that you should skip until kids are ready to absorb details of military strategy. The Cyclorama Center is a gorgeous anachronism, both in its high-modern, 1962 circular design and as a primitive "interactive experience." A 360-degree, century-old oil-on-canvas panorama of the Gettysburg battlefield is wrapped around a circular auditorium, effectively placing viewers in the midst of Pickett's Charge, the Confederates' doomed assault on Northern positions. A 20-minute light-and-sound presentation illuminates the scene. (The Electric Map and Cyclorama presentations each cost $3 for adults, $1.50 for ages 6-15, $2.50 for seniors.) A free, brief and clear 10-minute movie shown continuously downstairs provides a digestible overview, even for the preschool set, of what the fighting was about. Right off the Cyclorama's back porch is the start of what's called the High Water Mark Trail. This roughly follows the South's deepest penetration of Union defenses and provides (for strollers, wheelchairs and those less mobile) an easily accessible route to a good first dose of monuments, cannon and interpretive signage.

An inspired buff of nearly any age can find a week's worth of activities. There's the National Cemetery, final resting place of more than 6,000 war dead from Gettysburg (and subsequent conflicts). A monument marks the spot where Lincoln delivered his address during the cemetery's dedication, four months after the battle ended. There's an 18-mile auto tour, for which cassette tapes (available at most area gift shops for $10) provide a useful soundtrack. There are more than 1,300 monuments, statues and other commemorative items scattered on the battlefields, most erected by state and veterans' groups. Three strategically placed observation towers permit overviews of key battle areas, several preserved buildings and homesteads and miles of hiking trails.

Beyond the "official" attractions are several private-sector offerings on nearby properties that appeal to kids. Of the dozen-plus facilities, three are worth special attention. The must-do is the **NATIONAL TOWER** (717/334-6754; $5 for adults, $4.50 for seniors, $3 for ages 6-12), a 307-foot spectacle that hovers over the battlefield (and annoys many purists, who feel it violates sacred landscapes). The 1,016 steps make for a, well, memorable climb, but there also are elevators for easy access to the viewing levels, one open to the air and equipped with quarter-munching binocular viewers, another with a 12-minute narration sure to bore anyone under 12 but useful for those serious about understanding the three days of fighting. The **GETTYSBURG BATTLEFIELD THEATER** (717/334-6100; $5.25 adults, $3.25 ages 6-11, $4.75 seniors) offers an ambitious animated film and a "battlerama" of hand-painted miniatures. Finally there's the **NATIONAL CIVIL WAR WAX MUSEUM** (717/334-6245; $4.50 adults, $2.50 kids 13-17, $1.75 ages 6-12, $3.50 seniors), which, despite its wiggy feel, illustrates key moments of the war and the battle with life-size figures.

Included is a grisly-funny tableaux of Pickett's Charge and Lincoln delivering the Gettysburg Address, which is recited over and over through hidden speakers. The adjacent **EISENHOWER NATIONAL HISTORIC SITE** (717/334-4474; all one- to two-hour tours begin at the visitors center; $5.25 adults, $3.25 kids 13-16, $2.25 ages 6-12) preserves the private residence and farm of Dwight and Mamie Eisenhower, but you can safely put it at the end of your list. While historically significant — and a must-do for Presidential completists — the restored and preserved mid-century home offers little that appeals directly to children.

Words to the wise: *As with most popular National Park Service sites, try to avoid summer weekend visits. Fall and spring are much better bets.*

NOTES: Private tours with licensed guides are available for about $30 for a family; bus tours by two private firms (717/334-6274) range from $11-$15 for adults to $8-$11.50 for kids 6-11. **Food:** The Gettysburg community is loaded with dining options, from snack bars to up-market saloons to fast-food franchises (including the astonishingly ill-named General Pickett's Buffet); many are within walking distance of the visitors center. **Disabled access:** Although the visitors center and High Water Mark Trail can accommodate wheelchairs, access to the battlefields and some monuments is limited. Neither bus tour is wheelchair accessible.

Directions: *From the Beltway, take I-270 north to Route 15 North. Follow 15 past Catoctin Mountain Park and Emmitsburg and into Pennsylvania. Two miles into Pennsylvania you can exit at Business Route 15 north into Gettysburg or continue a few more miles to Route 134, Taneytown Rd., which takes you directly to the visitors center. From the nearest point on the Beltway, the drive is about 70 miles.*

Maryland

ANTIETAM NATIONAL BATTLEFIELD
Maryland Route 65, Sharpsburg Pike, Sharpsburg

HOURS: Daily 8:30-5 (summer until 6); closed major holidays. **COST:** $4 per family. **PHONE:** 301/432-5124. **WEB:** www.nps.gov/anti. &

This 960-acre battlefield, often taken in by car, was the site of the single bloodiest day of warfare in American history. More than 23,000 soldiers were killed or wounded as the Confederate Army, flush with victory at Manassas, tried to penetrate the capital's defenses from the north. You can view a 30-minute film about the battle at the small museum and visitor's center. Then rent the $5 audio tour, which takes you through an informative, 8.5-mile drive. Highlights include Burnside Bridge, a structure depicted in many war paintings, and Bloody Lane, where many soldiers died. In early December, there's a beautiful and moving illumination, as the roads of the driving tour are lined with candles.

Words to the wise: *Unlike Manassas, this battlefield isn't as accommodating to exploration on foot.*

NOTES: For **Food,** there's a sandwich place on Route 65, half a mile south of the visitors center.

Directions: *From the Beltway, take I-270 north to Route 70 west. Exit at Route 65 south (Sharpsburg) and continue for 11 miles. The battlefield is on the left at the intersection of Route 34.*

Virginia

MANASSAS NATIONAL BATTLEFIELD PARK
6511 Sudley Road, Manassas

HOURS: Daily sunrise-sunset; visitors center daily 8:30-5 (until 6 in summer); closed Christmas. **COST:** $2 adults (17 and up); annual pass $15. **PHONE:** 703/361-1339. ♿

This is the biggest draw locally for Civil War buffs. Much of the landscape remains as it was in 1861 and 1862, when Confederate forces decisively defeated Union troops along the banks of Bull Run. First Manassas is considered the first major battle of the war, the initial opportunity for the two sides to experience each other's military prowess. From June to September, rangers provide half-hour guided tours of the area (tours are sporadically given in other months, except December, January and February). Other times, self-guided walking tours, which take about 45 minutes and cover about a mile, are the best bet for families. A 12-mile, 90-minute, self-guided driving tour also is available. If your family members are enthusiastic hikers, a network of trails provides great exercise and a lot more battle detail around the 5,000-acre park.

The visual highlight of the park is a heroic equestrian statue of Stonewall Jackson: "There stands Jackson, like a stone wall," the legend reads. Kids love checking out the lines of cannon and other artillery, as well as the homestead that was caught in the crossfire. At 2 on summer weekends, there's a musket firing display. The visitors center has a six-minute slide-show-with-lighted-map narrative and a few exhibits, including a memorable display of how soldiers were outfitted in mismatched uniforms. At last report, a renovated exhibition area was expected to be open in 1999.

Words to the wise: *Avoid Memorial Day-to-Labor Day crowds. The guided tours provide a wonderful window on what happened here, but they are certain to bore kids under 10, who probably are better off just free-lancing around the property.*

NOTES: Wheelchair access to the field depends on weather conditions. **Food:** Old Town Manassas, five miles south, is filled with restaurants (and antique shops). **Nearby:** The Manassas Museum (9101 Prince William St., 703/368-1873; Tu-Sun 10-5 ♿), has displays on the area's history, including but not limited to the Civil War.

Directions: *From the Beltway, take I-66 west and follow signs to Exit 47/Route 234.*

BALL'S BLUFF REGIONAL PARK
Ball's Bluff Road, Leesburg

HOURS: Daily dawn to dusk. **COST:** Free. **PHONE:** 703/352-5900 or 703/729-0596. ♿

This under-visited, 170-acre park is a gem, perfect for family walks and a bit of human-scale history. Nothing of momentous magnitude happened here. In 1861 some Northern scouts crossed the Potomac and were chased back by Confederate sentries. But the simple signage illuminates how this very typical Civil War scuffle played out and how it affected the lives of the soldiers — particularly the half-dozen who are buried in a small cemetery in the midst of the park. The park's two-mile trail takes you up to the Confederate promontory and then down to the calm and beautiful river — hard to imagine as the same wide, urbane expanse you see just 25 miles downstream below Great Falls.

NOTES: For **Food,** you'll find restaurants in Leesburg. **Nearby:** White's Ferry (see p. 44**),** which permits delightful passage across the river either way.

Directions: *Take I-495 to Exit 10. Go west on Route 7 to near Leesburg. Take a right on Route 15 north, left on Ball's Bluff Rd. and follow the signs.*

WAR MEMORIALS

District of Columbia

VIETNAM VETERANS MEMORIAL
Constitution Avenue at 21ˢᵗ Street NW

HOURS: 24 hours; Park Service rangers on duty 8 am-midnight. **COST:** Free. **PHONE:** 202/634-1568. **METRO:** Foggy Bottom. **WEB:** www.nps.gov/vive. ♿

This eloquent tribute to the 58,000 men and women who died in the Vietnam War communicates powerfully with kids, who seem to absorb the gravity of the experience as they walk along the twin walls inscribed with the names of the dead. Because the events commemorated are so recent — and because many visitors are overcome with emotion at the wall — kids seem to understand that this memorial is different from the other historical markers they encounter along the Mall. Once children can grasp that each one of those engraved names represents a person just like them — and a family just like yours — war takes on a whole new meaning. The two sculptures — Frederick Hart's group of three soldiers to the west and Glenna Goodacre's three figures of the VIETNAM WOMEN'S MEMORIAL to the east — complete the tribute. You may want to point out the design's symbolic details: The walls point to the Washington Monument and the Lincoln Memorial, and the granite is reflective so visitors "see" themselves among the departed.

Words to the wise: *Like Arlington Cemetery, this isn't a place for kids who are giddy or too rambunctious.*

U.S. NAVY MEMORIAL AND NAVAL HERITAGE CENTER
701 Pennsylvania Avenue NW

HOURS: M-Sat 9:30-5 (10:30-5 in winter), Sun noon-4. **COST:** Free, except for movie. **PHONE:** 202/737-2300. **METRO STOP:** Archives/Navy Memorial. ♿

Don't expect anything like the Navy Museum at this small, downtown tribute. Outside, a handsome plaza features ship masts, a giant rendering of the globe designed to demonstrate how much of it is covered by water, and a rim of friezes depicting chapters in U.S. naval history. Kids will be briefly diverted. Inside, the only real attraction for youngsters is an absorbing Imax-style movie about life on an aircraft carrier ($3.75 for adults, $3 for kids 18 and under and seniors; the film generally is shown at 11 and 1).

Notes: For **Food,** a number of restaurants are in the area. **Nearby:** National Gallery of Art, FBI Building, Ford's Theatre, National Portrait Gallery.

KOREAN WAR VETERANS MEMORIAL
23rd Street and Independence Avenue NW

Phone: 202/619-7222. **METRO STOP:** Foggy Bottom.

The newest war memorial on the Mall, this set of 19 stainless-steel figures was dedicated in 1995 to those who lost their lives in the Korean conflict. It's a largely traditional rendering of war, and kids are likely to find the realistic figures, fully armed, dressed for foul weather and displaying a range of emotions, fascinating. Behind them is a wall bearing a mural and the inscription "Freedom Isn't Free," which could prompt some interesting discussion.

NOTES: For another fix on the location, the site is in West Potomac Park, south of the Lincoln Memorial Reflecting Pool.

Virginia

MARINE CORPS MEMORIAL
Off the George Washington Parkway, Arlington

HOURS: 24 hours (families should visit during daylight). **COST:** Free. **PHONE:** 703/285-1925. **METRO STOP:** Rosslyn. ♿

This realistic sculpture, dedicated to Marines who died in the service's many missions around the world, interprets the famous photo of World War II Marines struggling to raise Old Glory at Iwo Jima, the obscure Pacific Island where 6,800 Americans died. The park also is the site of summer concerts by the Marine Band (Tuesdays at 7:30 p.m., June-Aug.; see p. 121). Kids can get a dose of world history by reading the inscribed names and dates of the Marines' many global missions. On the same patch of ground is the NETHERLANDS CARILLON (703/285-2598), a Dutch gift to the United States for helping liberate that nation from the Nazis. The 49-bell instrument is played Saturdays from 2 to 4 (April-May), 6 to 8 (June-August) and 2 to 4 (September). Visitors can ascend the tower to watch the bell-ringer — and to absorb an even more impressive Washington cityscape.

NOTES: For another fix on location, the memorial is at Exit 75 off of I-66, just north of Arlington Cemetery. **Nearby:** The Newseum.

OTHER FACILITIES and TALES

District of Columbia

NAVY MUSEUM
Navy Yard, 901 M Street SE, Building 76.

HOURS: Weekdays 9-4 (until 5 Memorial Day-Labor Day); Sat & Sun 10-5. Closed major holidays. **COST:** Free. **PHONE:** 202/433-4882 or 202/433-2651 (recording). **METRO:** Eastern Market. ♿

The area's most impressive and kid-friendly collection of militaribilia is isolated in this compound in Southeast Washington, and it's worth the trip. The museum, which is housed in a former gun factory, offers a robust mixture of artwork (heroic seascapes of U.S. naval adventures), miniatures (ship models, some in bottles, some in glass cases, some out on a table) and full-size artifacts (a climbable, World War II-vintage antiaircraft gun, a replica of the Apollo space capsule). While it tells the story of the U.S. Navy from its creation to fight pirates through Operation Desert Storm, there's no fierce chronology or imposing text for kids to deal with. The collection is eclectic enough to sustain interest from toddlers and teens. Children also love the retired missiles and weaponry poised for display in the front yard. Afterwards, be sure to take a tour of the U.S.S. Barry (see p. 42).

Words to the wise: *The Marine Corps Museum and Combat Art Gallery also are within the Navy Yard complex, but the Navy Museum is the real draw for kids.*

NOTES: There's an on-campus McDonald's, but few other amenities are available in the neighborhood.

Directions: *From the Beltway, take I-295 south to I-395 (Southeast Expressway) and follow signs to the Navy Yard. Or take I-395 north from Virginia, follow as it turns into 395 east and follow signs.*

Maryland

UNITED STATES NAVAL ACADEMY
King George Street, Annapolis (or enter from Annapolis City Dock)

HOURS: Daily 9-5 (Jan. & Feb. 9-4), Sun grounds open at 11:30; closed major holidays. **PHONE:** 410/263-6933 (visitor information); 410/293-3109 (event recording). **WEB:** www.nadn.navy.mil. ♿

A visit to The Yard — the historic campus of the college that trains U.S. naval officers — is a pleasant diversion from Annapolis' often crowded City Dock, and it's worth a special trip for kids interested in ships, warfare and military history. The Armel-Leftwich Visitor Center is largely a gift shop and tour-departure site; its exhibits are thin and mostly promotional. The center, though, does afford a sweeping view of the Annapolis waterfront. A walk along the promenade is a great way to begin a visit. If you're doing the self-guided tour, focus on three sites: Bancroft Hall, the massive dormitory that holds an entire 4,000-member class of midshipmen. Its public and ceremonial spaces are impressive — note the illuminated ceiling — but aside from the building itself, few displays are likely to engage younger kids (two scale-model dioramas, for instance, are perched too high for them to see). Out front is Tecumseh Court (named for the bronze casting of the Indian warrior that adorned an early Navy warship), where the middies assemble to bugle and drums every weekday at 12:15.

The second highlight is the crypt of John Paul Jones, appended to the chapel. It's a spooky grotto where the body of Jones lies in a grand marble sarcophagus. In bays surrounding it are artifacts related to the career of the American Revolution's naval hero (and alleged coiner of the phrase, "I have not yet begun to fight"), including some war decorations, a sword he may have used in battle and models and paintings of ships he commanded. But if it's model ships and paintings you crave, head directly to highlight number three, Preble Hall, for a 35,000-item collection of artifacts, photos, maps and paintings — and, more likely to impress the kids, perhaps the largest fleet of handcrafted ship models in captivity, some dating from the 1600s. All around the campus are massive cannon, anchors and monuments, but the two biggest kid-pleasers are right across King George Street from the Visitors Center: a 1950s six-man submarine designed to launch clandestine frogman attacks in enemy harbors, and a mid-century Navy jet. No climbing is allowed, but kids love just touching the things.

> **Words to the wise:** *The guided tours ($5.50, adults, $3.50 grades 1-12, $4.50 seniors) take about an hour and a half and are too demanding for the 8-and-under crowd. But groups with older kids truly interested in the place will enjoy the extra detail. Hours and frequency vary with seasons and day of week (though in high season they usually depart hourly); call the information number for schedule. If you're seeking the spectacle of the daily mealtime assembly of middies, it's held weekdays only.*

NOTES: Disability access is good to each of the three attractions cited above, though the old buildings' elevators are a good distance from walking paths. **Food:** The Drydock restaurant in Dahlgren Hall is open to the public, and Annapolis has an array of eateries. Picnicking is not permitted on Academy grounds. **Parking:** Except during high season, visitor parking is available near Gate 1; other times, pay lots are your best bet.

Virginia

ARLINGTON NATIONAL CEMETERY
Off the George Washington Parkway and Memorial Bridge, Arlington

HOURS: Oct.-Mar. daily 8-5, April-Sept. 8-7. **COST:** Free, except for parking.
PHONE: 703/697-2131. **METRO STOP:** Arlington Cemetery. ♿

A cemetery is the one inevitable consequence of war. Arlington is an impressive one: somber but beautiful in the symmetry of its quarter-million graves, inspiring in the sacrifices made by those buried there (not all of whom necessarily died in battle). Why bring children? It's an important part of our nation's history, of course. It's also an introduction to the sort of duty and commitment children aren't often exposed to these days. This is most evident at the Tomb of the Unknowns: It's guarded 24 hours a day, a ramrod straight sentinel pacing a precise 21 steps in front of it before pausing for 21 seconds and retracing his steps. ("Why?" your child may ask, a question you may have trouble answering.) Famous Americans are buried here — John and Robert Kennedy, Joe Louis, Richard Byrd, Pierre L'Enfant — and the visitors center has good maps to help you find their grave sites. (To find a veteran buried in Arlington, you'll need the name, branch of service and year of death.)

Also here is **ARLINGTON HOUSE,** the Robert E. Lee family home that the Union commandeered during the Civil War (the burial of Union and "Colored" troops in his front yard being a not-so-subtle insult to the general and the start of Arlington Cemetery). Arlington House is now a memorial to Lee, and one of the better views of Washington can be had from this spot, though it's a bit of a hike up the hill. (If you think you'd rather be driven around in narrated comfort, the cemetery is a stop on Tourmobile's route.)

The cemetery's **WOMEN IN MILITARY SERVICE TO AMERICA** memorial is a cool bit of architecture that addresses contributions women have made to our nation's security. But since it's more memorial than museum, there are no exhibits to enlighten the kids. There are a few displays of memorabilia from women soldiers — uniforms, gas masks, photos of female pilots — but just as prominent are displays on the construction of the memorial itself, certain to bore most children. Parents of daughters, especially, may wish that there were a little more can-do attitude on display. There's a gift shop, though, where you can pick up neat reproductions and postcards of historic posters ("Every Girl Pulling for Victory" says one).

Words to the wise: *Most kids won't need reminding, but running, laughing and general foolishness are inappropriate here.*

Nearby: Pentagon, Iwo Jima Memorial.

Directions: *From Washington, go across the Memorial Bridge. From elsewhere, take the George Washington Parkway.*

STONEWALL JACKSON MUSEUM AT HUPP'S HILL
Route 11 North, Strasburg

HOURS: M-Sat 10-5, Sun 12-5. **COST:** Adults $3.50, $2 6-17 and seniors. **PHONE:** 540/465-5884. ♿

Although this facility is farther away from the Washington area than most places in this book, it's so specifically tuned to children's needs that it's worth the haul. In fact, if battlefields bore you and you can stand only a single Civil War trip with small kids, make this the one. Half the building is given over to an intimate museum highlighting the back-and-forth Battle of Cedar Creek, whose resolution in favor of the Union kept the Shenandoah Valley under Northern control. It also celebrates the museum's namesake, who became a legend for his military maneuvering at Manassas and elsewhere in these parts.

More important, the back half of the museum is a kid zone, featuring boys' and girls' period costumes, tiny encampments with tents where the kids can hunker, and a pair of saddled wooden horses they can mount. There are all sorts of real and replica artifacts to play with, from soap dishes to scabbards. The kids easily can kill half an hour here, and the play-acting invites them to view the war from a participant's point of view. The artifacts on display under glass are also memorable — terrifying medical and dental tools, stamps and coins, pens and letters and, of course, weaponry. The kids can touch primitive artillery shells and even some rifles. The grounds outside are pitted with trenches and "lunettes," earthworks used as cannon mounts, which again invite kids to see the war as something that really happened *right here* and, as the landscape reveals, not all *that* long ago.

Words to the wise: *The signage for the museum proper is insidery and nearly impenetrable. Unless your group includes a serious buff, don't expect to understand much about the Cedar Creek campaign.*

NOTES: For **Food,** the Hotel Strasburg has an elegant dining room; if you're flush and the kids can be respectful, it's a special place for dinner. There are less expensive Strasburg choices as well. **Nearby:** Many Civil War sites, including the Battle of Cedar Creek Battlefield and the Old Hupp Homestead (call 703/465-9197). The Museum of American Presidents (540/465-5999), with a modest collection (a lock of Washington's hair, James Madison's desk), also is close by.

Directions: *From the Beltway, take I-66 west to I-81 south. Get off at the first Strasburg exit (Exit 298/Route 11). Turn left on Route 11 south. The center is about a mile down on the right.*

NATIONAL MUSEUM OF JEWISH MILITARY HISTORY
1811 R Street NW

HOURS: Weekdays 9-5, Sun 1-5; closed Sat. **COST:** Free. **PHONE:** 202/265-6280.
METRO STOP: Dupont Circle.

One of the more obscure slices of U.S. military history is explored in the exhibits in this townhouse. Displays focus on Jewish military contributions from World War II to Desert Storm. This could make an interesting follow-up to a visit to the B'nai B'rith Klutznick National Jewish Museum (see p. 23).

MILITARY BANDS

ALL FOUR BRANCHES of the military have crackerjack bands that give free performances around Washington. They rotate from mid-June to August, with different branches playing different nights at different places. Two key venues are the Sylvan Theater, on the grounds of the Washington Monument, where bands perform Tuesday, Thursday, Friday and Sunday evenings, and the East Terrace of the U.S. Capitol, where they hold forth Monday, Tuesday, Thursday and Friday evenings. Call each branch for information on who's where when: Air Force, 202/767-5658; Army, 703/696-3399 (www.army.mil/armyband); Navy, 202/433-2525, and Marine Corps , 202/433-4011. In addition:

MARINE BARRACKS PARADE
This Marines' weekly concert and parade is one of Washington's great spectacles of tradition and military showmanship, with martial music, precision marching and a silent drill team. The parade is held Fridays at 8:45 p.m., May through September. You need reservations, at least three weeks in advance. Send your   request in writing (with desired date, an alternate date, number in the party, return address and phone number; it will be confirmed by return mail) to: Adjutant, Marine Barracks, Eighth and I streets SE, Washington, DC 20390-5000. For information, call 202/433-6060. (Can't get tickets? Go to one of the bands' shorter Tuesday summer shows at the Marine Corps Memorial.)

TWILIGHT TATTOO
A similar display, with the U.S. Army Band, a fife and drums corps and precision drill team, takes place on the Ellipse grounds, near the White House, every Wednesday at 7 p.m. from mid-July to August. Call 202/685-2851 or 703/696-3399.

10

LIVING HISTORY

THIS CHAPTER EXPLORES the past in varied forms, from homes of famous Americans to discursions on how ordinary Americans lived and played (especially played) to the devastating effects of human prejudice. Our criteria for inclusion have been fairly loose, including hands-on archaeology, some fussy historic homes and museums bursting with historic artifacts. (If you're after model farms of yesteryear, though, they're in Chapter 7.)

Some places here are not for all kids. The heavily visited U.S. Holocaust Memorial Museum, for example, demands careful parental judgment on whether children are ready to cope with that enormous tragedy. Similarly, Baltimore's Great Blacks in Wax Museum has one exhibit on the tortured occupants of a slave ship and another on lynchings, which parents may find too disturbing for some children.

In less difficult cases, some kids simply may be bored by static displays of rusty tools or musty furniture or old-fashioned clothing. Many sites feature docents dressed in what is invariably referred to as "period garb," acting as if the cotton gin was never invented and penicillin never discovered. It can be more than a little precious when some lady in a mobcap asks you what a digital watch is, but many children connect with what is essentially play-acting.

Because of the central roles that slavery and racism have played in American history, we've separated out explorations of African American history, even though a planned Washington museum addressing the subject has unfortunately not yet been built. Since Alexandria — once the most bustling and cosmopolitan town on the Potomac — is basically one big piece of living history, we've organized it separately as well. Finally, water was the fossil fuel of the 18th Century, and the Washington region is awash in one of the prominent water uses of those days: grist mills. We review them here, too.

The attractions discussed can, of course, be visited in any season, but timing a visit to coincide with when your child is learning about a particular historic period at school might be more rewarding for both of you.

District of Columbia

NATIONAL MUSEUM OF AMERICAN HISTORY
14th Street and Constitution Avenue NW

HOURS: Daily 10-5:30. **COST**: Free. **PHONE**: 202/357-2700 (TDD: 202/357-1729). **METRO STOP**: Federal Triangle. **WEB**: www.si.edu. ♿

"In most families, there's someone who hates to throw anything out." So begins an official publication on the National Museum of American History, proud pack rat of these United States. This is a place to return to again and again as children advance in school and develop new interests. Like the National Museum of Natural History, though, it can get crowded, so try planning a winter visit, and don't expect every room, display case or bit of memorabilia to engage every child every time.

For many year, the first thing you saw when entering from the Mall nicely summed up the museum's two-pronged mandate: the massive Star-Spangled Banner, with a Foucault pendulum swinging entrancingly in front of it. That's a bit of American history and a bit of science. It's something a little static with something a little active. The pendulum is still there, its 204-pound bob illustrating the Earth's rotation by knocking down tiny red pegs (one every 23 minutes in case you *just* missed one). But the flag has moved to the southwest corner of the second floor, where in early 1999 it was to begin being restored under the watchful eyes of museumgoers, who can peer through a 50-foot-long glass window like sidewalk foremen.

The second floor, which is where you'll be if you enter from the Mall, is mostly culture and history. The First Ladies hall is more than inaugural ball gowns. Yes, there are those (and non-inaugural frocks as well), but the exhibit also attempts to cover the social and political roles of presidential spouses, especially such activists as Eleanor Roosevelt, whose recorded voice is heard making a radio announcement on December 7, 1941 at a "very serious moment." The contributions of less famous women are noted in "From Parlor to Politics," which explores women's battles in such areas as improving public health, gaining access to higher education and winning the right to vote. "Field to Factory" traces the migration of African Americans from the agricultural south to the manufacturing jobs of the north. Many exhibits here and elsewhere are of the frozen tableau school, larded with historic objects and explanatory wall text. Don't expect kids to read every syllable or to dwell on every attraction. Exceptions are the interactive Hands-On History Room (see accompanying box) and the Hands On Science Room (see p. 51).

The museum's first floor, which is what you enter from Constitution Avenue, has a more technological focus. "A Material World" is a jumble of manmade objects, from bricks to transistor radios. Children who are into big machinery will like the agriculture and transportation exhibits, whose holdings include tractors, a Conestoga wagon,

TOUCHING TIME

HANDS ON HISTORY ROOM,
NATIONAL MUSEUM OF AMERICAN HISTORY
14th Street and Constitution Avenue NW, 2nd Floor

HOURS: Tu-Sun noon-3. **COST:** Free. ♿

Looking at an object through a sheet of glass just isn't the same as handling it. Here, handling is required. Docents guide kids 5 and up through activities designed to flesh out different exhibits in the larger Smithsonian museum. The history is soft-pedaled, not so overpowering that younger kids will lose interest but there for the grasping if they want to learn. Although the Hands-On History Room is popular, you shouldn't be too mobbed once you're in there. That's because the museum limits visitors to 35 each half-hour. The 30-minute window means that you won't have enough time to do everything. Pick a few activities and stick with them. Kids like climbing atop a highwheeler bicycle, turning the crank on a cotton gin, making rope (and taking home their own length), tapping out messages (or gibberish) on a telegraph key, sorting mail in a 19th Century efficiency test, running a treadle sewing machine and unpacking a Colonial-era girl's trunk, comparing what she cherished with what they own today.

> **Words to the wise:** *To control the crowds, (free) tickets are handed out starting at noon during busy times. They're often gone by 1. Also, they mean it when they say ages 5 and up. Littler kids just get in the way.*

bicycles and a rare Tucker automobile. The railroad hall is the nicest, an airy space punctuated by the recorded chugging of a steam locomotive. Dominating the scene is a massive green locomotive (which, unfortunately, kids can't climb). The maritime hall has re-creations of a 1920s engine room and a Mississippi towboat pilothouse (you can sit behind the wheel and call up videos on exactly what a towboat is), plus lots (and lots) of ship models. Your charges, though, may be most impressed by a replica of a tattoo parlor, with a well-illustrated sailor mannequin sitting in the chair. Other exhibits here probably will appeal only to kids with specialized interests (for instance, tiny dioramas in the civil engineering area, which somehow manage to diminish such massive endeavors as tunneling and bridge building).

Also worth a stop is "The Information Age," a big, interactive exhibit tracing the collecting, organizing and transmitting of information, from the telegraph to the World Wide Web. There's a model of the first transistor, displays of old TVs and hi-fi culture equipment (TV screens get bigger as stereos get smaller), an assembly-line robot that dances around an automobile and the prototype Apple computer. Get a barcode-bearing brochure at the exhibit's entrance and you can scan it at various stops along the way, getting a satisfying "beep." At other interactive stations, you can offer up your fingerprints and learn how the FBI uses computers to store and retrieve the loops and whorls, punch in your ZIP code to see what direct marketers think of your neighborhood, or print out a detailed account of your visit. ("As visitor 2,235,950 you were in our network from 11:56 a.m. until 12:11 p.m. on June 16." Scary.) You also can surf a few carefully selected Web pages just before you leave the exhibit. Some interactive stuff is bound to be on the blink when you visit, but then it wouldn't be an accurate evocation of the information age if it were otherwise. The museum's top floor probably has the least to offer kids, though it does have the ruby slippers worn by Judy Garland in "The Wizard of Oz," a "Star Trek" phaser, Indiana Jones' hat and jacket, and Michael Jordan's jersey. Kermit the Frog is near the escalators outside the "Information Age" exhibit. These are just some of the popu-

NOTES: For **Food,** American History has two cafeterias, one specializing in ice cream.
Nearby: Natural History Museum, Old Post Office Pavilion, National Aquarium.

UNITED STATES HOLOCAUST MEMORIAL MUSEUM
100 Raoul Wallenberg Place SW (near 14ᵗʰ and Independence Avenue)

HOURS: Daily 10-5:30; closed Yom Kippur, Christmas. **COST:** Free (see **Notes** for details on getting tickets). **PHONE:** 202/488-0400 (TDD: 202/488-0406). **WEB:** www.ushmm.org. &

This heavy-demand museum memorializes an immense tragedy and is necessarily graphic. The three-story permanent exhibition is not appropriate for anyone under 11. Even then, you should be sure your child can deal with exhibits that often deeply disturb adults, recounting as they do the systematic Nazi extermination of six million Jews and millions of others, including up to 1.5 million children. (Parts of the museum, including "Daniel's Story," are suitable for ages 8 and up, and access to them doesn't require the timed-entry tickets needed for the permanent exhibition.)

If you deem your charges ready, head first to "Remember the Children: Daniel's Story," an artfully told narrative of what it was like to be a Jewish child in Germany as the world turned upside down. It opens with a five-minute film composed of a series of photographs from before and during World War II. The narrator is the adult Daniel, who makes it clear that he and his father survived the Holocaust but that his sister and mother perished. Visitors wend their way through re-creations of Daniel's house, the sounds of laughter and family chatter playing over speakers. Pages from Daniel's diary are mounted in the various rooms, describing the accumulation of slights he endures (his friends won't play with him, he can't go to the pool). Things gradually worsen (his father's store is destroyed), and the light, almost fairy-tale design of the early parts of the exhibit starts to darken as Daniel's family is sent first to a ghetto — boarded up windows, tattered suitcases, letters that children can pull down and read — and then to a concentration camp ("an awful place with barbed wire and guards and hardly any food," says Daniel). The background sounds now turn to crying, with desperate conversations of women heard.

Throughout this exhibit, the Holocaust is described in terms children can understand. "Have you ever been punished for something you didn't do?" the narrator asks in the introductory film. "We were." As you leave the exhibit, you enter a room with phone kiosks playing recorded questions and answers ("What was the Holocaust?" "Who were the Nazis?"). Markers and paper are available for children to write down reactions to the exhibit, some of which are posted.

The museum offers a great deal else to see and hear and watch. For children, another fine attraction is the orientation film in the Meyerhoff Theater. While it contains quite a bit on the development and architecture of the museum itself, the 14-minute film also concisely outlines, in a non-graphic way, the rise of the Nazis, the implementation of the Final Solution and the eventual end of the war. Older kids, especially those who can learn at their own pace or are working on homework assignments, might benefit from a visit to the second-floor Wexner Learning Center. There they can call up all sorts of Holocaust-related information using touch-screen computers. Most information is displayed in multimedia form (with music selections, photos and witness interviews) and hot links, so that a child exploring a major subject (such as "Anti-Semitism," "The Camp System" or "Children") can veer off into related topics.

Before you leave, your family should visit the Hall of Remembrance, a somber but light- and candle-filled memorial to Holocaust victims, and the Wall of Remembrance, which is covered with tiles hand-painted by more than 3,000 American schoolchildren. The tiles create an explosion of color that is at first jarring in this melancholy museum, but the simple images and earnest sentiments on them probably express what your kids will be feeling.

Words to the wise: *This is an important museum, but it's not one to wander into blithely. Prepare beforehand with a trip to the library or a visit to the Holocaust Museum's excellent Web site. It includes a brief history of the Holocaust and smart guidelines for teaching about it.*

NOTES: Passes are needed for the permanent exhibition. Same-day passes are at the first-floor Pass Desk, 14th St. entrance. They are understandably harder to get on weekends than weekdays. For advance passes, call Protix, 703/218-6500 or 800/400-9373 ($1.75 per pass and $1-per-order service charge). **Food:** A cafe serves salads, sandwiches and some kosher entrees. **Nearby:** Bureau of Engraving and Printing, Ronald Reagan International Trade Center, Washington Monument, Jefferson Memorial, Tidal Basin, attractions on the Mall.

FORD'S THEATRE
511 10ᵗʰ Street NW

HOURS: Daily 9-5; closed Christmas. **COST**: Free. **PHONE:** 202/426-6924 (TDD: 202-426-1749). **METRO:** Metro Center, Gallery Place/Chinatown. **WEB:** www.nps.gov/foth. 🦽

The theater where Abraham Lincoln was fatally shot on April 14, 1865 is more active and compelling than most historic sites. It looks much as it did when Lincoln was assassinated by John Wilkes Booth (and is a working live theater today). You can enter the balcony area and get a Booth's-eye view of the rocking chair Lincoln occupied during the fateful performance of "Our American Cousin." The box looks precisely as it did that night. All day, at 15 minutes past the hour, visitors occupy theater seats in the balcony or orchestra and listen to Park Service employees explain the events surrounding that night. Afterward, you can go downstairs to the Lincoln Museum to see the topcoat Lincoln wore that night (its arm torn off by souvenir hunters), the gun and dagger Booth used in his attack and a pillow stained with Lincoln's blood. You'll get enough context about Lincoln's life and times to satisfy without overwhelming. Then you can cross the street to PETERSON HOUSE, where Lincoln died the next morning. The house offers a brief tour, remarkable mostly for how small the (replica) bed seems for a man 6 feet, 4 inches tall. If there's a long line, it's safe to skip it.

Words to the wise: *You can't visit when rehearsals or matinee performances are being staged, on a Thursday, Saturday or Sunday. If you plan to visit on one of these days, call ahead. Go early if you can; two or more tour buses can overwhelm the place. January and September are "low season" for tourism — and prime time for locals to visit.*

NOTES: While there's access for the disabled to the theater (via the front door) and to the museum (via a chair lift in the rear), there's no access to the balcony. **Food:** A Hard Rock Cafe is next door and Planet Hollywood is on the next block, but tour groups often crowd both. Other restaurants are close by. **Parking**: Numerous pay lots are in the neighborhood; street parking is very limited. **Nearby:** FBI Building, National Portrait Gallery, Old Post Office Pavilion and Tower, MCI Center.

ARTS AND INDUSTRIES BUILDING
900 Jefferson Drive SW

HOURS: Daily 10-5:30. **COST**: Free. **PHONE:** 202/357-2700 (TDD: 202/357-1729). **WEB:** www.si.edu. **METRO:** Smithsonian.

The second building constructed by the Smithsonian (the Smithsonian Castle was the first), the Arts and Industries Building originally contained wonders displayed at Philadelphia's Centennial Exhibition in 1876. It still contains many of those wonders, except now they're more than 100 years old. The building's formidable architecture appeals to many children — it's almost as castle-like as the Castle, and it has an ornate tile interior and a fountain — but it houses a collection that's frankly pretty musty. There are large examples of industry (a Baldwin locomotive, various massive tools) and small examples (women's clothes of the period, some artfully arranged files). Unless your kid is really into High Victoriana, this museum isn't worth more than a walk-through on the way to Discovery Theatre (which is housed here). While the collection is mostly static, Arts and Industries does mount rotating exhibits on the African American experience. Past ones have examined the black church and black women sculptors.

Nearby: Smithsonian Castle and Visitor Information Center, Hirshhorn Gallery, National Air and Space Museum, Sackler Gallery, National Museum of African Art, Freer Gallery.

DAR MUSEUM
1776 D Street NW

HOURS: M-F 8:30-4, Sun 1-5. Tours: weekdays 10-2:30, all day Sun. **COST:** Free. **PHONE:** 202/879-324. **METRO** : Farragut West. **WEB:** www.dar.org/museum/index.html. &

The Daughters of the American Revolution's museum has a nice collection of Colonial-era artifacts and furnishings and mounts surprisingly good special exhibits on life (especially women's lives) in pre-20th Century America. Hour-long tours take visitors past 33 rooms decorated in various period styles. (The toy-filled New Hampshire Attic is a favorite, as is an area where youngsters can paw the merchandise.) But a tour isn't the best approach to this place, especially since you can't cut out if your kid's eyes glaze over. Try to make reservations (202/879-3239) for the "Colonial Adventure." Offered the first and third Sundays of the month at 2, it invites children ages 5 to 7 to dress up along with a similarly garbed guide and tour the museum in a more fitting style.

Nearby: Lincoln Memorial, White House.

WASHINGTON DOLLS' HOUSE AND TOY MUSEUM
5236 44th Street NW

HOURS: Tu-Sat 10-5, Sun noon-5. **COST:** $4 adults, $2 under 11, $3 seniors. **PHONE:** 202/244-0024; 202/363-6400. **METRO STOP:** Friendship Heights.

This is a captivating collection of mostly Victorian dollhouses, miniatures, games and other toys, a place for toy lovers intrigued by a time before Power Rangers and Tickle-Me Elmo roamed the land. The dollhouses range from elaborate three-story mansions to an incredibly detailed kitchen, its shelves groaning under the weight of pots and pans. It's the sort of stuff that puts today's pink, plastic Barbie bungalows to shame. Befitting the collection, the museum is relatively small, but lots of items are crammed into a modest space. Dolls and dollhouse ephemera are for sale in the museum shop.

> **Words to the wise:** *Everything's behind glass, and kids who haven't quite come to terms with "look but don't touch" may feel frustrated. They can get a little more interactive in the Edwardian Tea Room, a nice place for tea party-loving birthday celebrants.*

PRESIDENTIAL MATERIAL

EVERY U.S. PRESIDENT with the exception of George Washington has lived in the White House, but around town you will of course find memorials, monuments and tributes to many of Washington's successors. Not all are worth a trip unto themselves, but any of them can make informative, sometimes fascinating stopovers during other outings. We examine those that are of most interest to parents and kids.

GEORGE WASHINGTON. If the kids are getting a dose of the alleged cherry-tree-chopper in school, you can visit several places for more insight into the Father of Our Country. First should be **MOUNT VERNON** (see p. 135). The 555-foot-high **WASHINGTON MONUMENT** (the Mall, 202/426-6840; www.nps.gov/wamo), despite its skyline prominence, is one of the city's more disappointing attractions, usually with a long wait to ride a cramped elevator to sample views that, while impressive, are clouded by thick, awkwardly placed lenses. At this writing, the momument was closed for renovations. Tours were to resume in December 1998 while exterior stonework continued, though some scheduling disruptions were possible. But you'd be unwise to stand in a long line to visit this memorial. Our recommendation: Save it for a summer evening, when there are extended hours (to near midnight from April through Labor Day), the crowds have thinned and you can take in a Washington sunset from all four directions. You can get free timed tickets at the monument's kiosk or in advance through TicketMaster (800/505-5040; modest service charges).

For a view of the first president as engineer and entrepreneur, visit the museum and grounds of Virginia's **GREAT FALLS PARK** (see pp. 102-104) which tells the story of his ill-fated Potowmack Canal Company. For a stranger and intimate view into Washington the Freemason, visit the **GEORGE WASHINGTON MASONIC NATIONAL MEMORIAL** in Alexandria (see p. 142). And when you're in Baltimore, the other **WASHINGTON MONUMENT** (Charles Street and Mount Vernon Place; 410/396-0929) makes a great side trip. For a $1 donation, you can climb the steps of the 178-foot-tall monument (described as the nation's "first formal" monument to Washington, dating from 1831) for a breathtaking view of one of the Baltimore's most urbane neighborhoods.

THOMAS JEFFERSON. The **JEFFERSON MEMORIAL,** at the southern end of the Tidal Basin (daily 8 am-midnight; 202/426-6821; www.nps.gov/thje), creates a powerful impression of our third president, credited with authoring the Declaration of Independence (viewable at the **NATIONAL ARCHIVES;** p. 178) and viewed as America's greatest Renaissance man. Its neoclassical form recalls the amateur architect's personal tastes, as well as his self-designed home near Charlottesville (during your visit, you may want to grab a nickel, whose back carries an image of Monticello and front a portrait of Jefferson). Inside is a big open space surrounding a three-times-life-size statue of the man. Excerpts from his writings are engraved, including, in a grand sweep around the dome: "I have sworn upon the altar of God eternal hostility against every form of tyranny over the mind of man." If you can sufficiently explain the nuances of that one to your kids, they — or at least you — may qualify for AP credits. This is another site that gathers power during a nighttime viewing.

ABRAHAM LINCOLN. The LINCOLN MEMORIAL (daily 8 a.m.-midnight; 202/426-6895; www.nps.gov/linc), anchoring the West end of the Mall, is our hands-down favorite memorial for kids and perhaps the closest thing Washington has to a patch of sacred ground. Every visitor, even a baby in a backpack, seems to sense the power of the place. As you walk up the front steps, the statue of a seated, brooding Lincoln looms larger with every stride (seated, he's 19 feet tall, like Jefferson, but if the figure were to stand it would be 28 feet tall). There are plenty of details to engage kids. Across the top frieze you'll find the names and admission dates of the 36 United States at the time of Lincoln's death; just above are the names of all 48 states (lacking only Alaska and Hawaii) that were in place when the memorial was dedicated in 1922. Along the interior walls are two works of Lincoln's prose worth absorbing with older children: the vaunted Gettysburg Address and, more powerful thanks to its relative obscurity, the second inaugural address. Turn your back on the Lincoln statue and the view of the Mall, with the 2,000-foot reflecting pool and the Washington Monument rising behind, is stunning. Walk around back and look across the Potomac River at ARLINGTON CEMETERY (see p. 119), where you can see both ARLINGTON HOUSE (the final resting place of Confederate leader Robert E. Lee, a former Union general until he signed up with his native Virginia during the Civil War) and the gravesite, with the eternal flame, of John F. Kennedy. In the base of the memorial is an informative mini-museum highlighting the role of the memorial as center in the struggle for civil rights. Other Lincoln sites around town include FORD'S THEATER AND LINCOLN MUSEUM and, directly across the street, PETERSON HOUSE (see p. 128 for both). Like the Jefferson and Washington memorials, Lincoln's is best visited at night, when dramatic interior lighting and the lighted rippling image on the reflecting pool leave potent impressions.

THEODORE ROOSEVELT. On ROOSEVELT ISLAND (see p. 94) you'll find a statue and inscriptions honoring the 26th president, a fitting tribute to the hearty outdoorsman, rugged individualist and military man.

FRANKLIN DELANO ROOSEVELT. The newest presidential tribute, the FRANKLIN D. ROOSEVELT MEMORIAL (202/619-7222; www.nps.gov/fdrm), is also one of the most innovative. Composed of four "rooms" (suggesting FDR's four terms), it provides more of a narrative about the man and his times than any other presidential memorial. It's also huge (7.5 acres) and filled with waterfalls, fountains, sculptures, gardens and various contemplative nooks. It offers plenty to engage kids and get them thinking about the depths (the Depression) and heights (victory in World War II) of the American Century. The first FDR tribute, located in front of the National Archives at Ninth Street and Pennsylvania Avenue NW and dedicated in 1965, bears only his name and birth and death dates. (FDR said he wanted a memorial the size of his desk, and so it is.)

JOHN F. KENNEDY. The 35th president's gravesite at ARLINGTON CEMETERY has burned with an eternal flame since his burial here in November 1963; the headstone is Cape Cod slate, and the marble plaza features quotations from his inaugural address. Nearby is a simple cross marking the grave of his brother Robert F. Kennedy, who was assassinated in 1968, the grave of Jacqueline Kennedy, buried here in 1994, and a tiny marker for the baby the Kennedys lost in 1961. The sweeping view of Washington across the river is one of the best. A living tribute to JFK is the JOHN F. KENNEDY CENTER FOR THE PERFORMING ARTS, containing a mid-century-style bust of Kennedy in the lobby.

If older kids want to indulge in local presidential obscurities, they have some choices. The **Grant Memorial**, on the West front of the Capitol, is a huge equestrian tribute to Ulysses S. Grant as Civil War hero (kids are certain to be amused by the lions, and the lesser soldiers, surrounding him). Near the reflecting pool is a modest remembrance of **James A. Garfield**, who served only four months in the White House before being assassinated. **William Howard Taft**, the 27th president, is buried at Arlington (in a grave located en route to the Kennedy site), and the massive, scenic span of Connecticut Avenue bridging Rock Creek carries his name.

Near National Airport, alongside the George Washington Memorial Parkway en route to National Airport, you'll find the **Lyndon Baines Johnson Memorial Grove**, 15 acres of gardens fronting a freeway and a rather unpleasant waterfront; there's a big chunk of Texas granite and some of that President's less colorful quotes (it's part of the larger Lady Byrd Johnson Park, a tribute to her role as beautifier of the U.S. landscape; Web: www.nps.gov/lyba). And the **Woodrow Wilson House** (2340 S St. NW; 202/387-4062) home of the 28th U.S. president (the only one to choose to live here after his presidency) may be a worthy stop for curious students 12 and up. The admission price ($5 adults, $4 seniors, $2.50 students) provides a movie and a tour; the kitchen is a time capsule of 1920s upper-class domestic life, and the library is full of souvenirs from Wilson's travels. Wilson, disabled by a stroke in 1919, used the vintage 1915 elevator to maneuver between the floors. Wilson is the only president buried in the District of Columbia; you can visit his tomb, adorned with the sword of a crusader, at WASHINGTON NATIONAL CATHEDRAL (see p. 198).

Finally, the area's largest collection of presidential portraiture is at the NATIONAL PORTRAIT GALLERY'S HALL OF PRESIDENTS (see p. 19). Not to be missed: Norman Rockwell's Richard Nixon, so pure and idealized that it makes you want to re-evaluate your opinion of both the subject and the artist.

Maryland

CHILDREN'S MUSEUM OF ROSE HILL MANOR PARK
1611 N. Market Street, Frederick

HOURS: Apr.-Oct: M-Sat 10-4, Sun 1-4; weekends only Nov.-early Dec.; closed Jan.-Mar. **COST:** $3 adults, $1 ages 2-17, $2 seniors. **PHONE:** 301/694-1648; 301/694-1646 to register a group. ♿

Rose Hill Manor, a fine Georgian residence that served as retirement home for Maryland's first elected governor (trivia quiz answer: Thomas Johnson), has been restored as a place where kids can learn about 19th Century life. It's one of the most hands-on of the area's many historic homes, a refreshing and useful departure from the look-but-don't-touch ethos of many historic properties. It's also unusually well equipped for young visitors (with a diaper-changing station in the women's rest room and footstools in the bathrooms). One of the nicest features is a period-outfitted playroom where kids can mess with antique toys such as a 100-year-old rocking horse, an old checkers set and handmade wooden dolls and dollhouses. Parents can just sit and relax. Enthusiastic docents lead tours, which focus on everyday life in 19th Century Maryland. There's a kitchen with a "beehive" brick oven, a sewing room, a blacksmith shop, a log cabin, a carriage museum, period herb and vegetable gardens and more. Along the way, kids are encouraged to touch some items and do things like card wool, spin thread, taste the popcorn families would eat for breakfast (that's right, popcorn) and lie down on the log cabin's bed.

Words to the wise: *The docents are well prepared to handle the 8-and-up crowd, but younger visitors may be bored. If you can, call ahead to make reservations.*

NOTES: The first floor and much of the grounds are easily accessible, though certain areas won't accommodate wheelchairs very easily. Call for specific advice. **Food:** There are plenty of places for lunch (as well as antique hunting) in Frederick.

CLARA BARTON HOUSE
5801 Oxford Road, Glen Echo

HOURS: Daily 10-4 (only by guided tour); closed major holidays. **COST:** Free. **PHONE:** 301/492-6245.

This 1891 wood-frame house, on the rim of Glen Echo Park, served as headquarters for the American Red Cross and as the retirement home of its founder, Clara Barton. You can see a pair of grand salons where Barton — humanitarian, suffragist, early equal rights advocate and, apparently, recurrent victim of clinical depression — greeted dignitaries. The huge central atrium is ringed by balconies and is topped by a large central air vent, which helped with air circulation and provided some heat relief in those pre-air-conditioned days.

Perhaps the most interesting part is the back office, a reconstruction of the places where Red Cross volunteers labored with early office machines (including a funky early copier) and some typewriters that were operated only by men, so physically taxing were they to use. As in most National Park Service facilities, docents are very familiar with the house's history and its most famous resident.

Words to the wise: *The Clara Barton House is likely to bore small children and isn't accommodating to strollers. Parents with kids in backpacks may not want to navigate the upper floors.*

NOTES: There's a ramp to the first floor. Upper floors, which get very hot in summer and are accessible via narrow stairs, may challenge some visitors. **Nearby:** Glen Echo Park.

BALTIMORE MUSEUM OF INDUSTRY
1415 Key Highway, Baltimore

HOURS: Summer: daily noon-5 (extended hours W), Sat 10-5. Labor Day-Memorial Day: Th-F, Sun noon-5, Sat 10-5, W 7 pm-9 pm. **COST:** $5 adults, $3.50 ages 6-18 and seniors, under 6 free; $17 group rate. **PHONE:** 410/727-4808. &

Think of this place as the Industrial Revolution equivalent of a farm museum: It helps children grasp how most urban Americans spent their days in the 19th and early 20th centuries — turning raw materials into manufactured goods in factories and craft shops. This transformed Baltimore cannery has hand-on exhibits of a machine shop, a sewing loft, a printing press and an assembly line. Not a place with slick multimedia demos, it offers mostly satisfying, turn-the-crank exploration. Special weekend activities, for $1 to $2 extra, let kids work at canning oysters (Sat 11, 2:30; Sun 2:30) and making small model cars (Sat-Sun 1).

NOTES: Nearby is Fort McHenry. For **Food**, your best bet is a quick drive to the Inner Harbor area.

Directions: *Take I-95 north to Exit 55 (Key Hwy./Fort McHenry National Monument). Make a left at the first light, cross under the roadway, and turn left again on Key Hwy. The museum is on the right.*

SANDY SPRING MUSEUM
17901 Bentley Road (off Route 108), Sandy Spring

HOURS: M, W & Th 9-4, Sun 12-4. **COST:** Free. **PHONE:** 301/774-0022. &

This tiny Montgomery County village is blessed with a new structure devoted to its history. Inside the airy facility is an assortment of old stuff: a Model T Ford, a re-creation of a country store (complete with checker board on a barrel), a large brick hearth and wrought iron cooking implements. Kids may enjoy trying their hand at a real loom. It's a modest collection of artifacts, more appropriate for older children. The younger set might enjoy occasional special programs.

Virginia

MOUNT VERNON
George Washington Parkway (eight miles south of Alexandria)

HOURS: Apr.-Aug.: daily 8-5; Sept. and Mar.: 9-5; Nov.-Feb.: 9-4. **COST:** $8 adults, $4 ages 6-11, $7.50 seniors, under 6 free. **PHONE:** 703/780-2000. **WEB:** www.mountvernon.org. ♿

While adults enjoy touring George Washington's plantation house, the long wait to get inside — and the subtlety of the period furnishings and details — often leave young children distracted and cranky. If you're visiting with the 10-and-under set, you may want to skip the main house (at least if there's a considerable line) and take the family to the wonderful outbuildings and grounds instead. The Colonial "campus" includes various preserved and reconstructed buildings illuminating life in the Colonial era: a smokehouse, a wash house, stables, various kitchen and food-preparation buildings and, not least, the slave quarters. Children tend to love the maze-like geometric gardens and the spooky George and Martha crypt.

Be sure to follow the trail downhill toward the river, where you'll find a wonderful recent addition that puts Mount Vernon solidly on the kids-places A-list: a hands-on, four-acre Colonial-era farm demonstrating George Washington's role as an innovative agriculturist. Docents smoke hog and show how tobacco was dried, animals kept, corn milled and so on. The highlight is a replica of Washington's 16-sided barn and a wheat-threshing machine. Hands-on activities are available from March to November.

The downhill trail also leads to a dock that offers a nice spot to view the river. There are two gift shops, one on the estate and one in the Mount Vernon Inn, outside the front gate. A treasure-hunt map that's available is ideal for older children who want to explore everything and can run off on their own.

> **Words to the wise:** *Call or check the Web for special events, which often are wonderful for children. If you take the trail all the way down to the river, save energy for the climb back up. In summer, carry a bottle of water.*

NOTES: In good weather, a great bonus way to do Mount Vernon is to take the family on a ride with Spirit Cruises (p. 46) or Potomac Riverboat Company (p. 48), both of which include visits to Washington's estate. **Food:** The Mount Vernon Inn has cheerful folks in period garb serving Colonial-style dishes. A Quick Bite to Eat, with burgers, sandwiches and the like, also is outside the gate. **Nearby:** Old Town Alexandria.

Directions: *Take the George Washington Pkwy. south, past Alexandria, until it becomes the Mount Vernon Memorial Hwy. You can't miss Mount Vernon.*

AFTER MOUNT VERNON . . .

AFTER YOU'VE BEEN to Mount Vernon, consider other historic Northern Virginia estates. They can give your kids a sense of the interconnectedness of Colonial life in these parts and of the vibrant scene that produced so many historic figures.

GUNSTON HALL
Gunston Road (Route 242), Lorton

HOURS: Daily 9:30-5. **COST**: $5, $4 seniors, $1.50 grades 1-12, under 6 free. **PHONE**: 703/550-9220. [&]

George Mason, author of Virginia's Bill of Rights (whose words "all men are by nature equally free and independent and have certain inherent rights" struck a chord with another Virginian), built this plantation house. The interior is fancier than Mount Vernon, with wonderful carved wood details. You can see the house only as part of a tour, so for kids bored with decorating, explore the grounds, including a reconstructed schoolhouse (with a switch on the teacher's desk and a chamber pot under the bed of the sleeping loft) and kitchen yard. The impressive boxwood gardens tower over grown-ups, let alone children, and are fun to run through. Every family gets a "Plantation Detective" booklet that older kids may enjoy filling out. A big kite festival is held every March.

SULLY HISTORIC SITE
Route 28, Chantilly

HOURS: Mar.-Dec.: W-Mon 11-4. **COST**: $4, $3 students 16 and up, $2 children and seniors. **PHONE**: 703/437-1794. [&]

This was a Lee family outpost, home to Richard B., uncle of Robert E. It's a little less stuffy than some of the area's other historic houses, perhaps because it's not quite so showy and still has signs of being overrun by Lee children (one etched her initials on a windowpane 200 years ago). You'll need to be part of a tour to see the inside, including a room done up as a schoolhouse. The lawns are host to a big antique car show every summer, and frequent weekend programs let kids see what life was like back in the old days. **Note:** Wheelchair access is to the first floor only.

WOODLAWN PLANTATION
9000 Richmond Highway (Route 1), Mount Vernon

HOURS: Daily 10-4:30 (last tour 3:30); closed Jan.-Feb. **COST**: $6 adults, $4 students and seniors, under 5 free. **PHONE**: 703/780-4000. [&]

Another outpost of the Washington clan, Woodlawn was built for George's step-granddaughter, Nellie Custis, who married his nephew, Lawrence Lewis. Tours take visitors past children's bedrooms, where kids can make some comparisons. Nature trails run through the grounds. Woodlawn hosts a respected needlework show every March. Also on the grounds: the Pope-Leighey House, designed by Frank Lloyd Wright.
Note: Wheelchair access here, too, is to the first floor only.

MANASSAS MUSEUM
9101 Prince William Street, Manassas

HOURS: T-Sun 10-5. Closed Mondays except for federal holidays. Also closed major holidays. **COST:** $2.50 adults, $1.50 seniors, $2.50 ages 6-17, Tu free. **PHONE:** 703/368-1873.

This museum is dedicated not to the Civil War battlefield but to the small town after which the battle was named. Opened in 1991, the museum is handsome and well crafted but modest in scope. Its artifacts range from Native American spearpoints to tools used by the area's earliest European settlers (a rusty old meat cleaver is pretty memorable) to relics of the town's days as a major railway hub (which is why it became so important during the Civil War). It has some carefully calibrated displays about slavery and the lives of freed blacks in the region. There's a baby cradle from a family named Robinson, circa 1840, and an 1880 baby carriage with wheels bigger than a contemporary bicycle's. A vivid 10-minute video looks mostly at the impact the Civil War battles had on the town. After your visit, take a walking tour of Old Town (the museum has a brochure); the highlight for kids is **ROHR'S STORE AND MUSEUM** at 9122 Center Street. It has a hands-on local history museum — sort of like a grandparent's funky attic — that kids will love rooting around in. It's loaded with antique toys and household implements. Even better is the attached store, an anachronistic "five and dime" with wooden floors, tin ceilings and penny candy. (The store is open 9-6 M-Sat. Its museum is open noon-4 Sat and Sun and costs $2 for adults, $1 for kids.)

Words to the wise: *There's a small playground out back, useful if getting to Manassas requires a long drive. The exhibits will bore the 6-and-under crowd. If you'd like to take in the battlefield, the five-mile route between the two turns out to be significant in the story of First Manassas.*

NOTES: There's an Old Town Visitors Center at 9025 Center St. For **Food**, try one of the restaurants in downtown Manassas.

Directions: *Take the Beltway to I-66 west. Exit at Route 28 south, Centreville Rd. Follow that for 7.5 miles into Old Town Manassas. Centreville ends at Church St.; continue on Church until you hit Main St. Make a left, cross the railroad tracks, and take the first left at Prince William St.*

FROM SLAVES to HEROES

A MUSEUM OF African American history is planned for the Mall. Until it becomes a reality, you can find at least some parts of the sweeping story of African Amercians at various places. The **NATIONAL MUSEUM OF AMERICAN HISTORY'S** "From Field to Factory" exhibit (see p. 124) details the great migration that brought rural blacks from the South to such urban centers as Chicago. The **NATIONAL MUSEUM OF AMERICAN ART** (p. 19) holds major works by black artists in its collection, including paintings by William H. Johnson. The **ARTS AND IN-DUSTRIES BUILDING** (p. 128) often plays host to shows with an African American theme. The following places take a more active role in exploring black history:

District of Columbia

AFRICAN-AMERICAN CIVIL WAR MEMORIAL
Vermont Avenue and U Street NW

METRO STOP: U Street/Cardozo.

More than 200,000 black Americans fought in the Civil War, a conflict in which they had more than a little stake. This recently completed memorial, in Northwest Washington's Shaw neighborhood, recognizes their contributions. The centerpiece is "Spirit of Freedom," Ed Hamilton's impressive nine-foot sculpture of African American Union troops. Granite walls around a landscaped plaza bear the names of 208,943 black soldiers and their white officers.

ANACOSTIA MUSEUM
1901 Fort Place SE

HOURS: Daily 10-5. **COST:** Free. **PHONE:** 202/287-3369 or 202/387-3060. **WEB:** www.si.edu. &

In a black neighborhood and of a black neighborhood, this Smithsonian museum recounts contributions of African Americans in Washington. It also casts an eye to the south, whence many black immigrants came, and has mounted exhibits on Caribbean and Latin influences in Washington as well. Past exhibits have examined the role of the black church in American life, African American inventors and the Harlem Renaissance. The museum is a good place to visit for Kwanzaa and also for Juneteenth, the June date when Texas slaves learned of their emancipation. Free shuttle buses run Tuesdays and Thursdays in the summer between the Smithsonian Castle and the Anacostia Museum; call for details.

BETHUNE COUNCIL HOUSE
1318 Vermont Avenue NW

HOURS: M-Sat. 10-4. **COST:** Free. **PHONE:** 202/673-2402. **WEB:** www.nps.gov/mamc. **METRO:** McPherson Square, Farragut North.

The child of former slaves, South Carolina's Mary McLeod Bethune lived a remarkable life: tireless educator, president of the National Council of Negro Women, friend of Eleanor Roosevelt, advisor to four presidents. Her Logan Circle townhouse includes historic photos, period furnishings and explanatory wall text. Kids may squirm during the hour-long guided tours (on the hour, last tour at 3, and including a 30-minute video). Instead of a tour, walk around at your own pace or talk with the park rangers (especially the indefatigable Mary Perry, whose daughter married into the Bethune family). They bring Mary McLeod Bethune to life, pointing out, for example, that Bethune was able to pick 100 pounds of cotton a day — when she was 7. There's also a nice bookstore with kid-appropriate biographies of Bethune and others, including Rosa Parks, Marian Anderson and Oprah Winfrey.

FREDERICK DOUGLASS HOME
1411 W Street SE

HOURS: Mid-Apr. to mid-Oct.: daily 9-5; closes at 4 the rest of year. **COST:** $3 adults, under 6 free, $1.50 seniors. **PHONE:** 202/426-5961. **WEB:** www.nps.gov/frdo/freddoug.htm.&

Older kids who are studying American history and the role of slavery may benefit from a visit to the home of a truly great individual: slave, shipwright, autodidact, lecturer, author, newspaper publisher, civil servant . . . there's not much that Frederick Douglass didn't do. He settled in Washington after he already was well-known worldwide for his writing and his speeches, finally buying Cedar Hill, this Anacostia home with a commanding view of the city below. The house is much as it was in Douglass' time (90 percent of the furnishings are original); a rebuilt "Growlery" is a one-room structure where the abolitionist retreated to study. An introductory movie covers the highlights of his life. A well-stocked gift shop offers books in keeping with Douglass' philosophy.

Directions: *Take the Frederick Douglass Bridge to a left on W St. The home is four blocks on the right.*

Maryland

BANNEKER-DOUGLASS MUSEUM
84 Franklin Street, Annapolis

HOURS: Tu-F 10-3, Sat 12-3. **COST:** Free. **PHONE:** 410/974-2893.   &

Maryland has had a strange history with its black citizens. Called the "free state," it nevertheless was home to many Southern sympathizers during the Civil War. This Annapolis museum, housed in a former African Methodist Episcopal church, explores the lives and contributions of the state's African Americans from slavery to more modern times. Frederick Douglass, of course, was the Maryland-born former slave who settled in Washington. Benjamin Banneker was a Colonial-era engineer and surveyor (he helped Pierre L'Enfant in the design of Washington).

GREAT BLACKS IN WAX MUSEUM
1601 E. North Avenue, Baltimore

HOURS: Jan. 15-Oct. 14: Tu-Sat 9-6, Sun noon-6 (closes at 5 rest of year); closed M, except Feb., July and Aug., Martin Luther King Day and other federal holidays. **COST:** $5.75 adults, $5.25 students and seniors, $3.75 ages 12-17, $3.25 ages 2-11, under 2 free. **PHONE:** 410/563-3404.

More than 120 costumed wax figures crowd this homespun but unique museum in a former fire station. Children are entranced right in the small lobby, where Hannibal sits astride a life-size elephant and two wax hands are out for handling. Founders Elmer and Joanne Martin don't shy from the more horrific experiences of blacks in America. The first exhibit is a replica of a slave ship, holding terrified figures in chains, some being tortured, one being thrown to sharks. A special exhibit on lynching ($1 extra admission) is similarly graphic. The lynching exhibit is not recommended for anyone under 12, and parents may want to bypass the more violent parts of the slave ship. The less violent, but just as damaging, aspects of racism are also explored, in the figures of Rosa Parks, Martin Luther King Jr. and others. Black achievement is noted in the work of inventors, religious leaders and historical figures, from Civil War soldiers to astronaut Ronald McNair, from businesswoman Madame C.J. Walker to arctic explorer Matthew Henson. Each display has a label explaining the relevance of the wax mannequins. In addition to T-shirts, key chains and the like, the gift shop also has a nice selection of children's books on well-known black heroes such as George Washington Carver and such lesser-known figures as pioneering pilot Bessie Coleman. Not as slick as a Smithsonian museum, Great Blacks in Wax is nonetheless an opportunity to learn about black history — and American history — in a unique way.

NOTES: There is wheelchair access to first floor only.

Directions: *From I-95, take the I-395 exit for Downtown/Inner Harbor. Turn right on Pratt St. and left on Gay St., and follow Gay as it becomes Ensor and then Harford Rd. Turn right on North Ave. The museum is two blocks down on the right. You can park on the street or in the supermarket lot across from the museum.*

Virginia: ALEXANDRIA BLACK HISTORY RESOURCE CENTER (see next section on ALEXANDRIA).

THE ALEXANDRIA EXPERIENCE

YOU CAN'T WALK very far in Alexandria without stepping on something historic. The former tobacco port has been steeping itself in history since the days of Washington and Lee. Most attractions will be over the heads of the smallest children, Alexandria having a somewhat rarified and genteel approach to its complement of historic sights. Teens and precocious preteens may prefer simply to shop along King Street and down by the water. Be aware that the city's stock of historic buildings means that wheelchair access can be problematical.

THE LYCEUM
201 S. Washington Street
HOURS: M-Sat 10-5, Sun 1-5. **COST:** Free. **PHONE:** 703/838-4994. &

This is Alexandria's history museum and a good starting point for getting your bearings and picking up brochures about the town's other attractions. Exhibits recount the development of the town, starting with the original inhabitants (there's a neat assortment of Native American arrowheads), through Colonial days (silver, furniture, pots) and up to modern times.

ALEXANDRIA BLACK HISTORY RESOURCE CENTER
638 N. Alfred Street (entrance on Wythe Street)

HOURS: Tu-Sat 10-4. **COST:** Free. **PHONE:** 703/838-4356. &

Housed in what once was the first library built for the black community in Alexandria, this center explores the African American presence in town, from the days of slaves and free blacks (the two lived side by side in Alexandria) to today. Pick up a brochure here for a walking tour of Alexandria's black historic sites.

BOYHOOD HOME OF ROBERT E. LEE
607 Oronoco Street

HOURS: M-Sat 10-4, Sun 1-4; closed Dec. 15-Feb. 1. **COST:** $4 adults, $2 ages 11-17. **PHONE:** 703/548-8454.

The Civil War general lived here from the age of 5. The house is furnished in a manner not too dissimilar from that which he would have experienced.

CARLYLE HOUSE
121 N. Fairfax Street

HOURS: Tu-Sat 10-4:30, Sun noon-4:30. **COST:** Tours $4 adults, $2 ages 11-17, under 11 free. **PHONE:** 703/549-2997.

Younger kids probably won't be impressed by this, well, impressively grand 18th Century house, built in 1753 by a wealthy Scottish merchant. Various worksheets enliven a visit somewhat (find various shapes, answer questions about the house's furnishings, etc.), but the best bet is to take in a summer offering called "Playtime From the Past." Costumed teens lead children through such games as Nine Men's Morris and wooden hoop rolling, giving them an idea of what it was like to be a kid in Colonial times. **Notes:** Wheelchair access is to the first floor only.

GADSBY'S TAVERN MUSEUM
134 N. Royal Street, Alexandria

HOURS: Apr.-Sept.: Tu-Sat 10-5, Sun 1-5; Oct.-Mar.: Tu-Sat 11-4, Sun 1-4. **COST:** $4 adults, $2 ages11-17, under 11 free. **PHONE:** 703/838-4242.

Two adjoining buildings, a 1770s tavern and a 1792 hotel, are the site of this period hostelry. Customers included George Washington, Thomas Jefferson and the Marquis de Lafayette. Kids may squirm on the tour, which takes visitors past the taproom, bedrooms and a ballroom, all filled with that youthful enthusiasm killer: "period furnishings." A better bet is to visit during one of the museum's monthly Time Travel programs, when costumed docents do their thing ("Pray, what manner of conveyance is an automobile?"). Or have lunch at the tavern itself. Waiters wear breeches, and the food's pretty good, though children used to McDonalds fries may be disappointed by the round "tavern fries."

STABLER-LEADBEATER APOTHECARY SHOP
105-107 S. Fairfax Street

HOURS: M-Sat 10-4, Sun 1-5; closed W Nov.-Mar. **COST:** $2.50 adults, $2 ages 11-17, under 10 free. **PHONE:** 703/836-3713.

Considering the animus most children harbor against their medicine, it's hard to imagine any children being captivated by this small, historical site dedicated to the early days of pharmacology. Opened in 1792, the shop was patronized by the likes of George Washington and Robert E. Lee. The one-room apothecary looks much as it did in olden times, with shelves lined with glass jars and mortar and pestles resting atop counters. Adults may find the admittedly fascinating collection worth a look, but kids will wonder why you dragged them in there.

GEORGE WASHINGTON MASONIC NATIONAL MEMORIAL
101 Callahan Drive

HOURS: Daily 9-5. **COST:** Free. **PHONE:** 703/683-2007.   ♿

George Washington was one, and so was Harry Truman — U.S. presidents, of course, but also Masons — and this curious memorial is more about the latter than the former. There are artifacts from Washington's life, including the furniture from the Alexandria lodge where Washington was Grand Master and the bedchamber clock that was stopped the moment the first president died. There's also a scale model of a Shriner's parade; bigger than two pool tables, it creaks around in an oval. The architecture is interesting and the view from the balcony atop the memorial's spire is nice, but visitors must be part of a tour, which lasts more than an hour. And the tour's structure — you get on and off one of two tiny elevators as you rise level by level to alight in rooms devoted to different aspects of the Masonic movement — means that only the most well-behaved children (and adults) will keep from fidgeting. Fun fact: The elevators don't go straight up and down — they rise diagonally as they go up the building.

☼F WATER and BREAD

Few things are as anachronistic today as the grist mills that once were a staple of American life: huge, grooved stones turned by water, crushing grain. Yet they suggest how life used to be. A half-dozen area mills can show kids the work that used to go into making a simple loaf of bread. Many have special programs, such as cider-pressing or blacksmithing demonstrations, and most sell flour that's been ground the old-fashioned way. Note that the main attraction — a water-turned wheel — may not always be functioning. There needs to be enough water to make the thing work. Pierce Mill in the District and Colvin Run in Great Falls are the most convenient for most Washingtonians.

District of Columbia

PIERCE MILL. Tilden St. NW at Beach Dr. in Rock Creek Park. **Hours:** W-Sun 10-4 (shorter hours in fall and winter). The mill offers a 60- to 90-minute tour weekends at 11. **Cost:** Free. **Phone:** 202/426-6908.

Maryland

UNION MILLS. 3311 Littlestown Pike (Route 97), Westminster. **Hours:** May & Sept.: weekends 12-4, June-August: Tu-F 10-4, weekends 12-4. **Cost:** Tours of mill and house: $5 adults, $3 ages 6-12. **Phone:** 410/848-2288. **Disability Access:** Wheelchair access to part of the mill but not to the house.

WYE GRIST MILL. Route 662, just off Route 50 in Wye Mill (15 miles from the Bay Bridge). **Hours:** Mid-Apr. to mid-Nov.: weekdays 10-1, weekends 10-4. The mill grinds on the first and third Sat of the month. **Cost:** Suggested donation: $2. **Phone:** 410/827-6909.

Virginia

ALDIE MILL. Route 50, west of intersection of Route 50 and Route 15 in Aldie. **Hours:** Apr.-Oct.: Sun 12-5. **Cost:** Free, but donations appreciated. **Phone:** 703/327-6118.

BURWELL-MORGAN MILL. Route 255/723, a half mile north of Route 50/17 in Millwood. **Hours:** May-Oct.: Th-Sun 10-5. **Cost:** $3 adults, $1 under 12. **Phone:** 540/837-1799.

COLVIN RUN MILL HISTORIC SITE. 10017 Colvin Run Rd., Great Falls. **Hours:** Daily 11-5 except Tu. The big wheel spins the first and third Sun of the month, Mar.-Nov. At 1 on Th, there's a puppet show (that's correct) explaining parts of the mill operation. **Cost:** Most programs are $4 adults, $3 students over 16, $2 under 16. **Phone:** 703/759-2771. **Notes:** Wheelchair access to much of the site but not to the mill.

143

GROUNDS for PLAY

PLAY — THAT'S ALL kids want to do. Is it so much to ask? Many activities in this guide have playful elements. This chapter, however, focuses on those that are pretty much solely grounds for play — climbing kid structures, splashing in water parks, engaging in disc golf or bankshot basketball, pedaling boats, romping through amusement parks and more. We've divided them into attractions that are mostly outside (mega-playgrounds, go-kart tracks, miniature golf courses, batting cages and the like) and mostly inside (pay-as-you-play entertainment centers, or inside "playgrounds," rock-climbing walls, skating rinks, laser-tag emporiums). While there are other benefits for kids here, particularly the development of assorted skills, there's really one overriding aim — to have fun.

I. The Outside Crowd

MEGA-PLAYGROUNDS

IN THE 1980s, a new type of playground started sprouting. Gone were rusty swings, splinter-causing seesaws and metal slides that you could fry an egg on in summer. In their place came extensive wooden jungle gyms strung with heavy nets, towering and twisting tubular plastic slides in a rainbow of colors, and tot lots with soft surfaces underfoot. The reaction of parents upon seeing these mega-playgrounds: "Why didn't they have these when *I* was a kid?"

You hardly need help finding the smaller neighborhood playgrounds that have a few of these attractions, or even the most facility-rich regional ballfield/picnic pavilion/hiking trail zone. But the Washington area has a handful of outdoor play facilities that are so ambitious and kid-friendly that they are destination-quality — places worth a ride around the Beltway to visit. Unless otherwise noted, all are free and open from dawn to dusk.

Maryland

CABIN JOHN REGIONAL PARK. 7400 Tuckerman Lane, Rockville. **Phone:** 301/299-4555. The draws here are two huge play structures, one for older kids and one for younger, both filled with challenges like rope-walks, tube-slides, tire-climbs and much more. It's a great place for two or more families to take their kids for a group play-plus-picnic. Remarkably, just across the path the county still maintains vintage climbables from the '50s and '60s: Cinderella's pumpkin coach, the Old Lady's shoe and a couple of Sputnik-age space vehicles, among others. These older structures are not as wisely designed as the newer ones, so take special care with preschoolers. There's also a seasonal miniature train, a skating rink and many acres of hiking trails. **Directions:** *From the Beltway, take Old Georgetown Rd. north. Turn left on Tuckerman Lane and continue until you see parking lot signs on the right.* ♿

LAKE WATERFORD. 830 Pasadena Rd., Pasadena. **Phone:** 410/222-6248. This Anne Arundel County park has one of the area's handful of wooden, Robert Leathers-designed playgrounds. Leathers is noted for both his creations and his construction methods: The community builds the thing in an Amish barn-raising sort of spirit. The park has dinosaur toys, a castle, tunnels, swings, a maze and more. Lake Waterford also has ducks and plenty of fishing. **Directions:** *From the Beltway, take Route 50 east to Route 2 north to a right on Pasadena. The park is a mile up.* ♿

OPPORTUNITY PARK. 3330 Northview Dr., Bowie. **Phone:** 301/262-6200. This was the first fully featured U.S. park designed to be accessible to everyone, regardless of physical limits. It has playgrounds for toddlers and bigger kids, both accessible to those in wheelchairs, plus a sensory trail, a wildlife trail, an exercise course and a fishing pond. **Directions:** *From the Beltway, take Route 50 east toward Bowie. Take Exit 11 to Route 197 south, Collington Rd. Turn right at Northview Dr. The park is one mile up on the right.* ♿

WHEATON REGIONAL PARK. 2000 Shorefield Rd., Wheaton. **Phone:** 301/946-7033. A tot lot that's the perfect scale for toddlers, challenging climbs for older kids and lots of slides, swings and sand boxes make this a dream destination for families. Wheaton has plenty of other kid-magnets — hiking trails, carousel, miniature train — and it's adjacent to the spectacular Brookside Gardens (see p. 102), a wonderful place for a family stroll with anyone from the tiniest infants to pre-teens. There also are lots of picnic tables and covered pavilions, which must be reserved if you're planning an event. **Nearby:** Brookside Gardens, Brookside Nature Center, Wheaton Ice Rink. **Directions:** *From the Beltway, take Georgia Ave. north. Go past University Blvd. and turn right on Shorefield Dr.* ♿

Virginia

TUCKAHOE PARK AND PLAYFIELD. 2400 Sycamore St., Arlington. Two big, colorful play structures, obviously designed by fun-loving architects, feature long slides, safe, high platforms, a variety of climbing activities and a wonderful chain-link maze unique to the area. It's a perfect bring-a-book-and-let-the-kids-have-a-blast park. Best for ages 7-12; ages 6 and under require adult supervision, and it's not for toddlers. **Directions:** *Take the Beltway to I-66 east, follow that to Exit 69, Sycamore St./Falls Church. Go right, cross Lee Hwy., and the park is on the left.* ♿

SOUTH RUN REC CENTER. 7550 Reservation Dr., Springfield. **Phone:** 703/ 866-0566. The playground outside this recreation center was designed with special-needs children in mind. Wide steps on the play equipment give children with walkers or crutches room to maneuver. Those in wheelchairs can negotiate the jungle gym via bridges, scoot into large swings and grab onto low bars. **Directions:** *From the Beltway, take I-95 south to Fairfax County Pkwy. west. The center is right off the parkway.*

District of Columbia

MONTROSE PARK. R and 30th streets NW. **Phone:** 202/426-6827. The play equipment is not spectacular here — swings, toddler swings, monkey bars, sandbox — but if you're in Georgetown, this park has a lot of open space and a boxwood maze that kids enjoy. **Nearby:** If the season, days and hours favor you, you can enjoy to the spectacular Dumbarton Oaks right next door (see p. 97).

GO-KART TRACKS

EVERY PARENT DREADS the day children get drivers' licenses. You can start that worrying now — at a go-kart track. Low-horsepower gasoline engines power tiny karts around the track. There's a steering wheel, a gas pedal and a brake. Age, and sometimes height, restrictions apply. Typically, children must be at least 8 years old (or 54 inches high) to drive solo. Some tracks have wider, double go-karts, which an adult can drive with a passenger as young as 2 or 3. More challenging slick tracks or grand prix-style tracks may require that drivers be 12. Prices are about $2 to $4 for a ride that usually lasts three to five minutes (more for slick tracks). Discount ticket books are available.

Maryland

FAST TRACK RACEWAYS. 5726 Buckeystown Pike/Route 85, Frederick. **Phone:** 301/663-9605. Figure-8 and slick track.

GO-KART RACEWAY. 1050 Route 3 South, Crofton. **Phone:** 301/261-6566. Half-mile asphalt road course with 27 turns.

SKELTERAMA GO-KART TRACK. 4300 Kenilworth Ave., Bladensburg. **Phone:** 301/864-0110. This go-kart track, the oldest in the area, is an asphalt road course.

WALDORF 500. U.S. 301 and Acton Lane, Waldorf. **Phone:** 301/870-7717. Eighth-mile asphalt track and slick track.

Virginia

ALEXANDRIA GO-KART RACEWAY. 400 Hooffs Run Dr., Alexandria. **Phone:** 703/548-5100. Half-mile asphalt road track.

CHAMPIONS. 13585 Minnieville Rd., Woodbridge. **Phone:** 703/730-3866. Half-mile grand prix track and slick track.

LOCAL WATER PARKS

WHILE CREATIVE water-play areas once were the province of the big amusement parks, local recreation departments have seen the wisdom of providing them for area citizens. The industry calls them "leisure pools" (as opposed to lap pools), and Northern Virginia is especially blessed with splash parks that even the smallest or most water-averse children are likely to enjoy. Hours can vary almost daily, so call ahead for details.

Virginia

BULL RUN REGIONAL PARK. 7700 Bull Run Dr., Centreville. **Hours:** Pool open Memorial Day-Labor Day. **Cost:** $4 adults, $3.50 ages 2-11. **Phone:** 703/631-0550. Water slides, tubes, toddler pool, a shipwreck and "Coconut Island" make this popular with families. Also in the park are miniature and disc golf courses. **Directions:** *From Beltway, take Route 66 west to Exit 52/Centreville. Stay right and take Route 29 south for 3 miles. The park is on the left.* ♿

CAMERON RUN REGIONAL PARK. 4001 Eisenhower Ave., Alexandria. **Phone:** 703/960-0767. **Hours:** Memorial Day-Labor Day, 10-8. **Cost:** Weekends $10 adults, $9 children (under 4 feet); weekdays $8 and $7. Cameron Run's claim to fame is its wave pool, capable of creating four-foot swells. There's also a twisting, three-flume waterslide, water playground and lap lanes. (Note: Only strong swimmers should venture beyond their waist.) Also in the park is a mini-golf course and batting cages. **Directions**: *From Beltway, take Exit 3A. Take a right at the light onto Eisenhower Ave. The park is a mile down on the right.* ♿

LAKE FAIRFAX. 1400 Lake Fairfax Dr., Reston. **Phone**: 703/471-5415. **Hours:** Memorial Day-Labor Day, 10-8. **Cost:** $9.95 adults; under 48 inches $7.95; under 2 free; $4.95 after 5 pm. The Water Mine Family Swimmin' Hole is a "themed water playground" that features a slow-moving "lazy river" on which you can float on a raft, slides, floating toys, devices that squirt water and gradual, "zero-depth" play areas. Also in the park is a carousel and a miniature train. **Directions:** *From the Beltway, take Route 7 west (Exit 10B). Turn left on Baron Cameron Ave. and left on Lake Fairfax Dr. Park is on the left.* ♿

SPLASH DOWN. 7500 Ben Lomond Park Dr., Manassas. **Phone:** 703/361-4451. **Hours:** Memorial Day-Labor Day. **Cost:** $11.50 for those over four feet tall, $8.50 under four feet, free for age 1 and under (call for information on $2-off coupons). In addition to a lap pool, Splash Down has a lazy river, water games, kiddie pool and slides, including two four-story tube slides. **Directions:** *Take Route 66 to Exit 47A. Follow Route 234/Sudley Rd. south and take a left on Sudley Manor Dr. Go 2 miles and turn left on Ben Lomand Park Dr. Proceed through the entrance of the park.*

WATER WORKS. 5301 Dale Blvd., Dale City. **Phone:** 703/680-7612. **Hours:** Memorial Day-Labor Day. **Cost:** $4.50, $3.75 over 60, 1 and under free, $3.25 after 4 weekdays. Water is manipulated in many fashions here (sprays, geysers, "fun bubblers"), and it also lends its slick presence to an enclosed "speed" slide, circular open slides and a floating hippo. **Directions:** *Take I-95 south to the Dale Blvd. Exit and follow Dale to the end. The park is on the left.* ♿

Maryland

MONTGOMERY COUNTY AQUATIC CENTER. 5900 Executive Blvd., Rockville. **Phone:** 301/468-4211. **Hours:** Call for complex times for kids' pool attractions. **Cost:** Montgomery County residents: $4.50 adults, $3.50 ages 1-17 and over 60; non-county residents $1.50 more. While not as flashy as its Virginia counterparts, this pool does have a long water slide and a shallow kids' pool with waterfall. (Also, this is one of the exceptions that's indoors, so it's open year round and bad weather needn't curtail your pool plans.) **Directions:** *From the Beltway, take Route 355/Rockville Pike north to a left on Marinelli Rd. Marinelli dead ends into the pool's parking lot.* ♿

ROLLINGCREST-CHILLUM SPLASH POOL. 6122 Sargent Rd., Chillum. **Phone:** 301/853-9115. **Hours:** Weekends 12-5, weekdays 6 am-9:30 pm year round. **Cost:** For Montgomery and Prince George's County residents, $4 adults, $3 ages 3-17 and over 60 (non-residents $5 and $4); under 2 free with paying adult. This inviting facility also is indoors, so it's a good destination on a rainy day. The children's pool features a regular playground — slides, stairs, tubes — right in the middle of the water. The family pool has various slides. Note: Kids over 48 inches can't play in the children's pool. Also, the pools close the first 15 minutes of every hour. The schedule for various features is complicated, so call before you go. **Directions:** *From the Beltway, take New Hampshire Ave. south to a left on East West Hwy./Route 410. Turn right onto Riggs Rd., then left onto Sargent. The pool is on the right.* ♿

SUMMIT HALL FARM PARK. 510 South Frederick Ave., Gaithersburg. **Phone:** 301/258-6445. **Hours:** Daily 11-8 Memorial Day-Labor Day (reduced weekday hours when school's in session). **Cost:** Non-residents $4.75 adults, $3.75 kids. Discounts for multiple-day and season pass. The highlight here is a 250-foot double waterslide (note: riders must be at least 4 feet tall, even on the "slow" lane), but there's also a stationary boat, water cannons, a raindrop umbrella, a lap swimming area and a kiddie pool, complete with frog slide, for the under-5 set. Both pools are zero-depth entry. Inside are plenty of family-friendly amenities, like changing tables, low-height toilets and complete locker room facilities. **Directions:** *Beltway to I-270 North to Shady Grove Rd.; exit right toward Route 355. From Shady Grove Rd. east, take a left at 355 (Frederick Ave.) headed north. The park is 1.5 miles on the left, sharing a driveway with Gaithersburg High School.*

DISC GOLF

It may never make it as an Olympic sport, but disc golf — in which players fling Frisbees (or other brands of flying discs) into chain-link baskets representing "holes" of a 9- or 18-hole course — is a great family diversion. The game's easy to learn, fun to play and a pleasant way to spend an afternoon at the park. As our observations of bandana-sporting teens during our outings suggest, it's possible to get quite serious about disc golf; players feeling the tug might want to check out www.discgolf.com for information on rules, clubs, courses and other details.

More likely, though, disc golf will be something you and the kids will do when you visit one of the parks noted here, each of which features an open-to-the-public disc golf course. The game's slightly more demanding of skill and attention than miniature golf. Five-year-olds can play, but the challenge really kicks in at around 7 and up. Smaller kids can have a blast simply following the throws of the older kids around the course. Bring a small pad and pencil for keeping score, if you're so inclined, plus a water bottle.

Maryland

CALVERT ROAD PARK. College Park. An 18-hole, 4,276-foot course. **Directions:** *From the Beltway, take Exit 23 to Route 201/Kenilworth Ave. south. Go about two miles and turn right onto Calvert Rd. Take the first right to the course.*

SENECA CREEK STATE PARK. Gaithersburg. An 18-hole, 4,500-foot course. There's a $4-per-car fee for Maryland residents, $5 for others. **Directions:** *From the Beltway, take I-270 north to Route 117/Clopper Rd. west (Exit 11B). Drive about three miles to the park on left, just past the Game Preserve Rd. sign.*

Virginia

BLUEMONT PARK. Arlington. A nine-hole, 1,779-foot course. **Directions:** *From the Beltway, take Exit 8 to U.S. 50 east (Arlington Blvd.). Drive about five miles to a left onto North Manchester. Go three blocks and turn right into the parking lot; the first tee is behind the basketball court.*

BULL RUN REGIONAL PARK. Centreville. An 18-hole, 3,145-foot course. There is a $4-per-car fee on weekends and holidays for non-Fairfax County residents. **Directions:** *Take I-66 west to Route 28 east. Take a right onto Route 28, go about three miles to Bull Run Post Office Rd. and turn left. Follow road about two miles; the course is next to a swimming pool.* ♿

BURKE LAKE PARK. Fairfax Station. An 18-hole, 3,699-foot course, with a $4-per-car fee on weekends and holidays for non-Fairfax County residents. **Directions:** *Take I-66 west to Route 123 south and drive about eight miles. The course is on your left.*

McLEAN CENTRAL PARK. McLean. A nine-hole, 1,950-foot course. **Directions:** *From the Beltway, take Exit 11 to Route 123 north. Drive about two miles to the first left past Old Dominion Dr., onto Ingleside Ave. Then turn left at the Dolley Madison Library. The course is behind the tennis courts.*

POHICK BAY REGIONAL PARK. Lorton. An 18-hole, 3,326-foot course, with a $4-per-car fee for non-Northern Virginia residents. **Directions:** *Take I-95 south to Exit 163/Lorton. Make a left on Lorton Rd. Then right on Armistead Rd., right again on Route 1 and left on Gunston Rd. The park is 3.2 miles on the left.*

BANKSHOT BASKETBALL

INVENTED AT A rehabilitation center in Israel as a way for patients to exercise, bankshot basketball is like regular basketball combined with miniature golf. There's no running. Instead, players take their shots from 12 fixed points, aiming the ball at crazily angled backboards. Physical ability isn't a guarantee of success, since there's as much geometry as muscle involved in scoring. It's a fun way for the disabled to compete on a relatively level playing field and for kids who are basketball crazy to stretch their skills. You'll find it at the Rockville Municipal Swim Center, 355 Martins Lane, Rockville, Md. **Phone:** 301/424-7403. **Cost:** In spring and summer, when the outdoor pool is open (daily 9-9), bankshot basketball is included in the price of pool admission: $5 adults, $4 ages 1-17. The rest of the year, it's free, but you have to bring your own ball.

Directions: *From the Beltway, take I-270 north to Route 28 east. At the first traffic light turn left onto Nelson St., which turns into Martins Lane. The pool complex is on the right.*

HORSEBACK RIDING

Owning a horse is a dream for many kids and a nightmare for many parents. You can get a taste of the action, if not the sky-high costs and punishing time commitments of horse ownership, by going on a trail ride. There are many trail-riding outfits in our immediate area and within a few hours' drive. Most cater to adults or older children. We list here generally those with a minimum age of 10, though a few will take all ages. Kids too small for their own horse (usually 4 and under) ride double with a grown-up.

Trail rides typically employ docile, well-trained horses that can amble along the prearranged route with no input from their human driver. Riders should wear long pants, and while hard-soled shoes with heels once were required, most places only prohibit sandals. Some provide helmets for youngsters; if you're at all concerned, don't hesitate to bring along a bike helmet.

While the outfitters here offer trail rides of varying lengths (half-day and full-day rides often include a packed lunch), children should stick to 60- or 90-minute rides when they're starting out. Reservations are a must, so call ahead.

District of Columbia

ROCK CREEK PARK HORSE CENTER. 5100 Glover Rd. NW. **Phone:** 202/362-0117. This is actually an exception to our 10-and-up rule, since trail riders must be 12.

(Those one-hour guided rides Tu-Th at 3, weekends at 12, 1:30 and 3; $21.) But Rock Creek also has pony rides. Children 30 inches and taller can ride weekends from noon to 3; it's $7.50 for 15 minutes.

Maryland

PISCATAWAY HORSE FARM. 10775 Piscataway Rd., Clinton. **Phone:** 301/297-9808. Guided trail rides are offered every day but Th for ages 10 and up; $20 an hour. They also offer pony rides for younger kids. Parents lead the ponies in a ring; $10 for 30 minutes.

WHEATON PARK STABLES. 1101 Glenallen Ave., Wheaton. **Phone:** 301/622-3311 or 301/622-2424. One-hour, $20 guided rides for ages 8 and up Sundays at 1, 2 and 3.

Virginia

FORT VALLEY STABLES. 299 S. Fort Valley Rd., Fort Valley. **Phone:** 888/754-5771, 540/933-6633. Guided rides for all ages; $20 an hour.

MARRIOTT RANCHES. 5305 Marriott Lane, Hume. **Phone:** 540/364-2627. Guided rides for ages 10 and up, Tu-Sun at 10, noon and 2; weekdays $26.50, weekends $28.50.

MOUNTAINTOP RANCH. Route 1, Elkton. **Phone:** 540/298-9542. Guided rides daily for all ages; $23 an hour.

West Virginia

ELK MOUNTAIN TRAILS. 921 Hoffmaster Rd., Knoxsville. **Phone:** 301/834-8882. One-hour guided rides for ages 6 and up (under 6 can ride with guide); $16.50 an hour.

MINIATURE GOLF

HERE'S AN IDEA: Hand kids a metal stick and ask them to hit a ball! The real difficulty, of course, comes in convincing your charges to pick up the ball after the maximum six strokes. Still, the brightly colored balls, the well-manicured indoor-outdoor carpet, the clown faces and windmills are appealing. Children under 4, though, may find the experience more aggravating than enjoyable. They definitely will aggravate any child-free foursomes who are stuck behind you.

Prices are about $3 to $4 for kids, slightly more for adults, with additional rounds at a reduced price. Miniature golf courses in county parks tend to be just one of many diversions. Head there if you also want to hike, picnic or even swim. For-profit concerns often also have video games, batting cages and other offerings. Courses at driving ranges allow mom or dad to hit a bucket of balls. We've also noted the handful of courses that are indoors and thus immune to bad weather.

District of Columbia

CIRCUS MINI GOLF PUTT-4-FUN. Hains Point, 970 Ohio Dr. SW. ♿ **Phone:** 202/488-8087. The oldest course in the area, this was built during the midget golf craze of the 1930s.

Maryland

FANTASY WORLD FAMILY ENTERTAINMENT CENTER. St. Charles Town Center Mall, Waldorf. **Phone:** 301/870-6613. This is an indoor course. ♿

LAUREL GOLF & RECREATION. 9801 Fort Meade Rd., Laurel. **Phone:** 301/725-4646. It also has batting cages and a driving range. ♿

MONTE MINIATURE GOLF. University Blvd. and Boteler Lane, College Park. **Phone:** 301/935-9821. With two 18-hole courses and a few holes that require a pitching wedge, this is one of the more interesting courses in the area. It's open only in summer.

PUTT PUTT. 130 Rollins Ave., Rockville. **Phone:** 301/881-1663. It also has arcade games and an ice rink. ♿

ROCKY GORGE MINIATURE GOLF COURSE. Route 29 and Old Columbia Road, Laurel. **Phone:** 301/725-0888. They have batting cages and a driving range here.

SUMMIT HALL FARM PARK. 508 South Frederick Ave., Gaithersburg. **Phone:** 301/258-6420. You'll find an inventive new 18-hole course with Astroturf "rough," embedded stone hazards, water holes and some ferocious banking in a large park. ♿

SWEET SPOT MINIATURE GOLF. 3601 Brinkley Rd., Temple Hills. **Phone:** 301/630-4653. It has a driving range as well.

WATKINS REGIONAL PARK. 301 Watkins Park Dr., Upper Marlboro. **Phone:** 301/390-9224. The park also has a playground, train and farm. ♿

WHITE FLINT GOLF PARK. 5451 Marinelli Rd., Rockville. **Phone:** 301/230-7117. There are two 18-hole mini golf courses and a driving range. ♿

Virginia

ALGONKIAN REGIONAL PARK. 47001 Fairway Dr., Sterling. **Phone:** 703/450-4655. You'll also find a driving range and "maxi golf" (an 18-hole course), plus pool, hiking trails and more.

BULL RUN REGIONAL PARK. 7700 Bull Run Dr., Centreville. **Phone:** 703/631-0550.♿

CAMERON RUN REGIONAL PARK. 4001 Eisenhower Ave., Alexandria.**Phone:** 703/960-0767. This garden-themed course was designed by the same fellow who does all those dinosaur and gorilla places at the beach. You also can enjoy a splash pool. ♿

CENTREVILLE MINI GOLF AND GAMES. 6206 Multiplex Dr., Centreville. **Phone:** 703/502-7888. An indoor playground, laser tag and arcade games are here as well.

CHAMPIONS. 13585 Minnieville Rd., Woodbridge. **Phone:** 703/730-3866. This one has go-karts, batting cages and bumper boats. ♿

CHANTILLY GOLF CENTER. 14531 Lee Rd., Chantilly. **Phone:** 703/802-6525. There's also a driving range. ♿

FOUNTAINHEAD REGIONAL PARK. 10875 Hampton Rd., Fairfax Station. **Phone:** 703/250-9124. ♿

JEFFERSON DISTRICT PARK. 7900 Lee Hwy., Falls Church. **Phone:** 703/573-0443. There's also real golf, picnic tables and horseshoes. ♿

LAKE ACCOTINK PARK. 7500 Accotink Park Rd., Springfield. **Phone:** 703/569-3464. You'll find a carousel here. ♿

LAKE RIDGE PARK. 12350 Catton Mill Dr., Woodbridge. **Phone:** 703/494-5564. Lake Ridge also has a 9-hole golf course, pedal boats, fishing and a playground.

LOCUST SHADE REGIONAL PARK. 4701 Locust Shade Dr., Triangle. **Phone:** 703/221-2159. You'll also find pedal boats and a batting cage here.

THE MAGIC PUTTING PLACE. 8902 Mathis Ave., Manassas. **Phone:** 703/369-9299. There are two, fountain-filled, 18-hole courses. ♿

POHICK BAY REGIONAL PARK. 6501 Pohick Bay Dr., Lorton. **Phone:** 703/339-6104. Also disc golf, boat rentals and hiking trails.

UPTON HILL REGIONAL PARK. 6060 Wilson Blvd., Arlington. **Phone:** 703/237-4953. Designed by the same fellow who did Cameron Run, this park also has a pool and batting cages.

WOODY'S GOLF RANGE. 11801 Leesburg Pike, Herndon. **Phone:** 703/430-8337. As the name tells you, there's also a driving range.

SPIN CONTROL: CAROUSELS

KIDS LOVE going around in circles nearly as much as running in a straight line. And if they're going up and down while going round and round, so much the better. The Washington area seems especially blessed with carousels. Those in parks usually are open Memorial Day through Labor Day. The cost is about $1 a ride.

District of Columbia
THE MALL. 1000 Jefferson Dr., SW, in front of the Smithsonian Castle. Phone: 202/357-2700. Open year round.

Maryland
GLEN ECHO PARK. 7300 MacArthur Blvd. and Goldsboro Rd., Glen Echo. **Phone:** 301/492-6282 or 301/492-6229.

WHEATON REGIONAL PARK. 2000 Shorefield Rd., Wheaton. **Phone:** 301/946-7033.

THE MALL IN COLUMBIA. 10300 Little Patuxent Pkwy., Columbia. **Phone:** 410/997-2142. Open year round.

INNER HARBOR. Key Hwy., next to the Maryland Science Center, Baltimore. **Phone:** 410/964-0055. Open weekends year round, daily in summer.

Virginia

BURKE LAKE PARK. 7315 Ox Rd., Fairfax Station. **Phone:** 703/323-6600.

LAKE ACCOTINK PARK. 7500 Accotink Park Rd., Springfield. **Phone:** 703/569-3464.

LAKE FAIRFAX. 1400 Lake Fairfax Dr., Reston. **Phone:** 703/471-5415.

LEE DISTRICT PARK. 6601 Telegraph Rd., Franconia. **Phone:** 703/922-9840.

SPOTSYLVANIA MALL. Route 3 and I-95, near Fredericksburg. **Phone:** 540/786-6600 or 540/786-6389. Open year round.

BATTING CAGES

SOCCER MAY BE overtaking baseball as the organized national pastime of America's youth, but there still are plenty of children who relish the crack of leather on pine. Or, more likely today, on aluminum. A batting cage is one way to practice what probably is the most enjoyable part of the game: making contact. The proprietors of the establishments below recommend that children be 6 or 7 before they step into a cage. You may also want to be standing behind them, grasping their hands and guiding their swing. Children must wear head protection. Beginners should stick to slow-pitch softball machines. The cost is about $1 for 18 pitches.

Maryland

LAUREL GOLF & RECREATION. 9801 Fort Meade Rd., Laurel. **Phone:** 301/725-4646. ♿

ROCKY GORGE. Route 29 at Old Columbia Road, Laurel. **Phone:** 301/725-8947. ♿

SPORT LAND. 9811 Washingtonian Blvd., Gaithersburg. **Phone:** 301/840-8404.

Virginia

CAMERON RUN REGIONAL PARK. 4001 Eisenhower Ave., Alexandria. **Phone:** 703/960-5714.

CHAMPIONS. 13585 Minnieville Rd., Woodbridge. **Phone:** 703/730-3866. ♿

DUG OUT. 13241 Braddock Rd., Centreville. **Phone:** 703/818-3331.

LOCUST SHADE REGIONAL PARK. 4701 Locus Shade Dr., Triangle. **Phone:** 703/221-2159.

NORTHERN VIRGINIA BASEBALL ACADEMY. 4000A-D Westfax Dr., Chantilly. **Phone:** 703/222-8837. 6750 Gravel Ave., Springfield. **Phone:** 703/922-5733.

OCCOQUAN REGIONAL PARK. 9751 Ox Rd., Lorton. **Phone:** 703/690-2121.

UPTON HILL REGIONAL PARK. 6060 Wilson Blvd., Arlington. **Phone:** 703/534-4580. ♿

WOODY'S GOLF RANGE. 11801 Leesburg Pike, Herndon. **Phone:** 703/430-8337. ♿

KID-FRIENDLY BIKE TRAILS

Riding the Schwinn up and down your street is fine for a while, but soon your kids (and you) will want to try pedaling through something a bit more scenic. The problem is that many parts of the area's better-known bike trails (Washington & Old Dominion, Mount Vernon) attract hardcore bikers who have little patience with slow, unsteady riders-in-training. You're better off going to a park that also has paved trails. One with a playground or some other kid-magnet will assure lots of other families (and something to do besides pedal). For an in-depth look at where to ride, check out John Pescatore's "Family Bicycling" ($10.95; EPM Inc.), an excellent guide to area trails. The Washington Area Bicyclists Association (202/628-2500; www.waba.org) also has information and maps on local trails and will mail you a free, well-written brochure called "Teaching Your Child to Ride a Bike."

Maryland

CAPITAL CRESCENT TRAIL. This bike trail links Bethesda with Georgetown. Start at Woodmont Ave. near Bethesda Ave. in Bethesda or at Fletcher's Boat House in Georgetown (4740 Canal Rd. NW, at Reservoir Rd.).

CENTENNIAL PARK. Route 108 and Centennial Lane, Ellicott City. **Phone:** 410/313-7303. Paved trails circle a lake at this multi-featured Howard County park.

LAKE ARTEMESIA. A paved path encircles this 36-acre, manmade lake created when the College Park Metro station was built. Park at the Mount Rainier Recreation Center, 4701 31st Pl., Mount Rainier. **Phone:** 301/924-2127.

SENECA CREEK STATE PARK. 11950 Clopper Rd., Gaithersburg. **Phone:** 301/924-2127. Besides paved paths, this Montgomery County park has boat rentals and picnic tables.

Virginia

BURKE LAKE. 7315 Ox Rd., Fairfax Station. **Phone:** 703/323-6600. Biking and hiking trails run through the park. There's also a miniature train and carousel.

LAKE ACCOTINK PARK. 5660 Heming Ave., Springfield. **Phone:** 703/569-0285. If you tire of pedaling on the bike trails here, you can put the same skills to use pedaling a boat. There's also a carousel and mini golf.

W&OD TRAIL. Phone: 703/729-0596. This flat, wonderful trail follows a railbed west from Shirlington to Purcellville. The eastern half, however, is heavily traveled, so go west, young men and women, and park at either Leesburg's Loudoun County High School (take Route 7 to a left on Catoctin Circle to another left on Dry Mill Rd.) or Purcellville's Loudoun Valley High School (Route 7 Bypass to a left on Route 278, a right onto Hirst Rd. and a left onto Maple St.). You can park there daily in summer but only on weekends during the school year.

PEDAL BOATS

It doesn't take much skill to pilot pedal boats, which is why they're perfect for pint-sized sailors. Area ponds and lakes typically put boats in the water starting around Memorial Day. They're often open weekends from then until the end of school, whereupon they're open daily until Labor Day. To rent, you'll need a refundable cash deposit and/or a driver's license. Most boats are for two people, both of whom furiously pedal (or not). In four-person boats, the two passengers in the back just enjoy the view. (Note: Some locations stock special boats for the disabled, powered by hand rather than by foot. Call for information.)

District of Columbia
THE TIDAL BASIN. 1501 Maine Ave. SW. **Phone:** 202/479-2426. Daily 10-6. Hourly rentals are $14 for a four-person boat, $7 for a two-person boat.

Maryland
ALLEN POND PARK. 3330 Northview Dr., Bowie. **Phone:** 301/262-6200. Daily 11-7:30. Four-person boat rentals are $5 for 30 minutes ($4 for Bowie residents). In the middle of Allen Pond Park is Opportunity Park, the completely accessible park for children with disabilities, complete with fishing, picnic areas, vending machines and other boat rentals.

CENTENNIAL PARK. Route 108 and Centennial Lane, Ellicott City. **Phone:** 410/313-7303. Weekends 9-5:30, daily after school closes for summer. Half-hour rentals are $4 for a two-person boat, $6 for a four-person boat. You'll also find basketball and tennis courts, playgrounds, picnic areas, fishing and a bike trail here.

COSCA REGIONAL PARK. 11000 Thrift Rd., Clinton. **Phone:** 301/868-1397. Th-Sun, noon-6:30. Rental for a two-person boat is $3.50 per half-hour and $6 per hour ($3 and $5 for Prince George's and Montgomery County residents). Four-person boats are $6 per half-hour and $10 per hour ($5 and $8). The park also offers fishing, hiking, tennis courts, the Clearwater Nature Center, a playground and a snack bar

LAKE KITTAMAQUNDI. 10221 Wincopin Circle, Columbia. **Phone:** 410/312-6332. F 5-9, weekends noon-9 late May-late July; closes 8 or 8:30 late July-late Aug. Hourly rates are $6 for a two-person boat ($8 after 7 pm) and $8 for a four-person boat ($10 after 7 pm). Canoe rentals, playgrounds and bike paths are also available here.

LAKE NEEDWOOD. 6700 Lake Needwood Rd., Derwood. **Phone:** 301/762-1888. Weekends 6:30-6, weekdays noon-6. Rentals are $4.50 per half-hour and $2.25 for each additional half-hour. Boats can hold two adults and one child under 5. The park also offers other boat rentals, a picnic area, two golf courses, fishing and pontoon boat rides on the weekends.

SENECA CREEK STATE PARK. 11950 Clopper Rd., Gaithersburg. **Phone:** 301/924-2127. Park open 8-sunset (boat rentals stop at 6 pm). Hourly rates are $5 for a two-person boat and $7 for a four-person boat. The park also offers trails, historic sites, other boat rentals, fishing, hiking, playgrounds and a golf course.

GREENBRIER STATE PARK. 21843 National Pike, Boonsboro. **Phone:** 301/ 791-4767. Rentals are $8 an hour per boat plus $2 per person to enter the park during the week ($3 on weekends). You'll find a sandy beach for swimming, plus fishing, hiking and snack bar.

Virginia

LAKE ACCOTINK PARK. 5660 Heming Ave., Springfield. **Phone:** 703/569-0285. Daily 10-8. Rentals are $4.50 per half-hour for a two-person boat. The 77-acre lake also offers hiking trails, miniature golf, a playground and a carousel.

LAKE FAIRFAX PARK. 1400 Lake Fairfax Dr., Reston. **Phone:** 703/471-5415. Daily 1-8. Rentals are $4.50 per half-hour for a three-person boat. The park also offers pontoon rides, a miniature train, a carousel and the Water Mine swimming hole (extra fees charged).

LAKE RIDGE PARK. 12350 Catton Mill Dr., Woodbridge. **Phone:** 703/494-5564. Weekdays 10-dusk, weekends 6 am-dusk. Four-person boat rentals are $5 an hour weekdays (in summer), $7 on weekends. The park also has a 9-hole golf course and lessons, a miniature golf course, fishing, canoe tours, a playground, a nature trail and a snack bar.

LOCUST SHADE REGIONAL PARK. 4701 Locust Shade Dr., Triangle. **Phone:** 703/221-2159. Sat-Sun 12-7:30. Rentals are $4 per half-hour for a four-person boat. The park also offers miniature golf, batting cages, a driving range, fishing, a picnic area, hiking and a small concession stand.

POHICK BAY REGIONAL PARK. 6501 Pohick Bay Dr., Lorton. **Phone:** 703/ 339-6104. Daily 10-6 starting in late June, limited hours before then. Rentals are $3 per half-hour for a two-person boat. There's a $4 park entrance fee if you're not from Northern Virginia. Also available are sailboat rentals, a swimming pool, an 18-hole golf course, miniature golf, disc golf, a picnic area and hiking trails.

AMUSEMENT PARKS

IN RECENT YEARS, amusement parks have figured out that not everyone wants to zoom on a roller coaster or be suspended upside-down from a re-creation of a Viking ship. So they've added more attractions for little kids. Many are of the tiny-car-that-goes-in-endless-circles variety, but others try a little harder. SESAME PLACE, about 3.5 hours from Washington in Langhorne, Pa., is the best bet for the under-7 crowd: Everything is kid-sized. There's a large selection of water activities, and costumed Sesame Street characters work the crowd. HERSHEYPARK, about 2.5 hours away in Hershey, Pa., appeals to kids for another reason: chocolate. While you're there you can visit CHOCOLATE WORLD (see p. 189) and munch on lots of the brown stuff. Kiddie rides are scattered through the park itself, and there's also a zoo. You can help sell a visit to Colonial Williamsburg with a stop at one (or both) of the amusement parks down there: BUSCH GARDENS and WATER COUNTRY USA. Adventure World has been redubbed Six Flags America and is promising $27 million of improvements when it reopens in May 1999. It's the closest to Washington, right near the Beltway in Largo, Md.

A day at an amusement park is not cheap. Admission prices range from $25 to $35 a person (rides are free). Factor in locker rental (if it's a water park), food and souvenirs as well. Some tips for getting the most out of your park visit:

❑ Call ahead for a map and schedule, so you can formulate your plan of attack. Note where kid-friendly rides are and times for special shows.

❑ To avoid crowds as much as possible, try arriving before the park opens. That way you also can leave earlier to escape long parking lot lines. If it's a water park, go straight to the lockers to stow clothes. Visit attractions at the farthest reaches of the park first, then work your way back toward the entrance.

❑ Drink plenty of liquids, take breaks and, of course, don't let kids go on any stomach-turning rides too soon after eating.

Here are details on large regional amusement parks:

SIX FLAGS AMERICA. 13710 Central Ave., Largo, Md. **Phone**: 301/249-1500. **Web**: www.sixflags.com. The old Adventure World is expecting $27 million of improvements from its new Six Flags owner, including a Looney Tunes movie play area and DC Comics-themed rides. **Directions:** *From the Beltway, take Exit 15A (Route 214 east) to the park.* ♿

PARAMOUNT KINGS DOMINION. 16000 Theme Park Way, Doswell, Va., 95 miles south of Washington. **Phone:** 804/876-5000. **Web:** www.pkd4fun.com. This is a good choice for children of mixed ages. Older kids might enjoy the James Bond/ 007-themed attractions, while younger ones can play in KidZville or the Nickelodeon-themed Splat City or Rugrats areas. They also can enjoy water games in Splash Island or eat at the Busytown Cafe, inspired by the popular Richard Scarry books. **Directions:** *Take I-95 South to Exit 98.*

HERSHEYPARK. Hershey, Pa., 2.5 hours from Washington. **Phone:** 800/ HERSHEY. **Web:** www.800hershey.com. This is a full-featured amusement park with roller coasters, water rides, a modest but quality selection of attractions for small kids (including a nice carousel), a zoo and a marine mammal show. **Directions:** *Take I-95 north to I-695 north to I-83 north to Harrisburg/Route 322 east and follow signs.* ♿

SESAME PLACE. N. Buckstown Rd., Langhorne, Pa., about 3.5 hours from Washington. **Phone:** 215/752-7070. **Web:** www.sesameplace.com. Lots of familiar strolling characters, a wave pool with kid-size waves, active attractions such as cargo nets and climbing areas and Twiddlebug Land (where everything is huge, making children feel like the eponymous bugs) make this an ideal destination for preschoolers. **Directions:** *Take I-95 north through Baltimore to Morrisville Exit 29A/Route 1 north to the Oxford Valley Exit. Turn right onto Oxford Valley Rd. and right again at the third traffic light.* ♿

BUSCH GARDENS. Williamsburg, Va., 3 hours away. **Phone:** 757/253-3350. **Web:** www.buschgardens.com. Do you have a kid who is into make-believe or who enjoys the Renaissance festival? Busch Gardens is an ersatz Ye Olde Europe. In addition to roller coasters and the like, it offers a petting zoo, an entertaining bird show and other animal attractions. **Directions:** *Take I-95 south to I-64 east to Exit 242 and follow the signs.* ♿

WATER COUNTRY USA. This Anheuser-Busch park also is in Williamsburg, **Phone:** 800/343-SWIM. **Web:** www.watercountryusa.com. Water obviously rules here, with flume rides, raft rides, etc. Kids' Kingdom has scaled-down rides for youngsters plus shows in the Minnow Matinee theater. H2O UFO is like a playground half-immersed in water. **Directions:** *Take I-95 south to I-64 east and follow the signs.* ♿

II. The Inside Set

INDOOR 'PLAYGROUNDS'

YOU EITHER LOVE self-contained indoor "playgrounds," or entertainment centers, or you hate them. And, as with so many things concerning parenthood, you can hate them and still frequent them. With their ball pits and cargo nets, hamster-trail tubes and quarter-sucking arcade games, they are sensory overload. Some people worry about sanitation or even question whether the places are detrimental to a child's creativity and socialization (this group seems to prefer the days when kids played with sock puppets and lengths of string). But most children love them, and you'll probably find yourself at one during your lifetime.

Our advice for getting the most out of your visit? First (yet again), get there early: The places become jammed later in the day, especially on weekends or rainy days. Second, while your child will know to wear socks and comfortable clothes, you should do the same: It is not unusual to have to kick off your shoes and head deep inside a plastic tube to perform an "extraction." Finally, set a limit ahead of time on how much you'll spend on game tokens.

Below are the main players in the local indoor-playground game. Remember, too, that many hamburger joints have similar, if smaller, play areas that are free.

DAVE & BUSTER'S
White Flint Mall, 11301 Rockville Pike, North Bethesda

HOURS: M-Sat 11-1am, Sun 11:30-midnight (under 21 must leave by 10 pm; summertime it's 11 pm). **COST:** Free admission, but assume you'll spend $10-$20 per player per hour on Power Cards. **PHONE:** 301/230-5151. ♿

D&B plays a different game from other indoor amusement venues noted here. It's largely designed for adults (those under 21 must be accompanied by someone over 25, and an adult can't bring more than three younger players). Also, activities aren't physically arranged for the preschool set. Still, Dave & Buster's can be a blast for kids 8 and up and a great place for kids and parents to play games together.

It has the area's best selection of "virtual reality" games (big-screen arcade games in which you fly, shoot, drive, hit baseballs etc.), and a huge choice of midway-style skill-and-luck games, complete with winners' tickets redeemable for prizes. There's a 3-D theater "ride," headset-based interactive games and a dark module that seems to shake its occupants like the hardware store paint mixer. The restaurant offers outsize portions of better food than you'd expect. When it's crowded (and it usually is), you can leave your name with the hostess, play for half an hour or so and then grab a meal. Or there's plenty to eat from the play area's drink-and-snack bar. An adult and child should expect to spend at least $40 for an hour or two of games, snacks, and enough tickets for only the most modest of prizes. Dress code: no T-shirts, tank tops or torn shorts. D&B would make a good "small" birthday party choice for a 10-year-old: lunch or dinner and a couple of hours of fun with, say, a best friend. But don't try to book your basic cake-and-play here.

Words to the wise: *Count on staying close to your charges; the staff won't let kids run around by themselves*

NOTES: Certain games can't accommodate those in wheelchairs, though several dining tables are reserved for disabled access. Food and beverages are available at typical chain-restaurant prices.

Directions: *From the Beltway, take Exit 34 to Rockville Pike north. White Flint is about 1.5 miles on the right.*

DISCOVERY ZONE Kid Zone

HOURS: Vary by location; call individual phone numbers below. **COST:** About $8 for 3 and up, $5 for 1-3, or under 38 inches; adults free. 🦽

DZ kicked off the nationwide pay-to-play chain craze, and it hasn't sat still since. At this writing, a number of the corporate locations (White Flint and Germantown are franchises) were in the midst of renovations to add such attractions as laser tag, a crafts room and kids' karaoke.

Maryland

ANNAPOLIS. Forest Plaza Shopping Center, 81B Forest Plaza. **Phone:** 410/ 573-1122.

GERMANTOWN. 11528 Middlebrook Rd. **Phone:** 301/540-2424.

GLEN BURNIE. South Dale Shopping Center, 46 Mountain Rd. **Phone:** 410/ 768-4386.

FREDERICK. 470 Prospect Blvd. **Phone:** 301/698-5040.

NORTH BETHESDA. White Flint Mall, Nicholson Lane and Rockville Pike. **Phone:** 301/231-0505.

Virginia

FALLS CHURCH. 5195 Leesburg Pike. **Phone:** 703/379-6900.

FAIRFAX. 3031 Nutley St. **Phone:** 703/207-7055.

MANASSAS. 7730 Stream Walk Lane. **Phone:** 703/369-4885.

JEEPER'S

HOURS: M-Th 10-9, F 11-10, Sat 10-10, Sun 11-8. **COST:** Prices for children vary by location. Adults free. **CENTRAL PHONE:** 800/JEE-PERS. **WEB:** www.jeepers.com. &

This indoor-play contender adds a few amusement park rides to the Discovery Zone formula. The two regular locations, both in Maryland, feature a tube-and slide-based climbing structure that the 4-to-8 crowd loves. They also have an area loaded with token-gobbling game machines (mostly non-violent) spewing tickets that can be redeemed for low-quality prizes, plus several amusement-park rides, ranging from a mild-mannered jungle jeep attraction to a modest roller coaster and bumper cars to a truly wicked scrambler. (Several games and rides are not wheelchair accessible.) All the activity revolves around the Tiny Rhino Diner serving Pizza Hut pizza and a few yuppie items like pasta and salads. Admission covers unlimited rides and play, but game tokens cost extra. A lot of kids seem to develop obsessions about the games, tickets and prizes, which can get expensive and annoying.

Maryland

ROCKVILLE. 700 Hungerford Dr. (Route 355); four miles north of White Flint Mall. **Phone:** 301/340-3308. **Hours:** M-Th 10-9, F-Sat 10-10, Sun 10-8.

GREENBELT. Beltway Plaza, 600 Greenbelt Rd., Greenbelt. **Phone:** 301/982-7073.**Hours:** M-F 10-9, Sat-Sun 10-10.

Virginia

FAIRFAX. Jeeper's Jr., a scaled-down version with less hardware, is located in the Fairfax Toys R Us KidsWorld at 13035 Fairlakes Blvd. **Hours:** M-Sat 9:30-9:30, Sun 10-6. **Phone:** 703/222-6620.

PLANET PLAY

HOURS: Usually 11-8, later in summer. **PHONE:** Individual numbers below. **WEB:** www.planetplay.com. &

This Northern Virginia-based group of four (mostly) indoor activity centers offers a combination of play structures, laser tag, fast food, redemption games and birthday parties. The Centreville location offers miniature golf, too, and

Springfield edges into Jeepers territory with bumper cars and a carousel. Offerings at each location vary, as do prices. Indoor play areas typically cost $2 for a half-hour or $3 to $5 for the entire day (older kids pay more). Laser tag runs anywhere from $3.50 for 10 minutes to $8.50 for 24 minutes.

Virginia

PLANET PLAY BURKE. K-Mart Town Center, 6030-G Burke Commons Rd., Burke. **Phone:** 703/425-0007. Laser Storm arena; 14-station indoor play zone including a moon bounce and ball pool; video, simulator and redemption games. Burger King food.

PLANET PLAY RESTON. Plaza America, 11674-B Plaza America Dr., Reston. **Phone:** 703/736-0580. The is the newest facility, featuring a four-level indoor play area with moon bounce, a LaserTron arena, separate tot play area, video games, simulator and redemption games. There's a Burger King downstairs.

PLANET PLAY SPRINGFIELD. Springfield Mall, lower level, across from McCrory's, Springfield. **Phone:** 703/313-6770. This one has the usual Planet Play amenities, plus indoor amusement rides, including bumper cars and a carousel.

CENTREVILLE MINI-GOLF AND GAMES. 6206 Multiplex Dr., Centreville. **Hours:** Daily 11-11. **Phone:** 703/502-7888. You'll find the widest range of activities at any Planet Play: (seasonal) outdoor mini-golf, a big game area, laser tag, indoor play area, moon bounce, fast food. ♿

INDOOR ROCK CLIMBING

INDOOR CLIMBING — in which participants scale nearly vertical surfaces studded with hand and foot holds, while safely tethered to an assistant called a "belayer" — requires a bit more planning, devotion and expense than most activities in this book. But for families with kids 6 and up, we think it's worth it. Wall climbing offers an unusual mix of gender-neutral physical challenge, opportunities to gain self-confidence and learn new skills, a chance for parents and kids to play together and sheer fun — all with more flexibility and less of an up-front commitment than, say, ballet or martial arts lessons.

The best place to start, we think, is with the commercial operation called Sportrock, which has Kids Nights every Friday. Call at least 24 hours in advance — they need a head count to adjust available staff — and then just show up. With no prior experience, kids slip on a harness and helmet and receive a brief introduction. Soon they're safely scaling 30-foot walls with the assistance of a trained instructor. Parents can marvel from the sidelines, relax in a small lounge or, better yet, take a Basic Skills class at the same time (grown-ups get a lot more background and prep about safety, skills and knot-tying) and join the kids later. Once you've learned to belay your kids (and your spouse), this can be a great once-in-a-while family activity — or, for some, a true passion that leads to serious outdoor adventuring.

Below is information on the area's two Sportrock facilities and other facilities that, after you've learned the ropes at Sportrock or some other venue, offer more affordable, though more limited, walls to climb. Both the Sportrock and Rockville facilities offer birthday parties.

Maryland

SPORTROCK I. 14708 Southlawn Lane, Rockville. **Hours:** Friday Kids Nights 6:30 to 8:30 (reservations required). General hours: Weekdays 12-11, Sat 11-8, Sun 12-8. **Cost:** Kids Night $17.50 per child, $28 for two children from the same family. Basic Skills classes, ages 14-adult, $27.50. All gear is provided. **Phone:** 301/762-5111. **Directions:** *Take Beltway to I-270 north to Exit 4A, Montrose Rd. east, and make a left on Tower Oaks Blvd. Then take a right on Wooton Pkwy. and a left on E. Gude Dr. Sportrock is in the second cluster of warehouses on the right.*

CITY OF ROCKVILLE CLIMBING GYM. F. Scott Fitzgerald Park, 603 Edmonston Dr. Climbers must pass a "climber's competency test" before using wall. Call for reservations, as capacity is limited. Classes for kids and adults are available through the City of Rockville, though not with the same flexibility as Sportrock. **Hours:** M-Th 6-10 pm; Sat 12-8, Sun 12-6. Weekend hours limited in winter. **Cost:** Admission $7 for Rockville residents, $8 for non-residents; $1 student discount; multi-use passes available. Gear rental $4-$9. **Phone:** 301/309-3226. **Directions:** *Take Beltway to I-270 north to Route 28 east. Continue past Route 355 (Rockville Pike) and stay with Route 28 (which requires you to take the first left after Route 355). Go four blocks and turn right at Baltimore Rd. Three streets later turn left on Edmonston Dr. Civic Center Park entrance is immediately on your right. Pass a mansion and continue downhill.*

EARTH TREKS CLIMBING CENTER. 7125C Columbia Gateway Dr., Columbia. For kids 6-12; no experience necessary. Call ahead for reservations. Parents or guardians of those under 10 must stay in gym for duration of session. If your kids get really inspired, this is the biggest and most challenging indoor climbing facility on the East Coast. **Hours:** Kids Klimbs are Sat 9-11 am. **Cost:** $13; shoes $2 more. **Phone:** 410/872-0060 or 800/254-6287. **Directions:** *From the Beltway, take I-95 north to Route 175 west. Take a right onto Gateway Dr., the third right onto Columbia Gateway Dr., and the fifth right into the parking lot.*

Virginia

SPORTROCK II. 5308 Eisenhower Ave., Alexandria. Hours, cost and reservation requirements same as at Rockville location. **Phone:** 703/212-7625. **Directions:** *Take Beltway to Van Dorn St. exit. Make a left on Van Dorn and a right on Eisenhower Ave. Sportrock II is about half a mile up on the right.* **Metro:** Van Dorn.

WAKEFIELD RECREATION CENTER. 8100 Braddock Rd., Annandale. **Hours:** Climbing wall Tu-Th 4-9. **Cost:** $6 (includes equipment). **Phone:** 703/321-7081. **Directions:** *Take the Beltway to Braddock Rd. west, and make a right into the park.*

ICE SKATING

THE EARLIER KIDS start learning to ice skate, the sooner they can go on to Olympic gold, followed by a lucrative contract with a touring ice show. Then they'll be able to take care of you when you're old and infirm. So sign up for lessons today! The schedules at most ice rinks — family skate versus adult skate, hockey practice versus group lessons — make those at community pools look like models of simplicity. Call before you lace up, lest the ice be already occupied. Admission for most rinks is about $4 to $6 for adults, slightly less for kids, with skate rental from $2 to $3. Outdoor rinks close in bad weather.

District of Columbia

FORT DUPONT ICE ARENA. 3779 Ely Place SE. **Phone:** 202/584-5007.

PERSHING PARK ICE RINK. 14th St. and Pennsylvania Ave. NW. **Hours:** Beginner ice safety lessons (how to get up, fall down, etc.) weekends 1-5, every hour on the hour. **Phone:** 202/737-6938.

Maryland

ARC ICE SKATING RINK. 50 Southlawn Ct., Rockville. **Phone:** 301/294-8101.

BETHESDA METRO ICE CENTER. Intersection of Wisconsin Ave. and East West Hwy. atop Bethesda Metro Center, Bethesda. **Phone:** 301/656-0588 or 301/656-0589.

BOWIE ICE ARENA. 3330 Northview Dr., Bowie. **Phone:** 301/249-2244.

CABIN JOHN REGIONAL PARK ICE RINK. 10610 Westlake Dr., Rockville. **Phone:** 301/365-0585 or 301/365-2246. Open year round.

COLUMBIA ICE RINK. 5876 Thunder Hill Rd., Columbia. **Phone:** 410/730-0322.

FREDERICK SPORT AND ICE ARENA. 1288 Riverbend Way, Frederick. **Phone:** 301/662-7362. Indoor rink open year-round.

THE GARDENS ICE HOUSE. 13800 Old Gunpowder Rd., Laurel. **Phone:** 301/953-0100 **Web:** www.thegardensicehouse.com. Indoor and open year-round. This is one of the nicest rinks in the area.

HERBERT WELLS ICE RINK. 5211 Paint Branch Pkwy., College Park. **Phone:** 301/277-0654 or 301/277-3719.

INNER HARBOR ICE RINK. Rash Field off Key Hwy., Baltimore. **Phone:** 410/385-0675 or 410/752-8632. "Tykes on Ice" children's sessions Sat 10-12. Drop-in group lessons Sun 5-7 (all ages, all levels). Registration on site.

PUTT PUTT GOLF, GAMES & ICE RINK. 130 Rollins Ave., Rockville. **Phone:** 301/881-1663.

TALBOT COUNTY COMMUNITY CENTER. 10028 Ocean Gateway, Easton. **Phone:** 410/822-7070.

TUCKER ROAD ICE RINK. 1770 Tucker Rd., Fort Washington. **Phone:** 301/248-3124 or 301/248-2508.

WHEATON REGIONAL PARK ICE RINK. 11751 Orebaugh Ave. (near Arcola Ave.), Wheaton. **Phone:** 301/649-3640 or 301/649-2250.

Virginia

FAIRFAX ICE ARENA. 3779 Pickett Rd., Fairfax. **Phone:** 703/323-1131 or 703/323-1132. Skating year-round. Registration for group lessons, which begin each week year-round.

MOUNT VERNON RECREATION CENTER. 2017 Bellview Blvd., Alexandria. **Phone:** 703/768-3224. Call 703/768-3223 for a taped announcement of times for public skating sessions, which change weekly.

PRINCE WILLIAM ICE FORUM. 5180 Dale Blvd., Dale City. **Phone:** 703/730-8423. Indoor and open year-round. One of the nicest facilities in the area.

RESTON SKATING PAVILION. 1830 Discovery St., Reston. **Phone:** 703/709-6300.

SKATENATION OF RESTON. 1800 Michael Faraday Ct., Reston. **Phone:** 703/709-1010. Indoor and open for skating year round. Registration for group lessons.

ROLLER SKATING

IN-LINE SKATES have taken over from those simple roller skates most of us wore as children. But there are still roller rinks where families can go round and round as a group. Most of these rinks rent the traditional quad skates, though some rent in-line skates or allow you to bring your own (provided the wheels and brakes are in good condition and the brakes aren't the kind that mark up the floor).

Like ice rinks and swimming pools, roller rinks have extremely complicated schedules. One night it's teen skate, the next it's gospel skate, the next pickup roller hockey. Many of the rinks we list below have special times for families or for young skaters. That's the time to go if you'd like to avoid a daredevil plowing through your group. Schedules are subject to change, so call before you go. Typical general admission is about $4, more on Friday and Saturday nights, less during special promotions. Skate rental is one or two bucks.

Maryland

BRADDOCK ROLLER RINK. 4604 Old Swimming Pool Rd., Braddock Heights. **Phone:** 301/695-4757. "Tiny Tots and Stroller Skate" for 8 years and younger, Sat 11-2. ♿

CALVERT ROLLER SKATING CENTER. Route 4 and Chaneyville Road, Owings. **Phone:** 301/855-6202 (D.C. line) or 410/257-7772.

CLINTON SKATING CENTER. 6805 E. Clinton St., Clinton. **Phone:** 301/868-6454. &

LAUREL SKATING CENTER. 9890 Brewers Ct., along Route 1, 2.5 miles north of Laurel. **Phone:** 301/725-8070.

PASADENA SKATING CENTER. 2318 Mountain Rd., Pasadena. **Phone:** 410/437-3636.

ROCKVILLE ROLLER SKATING CENTER. 1632 E. Gude Dr., Rockville. **Phone:** 301/340-7767. Matinee skating sessions geared toward families, Sat-Sun 1-4.

SEABROOK SKATING CENTER. 9901 Lanham-Severn Rd., Seabrook. **Phone:** 301/577-1733.

SKATE ZONE. 1082 Route 3 south at Capital Raceway Rd., Crofton. **Phone:** 410/721-7155. In fall and winter (M 10-12), parents can push strollers while kids ride their wheeled toys during "Trike, Tot and Roll." &

SKATE PALACE. 3132 Branch Ave., Marlow Heights. **Phone:** 301/894-8500. This is the only rink in the area with two skating surfaces, one of which is smaller and designed for beginners. Drop-in lessons are offered for all ages (Th 6:30-7:30, Sat 10:30-11:30). &

SPORTLAND OF MARYLAND. Rio Mall, 9811 Washingtonian Blvd., Gaithersburg. **Phone:** 301/840-8404. Though the rink is relatively small, skating is just one of the activities here. Others include batting cages, bumper cars and arcade games. &

SUPREME SPORTS CLUB. 7080 Deepage Dr., Columbia. **Phone:** 410/381-5355. &

WALDORF ROLLER SKATING CENTER. 3410 Leonardtown Rd., Waldorf. **Phone:** 301/843-1122.

Virginia

FRANCONIA SKATING CENTER. 5508 Franconia Rd., Alexandria. **Phone:** 703/971-3334.

PURCELLVILLE ROLLER RINK. 230 S. Nursery Ave., Purcellville. **Phone:** 540/338-5025. The rink is in a 1903 white wooden building owned by the town's fire department. &

SKATE AND FUN ZONE. 7878 Sudley Rd., Manassas. **Phone:** 703/361-7465. "Stroller and Trike Skates" are held 10:30 to 12:30 Thursday mornings in fall and winter for adults and children ages 6 and under. This skate center also has laser tag. &

LASER TAG

BANG-BANG, gotcha. Well, more like the light-sensitive electronic vest you're wearing has registered a direct hit. Laser tag takes shooting games into the 21st Century. Players divide into teams and scurry around semi-darkened, warehouse-type spaces trying to pinpoint each other with light-emitting pistols. The aim usually is to capture a flag, but most people simply like to get an "enemy" in their sights and pull the trigger. Games typically last 10 to 15 minutes. Prices range from $4 to $8 a game, depending on the day of the week. Some places sell discounted memberships for hardcore fans. Laser tag is not recommended for children under 6; some places also have size restrictions, excluding players under 44 inches tall. Call any location if your charges are close to these limits. In general, wheelchair access is difficult because of the twists and turns of the courses.

Maryland

LASER STORM. 5809 Buckeystown Pike, Frederick. **Phone:** 301/620-4199.

SPORT LAND. Rio Mall, 9811 Washingtonian Blvd., Gaithersburg. **Phone:** 301/840-8404.

Virginia

CENTREVILLE MINI GOLF AND GAMES. Centreridge Shopping Center, 6206 Multiplex Dr., Centreville. **Phone:** 703/502-7888.

LASER QUEST. Potomac Festival Mall, 14517 Potomac Mills Rd., Woodbridge. **Phone:** 703/490-4180.

PLANET PLAY. K-Mart Shopping Center, 6030-G Burke Commons Rd., Burke. **Phone:** 703/425-0007.

SKATE AND FUN ZONE. 7878 Sudley Rd., Manassas. **Phone:** 703/361-7465

BOWLING

KIDS ALREADY SPEND plenty of time flinging things around your house and knocking stuff down. Channel that innate urge at a bowling alley. Lanes with duckpin bowling — where you roll holeless, grapefruit-size balls at pint-size pins — are, of course, a better bet for little hands than muscling those big tenpin bowling balls. Also, most grown-ups seem to do no better than youngsters, making a duckpin game more fun for the whole family. Invaluable for the youngest bowlers are lanes that put out bumpers for children. The rubber bumpers cover the gutters, eliminating some of the disappointment that comes from rolling scoreless frame after scoreless frame. Games are in the $2 to $3 range, with shoe rental adding another couple of bucks. Birthday parties are big business on weekends.

Maryland

AMF BOWIE. Free State Mall, 15514 Annapolis Rd., Bowie. **Phone:** 301/262-5553. Bumpers available upon request during open bowling. ♿

AMF COLLEGE PARK BOWLING LANES. 9021 Baltimore Blvd., College Park. **Phone:** 301/474-8282. Bumpers available upon request during open bowling. ♿

AMF SOUTHWEST. 4991 Fairview Ave., Linthicum. **Phone:** 410/789-2400. Bumpers are available during open bowling.

BOWL AMERICA WESTWOOD. 5353 Westbard Ave., Bethesda. **Phone:** 301/654-1320. Bumpers are available by request during open bowling. ♿

GLEN BURNIE BOWLING CENTER. Beltway Crossing Shopping Center, 6322 Ritchie Hwy., Glen Burnie. **Phone:** 410/636-5904. No bumper bowling. ♿

RIVIERA BOWL. 8551 Fort Smallwood Rd., Pasadena. **Phone:** 410/255-3550. No bumper bowling. ♿

THURMONT BOWLING CENTER. 20 Frederick Rd., Thurmont. **Phone:** 301/271-2881. Bumpers available upon request.

TUFFY LEEMANS GLENMONT BOWL. Woodmont Shopping Center, 12345 Georgia Ave., Wheaton. **Phone:** 301/942-4200. Families should call a week or two in advance to reserve a bumper lane. ♿

VILLAGE LANES BOWLING CENTER. Village Shopping Center, 902 East St., Frederick. **Phone:** 301/662-1442. Call in advance to request a bumper, available during open bowling. ♿

WALKERSVILLE BOWLING CENTER. 44 Pennsylvania Ave., Walkersville. **Phone:** 301/898-3355. Bumpers available upon request.

WHITE OAK BOWLING CENTER. White Oak Shopping Center, 11207 New Hampshire Ave., Silver Spring. **Phone:** 301/593-3000. Bumpers are plentiful during open bowling.

Virginia

FALLS CHURCH BOWLING CENTER. 400 S. Maple Ave., Falls Church. 703/533-8131. Bumpers available upon request.

12

ᗪOING the FEDERAL SHUFFLE

WE MAY BE RAISING our families in or near the Nation's Capital, the Seat of Democracy, the Center of Power of the Free World, but let's face it: When it comes to entertaining most children, a little bit of the Federalist Papers goes a long way.

While you certainly should expose your offspring to the unique opportunities of federal Washington, we have found that this goes over best in small, occasional and age-appropriate doses. An Oklahoma family making its first visit to our nation's capital can be forgiven for sweltering in a summer line with a 5-year-old while awaiting a three-minute glimpse of the Supreme Court. A resident of Burke, Oxon Hill or Gaithersburg cannot (except when required to escort out-of-town visitors and their offspring).

That said, appropriate visits to sites in this chapter can convey some of the greatest benefits of D.C.-area residency: de-mystification of federal institutions, a heightened appreciation of the benefits and complexities of a democracy, and awareness of the striking range of the government's reach.

Two rules are in order here:

1. Try not to do federal Washington on summer days or major school vacations, when prime sites and comfort amenities are overwhelmed. The best times: weekends from October through March. Exception: summer evenings, between 7 and 8, when the heat and the crowds have dissipated.

2. Match the activity to the age. A 3-year-old is better suited to a romp on the Ellipse than to a tour of the White House. A 5-year-old will be underwhelmed by the gilded copy of the Magna Carta on display in the Capitol's Rotunda but may get a kick out of the Rotunda itself.

Following are highlights and appropriate age ranges for visiting major government institutions (for attractions on historic figures, such as presidential memorials, see Chapter 10 on Living History). It's a relatively brief list, picked because the sites are most accommodating to children.

THE WHITE HOUSE
1600 Pennsylvania Avenue NW

HOURS: Tu-Sat 10-12. **COST:** Free. **PHONE:** 202/456-704 (recordings), 202/619-7222 (Park Service). TDD: 202/456-2121. **WEB:** www.whitehouse.gov. **METRO:** McPherson Square, Federal Triangle, Farragut West (all require healthy walks).   ♿

If most White House tenants get decidedly mixed reviews, so do public tours of the place. Of course, just being able to say you were in the White House is a kick, even (maybe especially) for kids. But what you get to see for all your trouble can be disappointing.

If you take the regular, self-guided tour, you'll start by walking past a couple of roped-off, ground-floor rooms (a library, a room graced with portraits of recent First Ladies). Then you'll head upstairs and pass through the grand East Room (with the 1797, saved-from-the-British-burning portrait of George Washington by Gilbert Stuart) and a number of smaller rooms — Green, Blue and Red. These are filled with portraits and period pieces and are the settings of a few charming anecdotes that are likely to be lost on the pre-teen set. Last comes the State Dining Room, where (what else?) state dinners are held. You won't see the Oval Office, any family quarters, or offices where staffers carry out the executive mission. Even the press room is off limits.

In light of this, here are some age-appropriate recommendations and how-tos to help navigate your way.

- ❑ **6 AND UNDER.** Don't bother trying the tour. Walk around the mansion's front (Pennsylvania Avenue) and rear (Ellipse), and tell your daughters or sons that This Is Where the President Lives. Take out a $20 bill and show your child the rendering on the back (and explain that Andrew Jackson, the fellow on the front, lived there). Go to the White House Visitors Center (see p. 174), preferably after noon, when the crowds are gone, and take in some of the history and videos.

- ❑ **6 TO 12.** Take the public tour, but do so in late fall or pre-spring, when crowds are thinner and tickets aren't needed. Make sure you go to the White House Visitors Center beforehand (leave yourself at least half an hour), where videos, artifacts and displays put the tour in context. The White House Web site (www.whitehouse.gov) also is exceptionally informative and can be useful in preparing for a visit. The visit itself usually lasts 15 to 25 minutes, with taciturn Secret Service personnel at each doorway to answer questions and enforce sobriety.

- ❑ **12 AND UP.** Call the office of your U.S. Senator or Representative and request VIP tour tickets. You'll need to do this three to six months in advance, and you'll have to accept an available date and time. This will put you in a

YOUR TICKET to the WHITE HOUSE

Who needs tickets?

In general, anyone who wants to visit between mid-March and Labor Day (though you should call the information number for specific dates when tickets are required). If you visit from Labor Day to early March (which we recommend) you won't have to bother with passes.

If I'm visiting when we need tickets, how do I get them?

Same-day tickets are available at the White House Visitors Center on a first-come, first-served basis. (For advance VIP tickets, see **WHITE HOUSE** entry.) During high season, the line begins to form as early as 6 in the morning, and if you're not in line when the center opens at 7:30, you may be out of luck. If you arrive at 7, expect to wait an hour or so to get tickets. Each person can get up to four tickets, so if you're in a party of five, six or more, at least two of you will have to stand in line. The tickets are timed for tours that begin at 10 and end no later than noon. (Note that you may emerge at 8:30 with tickets for an 11:30 tour, so it's wise to have plans about how to use that time. The White House Visitors Center itself can happily consume 30 minute to an hour.) Before your tour, you'll assemble on bleachers set up on the Ellipse and wait for your number and time to be called; from there, a Park Service ranger will lead you to the White House. If the gods are smiling, a marching band will entertain you while you wait. There's nothing quite as inspiring, or heart breaking, as the sight of a hulking tuba player from San Antonio playing his heart out on Sousa marches in the capital's sweltering midday heat.

And if I'm going in the off-season, as you suggest?

It's still no walk in the park. You assemble at the Southeast Gate of the White House (on the right as you face the mansion from the Ellipse) as early as you can bear. The line often forms by 8. We recommend arriving no later than 9, but you're assured entry if you're in line by noon. An adult can hold a place for a family, who can run off some steam on the Ellipse or grab a snack from a vendor.

I'm still confused.

Call the recording phone number or hit the Web site; both are detailed and anticipate most questions.

group of 70 VIPs, and you won't have to wait for a timed ticket (though you'll still have to wait in a line). You'll also get a tour with a live guide (a Secret Service employee) and admission to several additional rooms (the China Room, the Map Room, the Diplomatic Reception Room). This is the best access that a commoner can get, but it's worth pursuing only with children who have sufficient interest in going and who can pay attention. And, yes, you should again be sure to hit the Visitors Center before your tour.

Words to the wise: *Strollers are not permitted on White House tours (they can be checked prior to entry). Tours are not available on Sundays or Mondays. Call ahead, as tours sometimes can be canceled with little or no notice due to presidential activity. No public bathrooms are available in the White House; the nearest ones are in the Ellipse Visitors Pavilion, near the bleachers. Also, since you'll be going through metal detectors, you might want to lighten up on coins, keys, pens and other objects.*

NOTES: Call for information on public events: garden walks, holiday candlelight tours, etc. **Parking:** It's spare and highly restricted. Either take public transportation or budget up to $10 to park in a private garage several blocks to the north. **Food:** There are numerous restaurants on and off Pennsylvania Avenue. **Disabled Access:** Those in wheelchairs (plus up to six others in their parties) can enter anytime from 9:45 until noon, without tickets and without waiting in line. The hearing- or sight-impaired can arrange for special tours in advance. Write to Visitors Office, White House, Washington, DC 20502, or call the TDD number above. **Nearby:** Washington Monument, other Mall attractions.

WHITE HOUSE VISITORS CENTER
15th Street and Pennsylvania Avenue NW

HOURS: Daily 7:30-4 (visitors center only). **COST:** Free. **PHONE:** 202/208-1631. **METRO:** Federal Triangle, McPherson Square.

This museumette in the Department of Commerce building (look for the blue awning and three flags) is where you pick up tickets (if you're planning to visit in high season, when they're required) and prepare for the tour (which you should do regardless of how and when you visit). The White House Visitors Center has inaugural portraits, history (kids are fascinated by the White House burning story), artifacts and videos of First Families in action. The center also has a gift shop, operated by the White House Historical Society. It's a place worth visiting in its own right, even if you don't have the time or inclination for a White House tour.

U.S. CAPITOL
East Capitol and First streets

HOURS: Memorial-Labor Day daily 9-8. **Tours:** Weekdays 9:30-7, Sat 9:30-3:30. Closed for major holidays. **COST:** Free. **PHONE:** 202/225-6827. **WEB:** www.aoc.gov. **METRO STOPS:** Capitol South, Union Station (both require a sizable walk to the Capitol Building). &

Kids will find the Seat of Democracy more interesting as they get older. But even toddlers can get something out of a visit to this extraordinary building.

- **6 AND UNDER.** Take the self-guided tour, which begins from the lower level of the East Front (the side not facing the Mall). You'll have plenty of time to absorb the immensity and beauty of the Rotunda — the grandness of the space, the sheen on the ancient stone floor and the epic scale of the oil paintings (kids can pick out George Washington easily). Also on this level you'll find Statuary Hall, a sort of limestone wax museum of minor historical figures likely to intrigue a toddler only briefly. (The gilded exotica of Hawaii's first "national" chief is worth seeking out.) On the first floor, the Crypt (nobody's buried there) has a star seal in the center of the hall; kids may get a kick out of knowing that they are standing at the epicenter of the dome and of Washington's four-cornered street grid. Head off to the "whisper room" — alleged to carry a whisper around its circumference effortlessly (though we suspect the acoustics aren't what they used to be). Take the elevators to the third floor, where (on weekends only) you can visit the empty House and Senate chambers (kids under 6 can't enter the Senate chambers). If you can manage to explain the difference between the House and Senate — and how all of this is different from the White House — consider yourself a gifted parent-educator and a true patriot.

- **6 TO 12.** Take the guided tour, which departs from the Rotunda (climb the big center steps to get to the second level) every 15 minutes from 9 to 3:45. (On Sundays, just during high season, there are tours that begin at 1.) The 25-minute tour takes in the highlights of the public areas, and the guides are pretty good at providing a digestible mix of history, personalities and political process. At this age, kids will be able to absorb the significance of some of the paintings and frescoes, as well as the historic display downstairs in the crypt. The models of the Mall and early plans for the Capitol are likely to be interesting. If the House and Senate are in session, you'll get a quick glimpse of the "action" on the floor — often a member of Congress delivering a speech to a hall populated only by a few bored aides and technicians (perhaps your child's first taste of "real" politics).

- **12 AND UP.** If you're planning a visit during the week, have your child call up your U.S. Senator or Representative's office (a minor civics lesson itself) and request special passes that permit you to observe the House or Senate in action. Then check *The Washington Post* (or its Web site: www.washingtonpost.com) to see what Congressional action is planned for the day of your visit. Your pass will permit you to hunker in the gallery longer than the guided tour allows. On the day of your visit, either before or afterwards, take the guided tour. If you're feeling lucky, find out which building your Senator or Rep's office is in and drop by. While it's not a sure thing — legislators' schedules can be hellish — it's possible your Person in Washington will make time for a quick hello and handshake. If your visit is on the weekend, forget the pass; just take the guided tour and allow time for lingering in the Crypt, exploring the funky ancient staircases and well-worn decorative treasures.

Words to the wise: *Parking is scarce. If you must drive, go early on a winter weekend when no major events or demonstrations are planned. Or park at Union Station (parking entrance is off North Capitol Street) and walk to the Capitol building — an invigorating and informative stroll. Here, too, you'd be wise not to have too much metal in pockets or purse because of the need to go through security detectors.*

NOTES: For disability access, approach through the lower entrance of the East Front. **Food:** Both the House and Senate have cafeterias. There are scattered restaurants on the Hill and plenty in Union Station. **Nearby:** Supreme Court, Library of Congress, Union Station.

FEDERAL BUREAU OF INVESTIGATION
935 Pennsylvania Avenue NW

HOURS: Weekdays 8:45-4:15; closed federal holidays. **COST:** Free. **PHONE:** 202/324-3447 (TDD: 202-324-1016). **METRO STOPS:** Metro Center, Archives/ Navy Memorial, Gallery Place, Federal Triangle. **WEB:** www.fbi.gov. &

This is one of the few local tours that really pays off for kids. A visit to the center of federal law enforcement makes strong impressions about the rule of law, the high price of a life of crime and the impressive assets that the Good Guys have at their disposal. The huge and artless edifice was designed partly to accommodate these public tours, which notorious FBI director J. Edgar Hoover saw as a valuable way to sell the agency to the public. All these years later, the event still carries a whiff of propaganda. For instance, as the tour begins you encounter a death mask of gangster John Dillinger, complete with the forehead bullet wound resulting from the 1934 shootout with the feds. The hour-long tour starts with an overview of the FBI's work and its 400 field offices and more than 11,000 special agents who carry it out. On the second floor, visitors take in stations explaining the FBI Academy, the history of gangsters and organized crime, the 10 Most Wanted Fugitives program, and the more topical threats of terrorism and espionage. A glass case displays booty seized from criminals, from jewelry to weapons. From the third floor you look down on the FBI's high-tech forensics lab, with its banks of computers, DNA equipment and scientific instruments for, say, identifying scraps of cloth and flecks of paint. Inevitably, someone in the tour group will ask where they keep the "X-Files" — the agency's top-secret files about investigations into extra-terrestrial contacts, upon which the popular TV series is based. The special agent's earnest insistence that such files are purely fictional, of course, serves only to verify their existence for some. The other major highlight comes at the end of the tour, when a special agent demonstrates agents' firearm skills by firing revolvers and automatic weapons, with alarming precision, at human-shaped paper targets. Subtle? No. But impressive.

Words to the wise: *In summer, lines for the popular tour can be insufferable. Only 30 people are admitted per half-hour, and those carrying*

"VIP" tickets will pass you in line, making your blood boil. The best bet is to become a VIP yourself by calling your Senator or Representative at least three months in advance and getting a special, timed reservation. (Federal employees can get tickets with just two weeks' notice.) If you must go sans reservation, try the first and last weeks of summer vacation — and skip the 6 a.m. sidewalk lineup. This is a rare attraction whose lines actually ease in mid-afternoon: They're often less than an hour long then, and visitors can kill time on reasonably comfortable shaded benches. Restrooms and vending machines are available while you wait.

NOTES: The tour entrance is on the E St. side, near Ninth Street. No picture taking is permitted. You can call in advance to arrange for a sign-language interpreter. **Food:** Restaurants are plentiful on both Pennsylvania Avenue and side streets. **Nearby:** National Archives, U.S. Navy Memorial, Old Post Office Pavilion.

BUREAU OF ENGRAVING AND PRINTING
14th and C streets SW

HOURS: Weekdays 9-2 except federal holidays. Ticket distribution starts at 8. **COST:** Free. **PHONE:** 202/622-2000. **WEB:** www.moneyfactory.com. **METRO STOP:** Smithsonian (Independence Avenue exit). &

Kids love this tour, not only because it's about something they already find fascinating (money) but because it's the closest thing federal Washington has to a large-scale "factory," where real stuff gets made by big machines. The 30-minute, self-guided tour leads through a maze of narrow corridors overlooking what is essentially a vast printing plant, where much of the nation's currency is created (there's another plant in Fort Worth, Texas). The plant also produces stamps and some government documents. Kids will see the essentials of moneymaking. In the laborious plate-making process, workers seem like 18th Century artisans ticking at blocks of metal with needle-like tools. At the big printing presses, sheets of 32 bills come running off. At the inspection area, eagle-eyed workers try to spot errors. At the cutter, bills are sliced neatly into blocks for shipment to Federal Reserve Banks. Amusing factlets: Bills are printed not on paper but on a material that's mostly cotton; the average $1 bill lasts a mere 18 months in circulation; 95 percent of bills printed here are replacements for those taken out of circulation by banks. The tour deposits you at a visitors center, where some of Washington's most memorable souvenirs, most of them versions of mulched bills that were rejected for one reason or another, are available.

The tour is quite popular, so avoid high tourist times. Tickets are required for all tours. The ticket office, on 15th Street (renamed Raoul Wallenburg Place in association with the neighboring Holocaust Museum), opens at 8. Regardless of season, try to get there before 9. May through September, tickets often are gone by 11.

Words to the wise: *If you're lucky enough to find parking nearby, it's likely to have a two-hour limit. Strollers are not permitted on the tour. Closed out of a tour? The Visitors Center is open without wait from 8:30 to 3:30 weekdays. It's not open on weekends.*

NOTES: Upon request, tours are available for the hearing and sight-impaired. **Food:** There are no choices in the immediate area, but it's a short drive to Pennsylvania Avenue or Capitol Hill eateries. **Nearby:** U.S. Holocaust Memorial Museum, Tidal Basin, Jefferson Memorial, Washington Monument, other Mall attractions.

NATIONAL ARCHIVES
700 Constitution Avenue NW

HOURS: Daily 10-5:30 (in summer until 9 pm). **COST:** Free. **PHONE:** 202/501-5000 (recording and event listings); 202/501-5500 (offices). **WEB:** www.nara.gov. **METRO STOP:** Archives/Navy Memorial.　♿

The wide steps leading up to this proud, neo-Classical structure — and the beauty of the massive rotunda, decorated with murals featuring Jefferson, Washington, Madison and other early American luminaries — make this a dramatic place that can instill awe even in a distracted toddler. Unfortunately, kids under 10 are unlikely to appreciate the importance of the Big Three Documents displayed there: the Declaration of Independence, the Constitution and the Bill of Rights. None is readable as presented — each lurks under a barrier of thick green glass, in an atmosphere of compressed helium — but kids enjoy hearing that all three are lowered into a vault every night for added security.

Surrounding the rotunda are various exhibition halls, where artifacts from the Archives' bottomless collection of government information are rotated in thematic or historical collections. Among the Archives' greatest hits, usually on display: a 13th Century copy of the Magna Carta (owned, oddly, by Ross Perot and on permanent loan); the Japanese World War II surrender documents; audio tapes of FDR's fireside chats; the Lousiana Purchase agreement signed by Napoleon Bonaparte; Mathew Brady's Civil War photos, and Richard Nixon's resignation letter. Any government document judged to have "enduring value" — somewhere between 2 and 5 percent of the paperwork generated — is maintained by the Archives. A facility in College Park, opened in 1993 and accessible from the main archives building by van, accommodates the overflow, plus many non-paper forms of documentation.

Kids 12 and up with a budding interest in research, history or politics may enjoy one of the Archives' twice-daily, 90-minute guided tours, which reveal the breadth and depth of the national collection. However, you'll need to sign up several weeks in advance. Students 16 and older can take advantage of the Archives' research facilities to access a stunning range of public documents; call 202/501-5400 for information about research opportunities. The College

Park facility (known as Archives 2, 8601 Adelphi Road, between University Boulevard. and Metzerott Road; 301/713-6800) is a high-tech architectural tour de force. While it is visitable and interesting, it lacks the majesty and heroic clout of the main building downtown. It is the place to go, however, if you want to listen to Richard Nixon's infamous White House tapes.

Words to the wise: *You needn't endure the rotunda's slow-moving line, which provides access to all of the displays around the perimeter. A shorter, brisker line provides access just to the Big Three — a fine dose for the under-8 crowd. If the two lines are not clear to you, just ask the guard.*

NOTES: Wheelchair entrance is on Pennsylvania Avenue; the handicapped parking lot is accessible via Ninth Street. **Food:** You can pick from area restaurants. **Nearby:** FBI Building, U.S. Navy Memorial, Old Post Office Pavilion.

LIBRARY OF CONGRESS
First Street and Independence Avenue SE

HOURS: See details below; closed major and federal holidays. Gift shops: M-Sat 9:30-5. **COST:** Free. **PHONE:** 202/707-5000; visits, tours, shops: 202-707-8000; current and coming exhibitions: 202/707-4604. **WEB:** www.loc.gov. **METRO STOP:** Capitol South, Union Station. &

The Thomas Jefferson Building is the centerpiece of this largest library in the world, and it's a gorgeous example of beaux-arts architecture. Unfortunately, its most inspiring space — the 125-foot-high octagonal reading room, festooned with delicate frescoes, heroic busts and marble columns — isn't open to anyone under 18 (it's where serious scholars work at desks and wait for library staff to deliver requested material). Still, the Great Hall (enter the side facing the Capitol) is a spectacular place to visit, even with small children. They are likely to be impressed by the Library's Gutenberg Bible (one of only three existing) and its semi-permanent "American Treasures" exhibition, an ambitious gathering of literary and cultural artifacts from the library's collection of 100 million-plus items. (An audio tour is available for $2.50 a person.) Kids 10 and up will likely appreciate the building's guided tours, offered weekdays and Saturdays at 11:30, 1, 2:30 and 4. They'll learn about the library's founding as Congress' information source; about how, when that collection was destroyed in the British burning of 1814, Jefferson offered his own 6,000-book collection to Congress; about how materials are selected and stored and much more. Visitors can observe the Main Reading room from an overhead gallery. The other library building to be sure to hit is the modern, six-story Madison Building (at Independence Avenue). Its visitors center offers a 22-minute film.

JEFFERSON BUILDING HOURS
The visitors center is open from 10 to 5:30 Monday through Saturdays; a brochure for a self-guided tour, the best option for the under-10 set, is available. A

12-minute, captioned video begins every 20 minutes. Guided tours, best for kids 10 and up, are offered at 11:30, 1, 2:30 and 4. Exhibition areas close at 5.

MADISON BUILDING HOURS

Open weekdays from 8:30 a.m. to 9:30 p.m. and on Saturday from 8:30 to 6. A 22-minute video is shown every half-hour in the first floor auditorium. Exhibition areas close at 5. Classic films are shown for free in the Madison's small Mary Pickford Theater (202/707-5677).

NOTES: For tours for the hearing impaired, call TDD 202/707-6362. **Food:** The Madison building's 6th floor has a fine cafeteria (202/707-8300) with great views (note that it does not accept credit cards). Otherwise, you can walk over to Union Station or find other eateries in the area. **Nearby:** U.S. Capitol, Supreme Court, Union Station.

NATIONAL POSTAL MUSEUM
First Street and Massachusetts Avenue NE

HOURS: Daily 10-5:30. **COST:** Free. **PHONE:** 202/357-2700 (TDD: 202/357-1729). **WEB:** www.si.edu. **METRO STOP:** Union Station. &

Even in this age of e-mail, nothing matches the heartwarming feeling of finding a personal letter stuffed in the mailbox or, better yet, of a package being delivered. This surprisingly engaging Smithsonian museum — housed in a glorious old Washington post office — tells the story of mail with just the right amount of detail. (It also has a nice helping of whimsy: Have your children look down and see what's interesting about the floor designs in the museum's main hall.) Start at "Binding the Nation," a look at how mail was moved in Colonial times. It re-creates an old post road at night, basically a route through darkened woods, complete with the spooky sounds of forest animals. Kids love it, even if more for the theatrics than the history. Older kids may enjoy a section on the development of the stamp (fun fact: stamp gum must be kosher). Two clear plastic columns filled with the microscopic circles from stamp perforations are a hoot. Elsewhere are air mail planes hanging from the ceiling, an actual mail train (its canvas bags sitting empty while old timers on video screens recall the old days) and touch-screen postcard printers visitors can use to create personalized mail. (Note that lines can be long at peak times.) "What's in the Mail for You!" is an aggressively interactive look at how direct marketers target their customers. A stamp shop sells the neat issues your local post office always seems to be out of and will seem like heaven to young philatelists.

Words to the wise: *Don't forget to bring the addresses of friends or relatives to whom you might want to send a post card.*

NOTES: For **Food,** Union Station, right next door, has diverse food courts and sit-down restaurants. **Nearby:** Union Station, U.S. Capitol.

DEPARTMENT OF THE INTERIOR MUSEUM
1849 C Street NW

HOURS: Weekdays 8:30-4:30. **COST:** Free. Adults must show photo ID. **PHONE:** 202/208-4743. **WEB:** www.doi.gov/museum. **METRO STOP:** A long walk from Farragut West. ♿

This curious little museum recounts the activities of the Department of the Interior, the agency in charge of keeping an eye on our natural resources. Interior also administers programs related to Native Americans, and some of the most interesting exhibits here include classic Pueblo pottery, Cherokee baskets and contemporary Native American art. An Indian canoe hangs from the ceiling, and a video speaks to the challenges of merging the traditional with the modern in Native American affairs. (A separate Museum of Native American history is planned for the Mall.) The bulk of the museum, however, has a school report feel to it, with topographic maps showing mineral deposits, examples of various types of rocks, a mounted bison head and other taxidermied animals. Children might enjoy running their hands over a small-scale model of Mount Rushmore or peering into the anachronistic dioramas scattered throughout (sponge fishermen, sheep farmers, a 1939 view of Washington, Juneau at night). Too bad most of the dioramas are up too high for younger kids to look into. Across the hall is the Indian Crafts Shop. Most of the merchandise is pricey jewelry, textiles and dolls, but all are authentic. There are a few sticker books and paper dolls, though, that are within a child's budget.

Words to the wise: *This one is chiefly for federal completists or Native American enthusiasts. For guided tours, call two weeks in advance.*

Notes: Food: There are no easy commercial choices close by. You may want to bring lunch and picnic on the Mall. **Nearby:** Vietnam Veterans Memorial, Korean War Veterans Memorial, Lincoln Memorial.

13
CHILDREN'S MUSEUMS

THERE ARE NOW more than 200 "children's museums" across the country. While each interprets its mandate differently, nearly all share the thought that kids can learn things while having fun, and vice versa. Washington's major entrant, the Capital Children's Museum, is not among the biggest, newest or most lavishly funded. Still, it's worth a trip, particularly for kids under 8.

But the concept of a children's museum is continuing to evolve. More "regular" museums are transforming themselves from static displays of objects and art into kid-friendly, interactive learning centers. Others are sprouting new kid-friendly wings, rooms or programs. At the same time, commercial enterprises are beginning to get involved with play-to-learn centers. The most wholesome and interesting examples of this are in Maryland, in Rockville and Columbia, at huge and bright pay-to-play activity centers called Imagine That! and ExploraWorld, respectively.

In this chapter we include the major places designed specifically to educate kids through structured play and exploration. We also offer references to facilities in other chapters that offer a significant interactive play element.

So where's the children's museum headed? Two developments are worth noting. The staid Smithsonian, which dominates the Washington museum scene, at last report was considering plans that would significantly update its scientific, identification and explanation-based presentations with more engaging and dynamic — and, yes, kid-friendly — exhibits. Don't hold your breath, however; the change still is controversial and likely to come slowly, if at all. Meanwhile, as this book went to press, there was an ambitious plan to open in 1999, in Baltimore, Port Discovery, a $35 million, 80,000-square-foot facility described by its promoters as the "second largest children's museum in the world." Walt Disney Imagineering was on board to design some attractions. For information on Port Discovery, keep your eyes on *The Washington Post*, call Baltimore information or search for Port Discovery on the World Wide Web.

The District

CAPITAL CHILDREN'S MUSEUM
800 Third Street, NE

HOURS: Daily 10-5, Easter-Labor Day 10-6. **COST:** $6, free under 2. **METRO STOP:** Union Station. **PHONE:** 202/675-4120. **WEB:** www.ccm.org. ♿

Children seem to react differently from grown-ups to this museum. Grown-ups wish it were a little nicer, the layout less meandering, the exhibits a little less tatty, the bathrooms not quite so leaky, the air conditioning a bit more powerful. The Smithsonian has spoiled adults, as have the children's museums of some other cities. Kids, though, seem to have a fine old time at the Capital Children's Museum, thank you very much. That's probably because the place looks played in. Most children seem immediately won over when they get off the elevator at the third floor (the recommended starting point) and encounter a room filled with bubble soap and paraphernalia, including one of those contraptions you can pull to enclose yourself in a glistening tubular bubble. Next door is a pair of mazes. At an animation exhibit, kids can make flip books and sit at light tables and trace the outlines of such characters as Bugs Bunny and Wile E. Coyote. They can sit in the front of a Metro bus or the back of a fire engine. The museum has a strong international bent, at least as it applies to two disparate countries, Mexico and Japan. A large exhibit on Mexico features a re-creation of a market, kitchen, corner store, log cabin and public square. A sandbox stands in for the beaches of Yucatan. Crafts abound here, and most kids leave with a tissue-paper flower, yarn art and a sip of hot chocolate they've made themselves. There's also a Japanese tatami room, though its hours are spotty and elements modest (among them a laminated copy of the Mini Page newspaper, some children's backpacks and hats, and a poster that points out that Japanese students go to school 240 days a year, compared with a paltry 180 days in the United States). A new chemistry exhibit is promising. Sponsored by the Chemical Manufacturers Association, it has the requisite "All these things are made of chemicals" pile o' stuff. Children over 6 can don lab coats and goggles and do things like testing the pH of various liquids. Entertaining chemistry demonstrations are given several times a day.

Words to the wise: *Go early or on non-school days. These buildings, originally designed as a convent and nursing home, don't lend themselves to the crowds they often draw, and school groups can clog up hands-on activities.*

NOTES: While elevators serve each floor, some attractions — including the mazes and parts of the "Changing Environments" exhibit — aren't easily maneuvered by those in wheelchairs. **Food:** Except for vending machines, there's no food at the museum. **Nearby:** Union Station.

184

Directions: *From Union Station Metro stop, walk towa_ the parking garage's tour bus/rental car level. Walk throu on H St., following the colorful mosaics over the bridge. the first intersection (Third and H streets).*

Maryland

IMAGINE THAT!
Congressional Plaza, 1616 E. Jefferson Street, Rockville

HOURS: Sun-Th 10-6, F-Sat 10-8. **COST:** All-day admission $7.99 children, $2 adults, free under 18 months. Late rate admission (M-Th 3-6, Sat 6-8, Sun 4-6) is $6 children, adults free. **PHONE:** 301/468-2101.   ♿

Imagine That! is an incredibly fun place to take kids. Imagine a massive open room (16,000 square feet) subdivided by low walls into distinct, thematic play areas. Each play area boasts the kind of cool stuff kids wish they had in their rooms. There is an actual fire truck (and airplane and race car). There's a closed-circuit TV studio where a kid can don a cheesy suit coat and be a news anchor. There's a wooden-floored dance studio with ballet slippers, tap shoes and tutus to try on. There's a room full of musical instruments and much else: a dentist's chair, an ambulance, an art area, a grocery store full of fake food and cash registers that go beep, a sandbox. Might kids learn something here, as they would at a museum? Perhaps. But what they spend most of their time doing is rushing from area to area in a mad dash, alighting in one for a while, then getting on the move again. This is pure play, and that's nothing to be ashamed of.

> **Words to the wise:** *For safety, Imagine That! insists that one adult accompany every four children.*

NOTES: There's a small restaurant inside.

Directions: *From the Beltway, take Route 355 (Rockville Pike) north. Go left on Halpine Rd., right on East Jefferson, right into second parking lot entrance.*

EXPLORAWORLD
6570 Dobbin Road, Columbia

HOURS: Sun-Th 9:30-6, F & Sat 9:30-8. **COST:** $2 adults, $6.95 ages 2 and up, $3.95 1-2, under 1 free. **PHONE:** 410/772-1540. **WEB:** www.exploraworld.com.

If you've been to Imagine That! (see preceding entry) you know what to expect from ExploraWorld: themed play areas spread over a large space, many with actual adult things, including a fire truck, an ambulance and cash registers. Kids can wear spangly outfits while dancing in front of a mirrored wall or singing along with karaoke. They can have fun with an assortment of bubble

ox, a rowboat, a large, castle-shaped climbing structure, a little
d mail carrier uniforms. ExploraWorld also has a puppet theater,
uter terminals loaded with a few kids' games, a plastic food-filled
store and more.

dig at Imagine That!, ExploraWorld calls itself "Maryland's largest activ-
ty center of its kind." At 23,000 square feet, the former pet-supply wholesaler's
warehouse is larger than its Rockville counterpart (reflecting cheaper real estate prices in Howard County, perhaps), but there isn't necessarily more to do
at ExploraWorld. The stuff is simply more spread out. It's not carpeted, so tiny
voices quickly rise to a din. And some of the equipment is frighteningly con-
sumer grade: You wonder how it will stand up to the assault of thousands of
little hands. That said, two little girls of our acquaintance spent *four hours*
here one Saturday. If you live in or near Howard County, you'll appreciate
being close to ExploraWorld. If you live in lower Montgomery County or the
District, Imagine That! is a shorter drive for a slightly better experience. If you
live in Virginia, you should try convincing some investors to open one of these
places down there.

Words to the wise: *You can save $2 off each person if you visit during
the last two hours of operation.*

NOTES: ExploraWorld requires an adult for every four children. While the facility is
handicapped-accessible, some attractions would be tough for kids in wheelchairs. No
strollers are allowed. **Food:** A restaurant serves yogurt and fruit as well as hot dogs,
pizza, sodas and candy.

Directions: *From I-95, take Route 175 west toward Columbia to a left onto Dobbin
Rd. (From Route 29, turn east on Route 175 and right on Dobbin.) ExploraWorld is
seven-tenths of a mile down, on the right.*

CHESAPEAKE CHILDREN'S MUSEUM
In Riva shopping center at 233-D Forest Drive, Annapolis

HOURS: Daily (except W) 10-4 (extended hours in summer). **COST:** $3. **PHONE:**
410/266-0677. &

This is more like a well-equipped playroom than a museum, but it does hold
younger children's attention. A shopping center storefront has been filled with
such playthings as dress-up clothes, a large climbable tugboat, a tabletop Brio
train set, a well-equipped art area and aquariums sporting lizards, a snake, a
turtle and a frog. Kids can play with a handful of computers and an actual
dentist's chair. Not nearly as large as the Capital Children's Museum, or nearly
as educational as anything by the Smithsonian, the Chesapeake Children's Museum is still fun, and you can feel virtuous as you watch other parents walk
right past it to the Chuck E. Cheese a few doors down.

Words to the wise: *Since it's rather modest, this place probably isn't worth a trip of any great distance. It's a better bet if you're heading for or live in the Annapolis area.*

NOTES: The shopping center offers plenty of food options.

Directions: *From the Beltway, take Route 50 east to Exit 22 to Riva Rd. Turn left at the first light and right at the next light.*

RELATED ENTRIES

For more interactive learning activities offered in places other than children's museums, see the following entries (also see other atttractions in the chapters on Science, Living History and Nature and the Outdoors):

NATIONAL MUSEUM OF AMERICAN HISTORY
❑ Hands On Science Room (p. 51)
❑ Hands On History Room (p. 125)

ROSE HILL CHILDREN'S MUSEUM (p. 133)

MARYLAND SCIENCE CENTER (p. 53)

DISCOVERY CREEK CHILDREN'S MUSEUM (p. 85)

14

$\mathcal{B}$EHIND THE $\mathcal{S}$CENES

CHILDREN HAVE a commendable interest in learning How Things Are Made and How Things Work. Since Washington is not a center for manufacturing much other than policies and pronouncements (and leaving aside whether anything works very well), you'll have to drive outside our general 40-miles-beyond-the-Beltway radius to get to most plant tours here. Also covered are fish hatcheries, postal facilities and grocery stores open to the public. They don't actually make anything at the Newseum, the neat interactive media museum, but it does offer a behind-the-scenes look at how news is reported. Several local newspapers also invite visitors to take a look.

FACTORIES

CHOCOLATE WORLD
Hershey Park Drive, Hershey, Pa.

HOURS: Open 9 am; closing times vary, from 5 to 10, by the season. **COST:** Free. **PHONE:** 800/HERSHEY. **WEB:** www.800hershey.com.　⌖

It's hard to visit this free attraction without dropping some cash on the amusements at next-door Hershey Park. But it's a good twofer. Chocolate World is Hershey's Disney-style exploration of how all those chocolate candies are made. Visitors hop into cocoa bean cars and are conveyed past faux assembly lines. As you get off, you're handed a free sample, then herded into a gift shop where you can buy everything from beach towels to coffee mugs with the Hershey logo.

Directions: *Take I-95 north to I-695 north to I-83 north. Exit at Harrisburg/Route 322 east, and follow the signs (approximately 3 hours).*

CRAYOLA FACTORY
30 Centre Square, Easton, Pa.

HOURS: Sept.-May: Tu-Sat 9:30-5, Sun noon-5. June-Aug.: Tu-Sat 9-6, Sun 11-6; open some Monday holidays. **COST:** $7, under 2 free, seniors $6.50, **PHONE:** 610/515-8000. **WEB:** www.crayola.com/factory.

They don't actually make the ubiquitous coloring, scribbling and marking implements at this "factory." As with Hershey, this is a stunning re-creation that provides insight into the production process, some fun and games, and another opportunity to shed some money in the pursuit of licensed products. The Crayola Factory is in Easton, Pa., about 4 hours from Washington. But since every kid has owned some piece of Crayoliana, it's worth a visit. Glass-walled areas highlight how various products are made, including crayons and markers (free samples, too!). Exhibits allow visitors to interact: There's a sidewalk area where you can play with chalk, glass walls where you can make a mark, a room where you can adjust colored spotlights. And Crayola's parent company, Binney & Smith, clearly hopes you don't forget the gift shop.

Directions: *Take the Pennsylvania Turnpike (Route 476) to Exit 33 (Route 22 east). Take that to Route 309 south/I-78 east, to Exit 22/Easton. Go left on Morgan Hill Rd., right on Philadelphia Rd. and left on St. Johns St. Then take Third St. to Pine St. and turn left (4 hours).*

HERR'S FOODS
20 Herr Drive, Nottingham, Pa.
HOURS: M -Th 9-4, F 9-12; closed weekends and major holidays. **COST:** Free.
RESERVATIONS: Suggested. **PHONE:** 800/637-6225. &

This tour explores the evolution of the potato chip (not to mention the birth of the pretzel and the lifecycles of the lowly corn chip and the mighty cheese curl). Visitors to this factory, just over the Maryland border, can watch giant mixers churning pretzel dough, corn chips being fried and potato chips being bagged and boxed. The best part: complimentary samples, including warm-from-the-fryer potato chips.

Directions: *Take I-95 past Baltimore and over the Severn River. Exit at Route 272 (North East, Md.). Go north 11 miles to Nottingham, and watch for signs (2 ½ hours).*

HARLEY-DAVIDSON FACTORY
1425 Eden Road, York, Pa.
HOURS: Weekdays 10 & 2. **COST:** Free. **PHONE:** 717/848-1177.

This plant makes the classic American motorcycle. The 90-minute tour, for ages 12 and up, includes a look at the assembly line and at a museum on the two-wheeler. While younger children can't go in the plant, they can visit the museum, which has 30-minute tours weekdays at 12:30 and Saturdays at 10, 11, 1 and 2.

Directions: *Take I-95 north to I-695 toward Towson. Exit at I-83 north and follow it into Pennsylvania. Exit at 9E (U.S. Route 30). The plant is on the left (2 hours).*

FISH HATCHERIES

TAKE EGGS, add milt, and mix. Before you know it, you've got some small fry. These hatcheries raise fish to be released in area rivers, streams and lakes. If you visit, you'll probably see ponds or "raceways" teaming with hungry finned beasts. While this isn't quite fish in their natural habitat, kids will get a close look at something that may end up at the end of their hooks. They doubtless will be impressed by the way the fish churn the water white. (Some hatcheries let kids feed breadcrumbs or unsalted canned corn to the fish. Call to make reservations before going. All visits are free.)

Maryland

ALBERT POWELL TROUT HATCHERY. Route 66, Hagerstown, Md. **Hours:** Daily 9-3:30. **Phone:** 301/791-4736. Beautiful rainbow trout are raised here. Access is restricted from November to February, when the most critical work goes on.

CEDARVILLE HATCHERY/JOSEPH MANNING HATCHERY. Cedarville State Forest, Brandywine, Md. **Hours:** Tu and Th 9-4. **Phone:** 301/888-2423. These Maryland State hatcheries are side by side. Cedarville raises such freshwater fish as bass, blue gill and sunfish. Manning raises saltwater species like rockfish and shad. Display aquariums in the visitors center give kids a good look at a variety of fish.

Virginia

FRONT ROYAL FISH CULTURAL STATION. Route 619, east of Strasburg, Va. **Hours:** Weekdays 7:30-4. **Phone:** 540/635-5350. The 22 ponds here contain everything from channel catfish to walleyes to the mighty muskellunge.

MAIL CALL

LET'S HOPE that e-mail never replaces "snail mail." If it did, our kids wouldn't be able to tour the places where all the cards, letters and packages are sorted. Visiting a room full of modems just doesn't sound all that interesting. The postal processing centers here welcome visitors. Call ahead, and also ask your local post office about tours.

District of Columbia

WASHINGTON PROCESSING AND DISTRIBUTION CENTER. 900 Brentwood Rd. NW. **Tours:** Weekdays at 10 (ages 6 and older). **Reservations:** Required. **Phone:** 202/636-2148. ♿

Maryland

SUBURBAN MARYLAND PROCESSING AND DISTRIBUTION PLANT. 16501 Shady Grove Rd., Gaithersburg. **Tours:** Weekdays (school age and up). **Phone:** 301/670-6062. ♿

SOUTHERN MARYLAND PROCESSING AND DISTRIBUTION CENTER. 9201 Edgeworth Dr., Capital Heights. **Tours:** Weekdays. **Phone:** 301/499-7424. Kids under 6 can visit, but strollers aren't allowed.

Virginia

MERRIFIELD PROCESSING AND DISTRIBUTION CENTER. 8409 Lee Hwy., Merrifield. **Tours:** Weekdays at 10 (ages 6 and older). **Reservations:** Required. **Phone:** 703/698-6519. ♿

DULLES INTERNATIONAL MAIL FACILITY PROCESSING AND DISTRIBUTION CENTER. Prentice Drive, Dulles. **Tours:** Tu-Th at 10 (preschoolers welcome). **Reservations:** Required. **Phone:** 703/406-6600. With enough advance notice, you may be able to meet the Customs canines that sniff out bad mail. ♿

THE MEDIA

THE NEWSEUM
1101 Wilson Boulevard, Arlington

HOURS: W-Sun 10-5. **COST:** Free. **PHONE:** 703/284-3544 or 888/639-7386.
METRO STOP: Rosslyn. **WEB:** www.newseum.org. ♿

The Newseum is to a real newsroom as Hershey's Chocolate World is to a real chocolate factory. But it's probably the best overall introduction to the media for young audiences, particularly those old enough to read on their own.

Cuneiform tablets, battered typewriters, reporters' notebooks and press passes, a curving, pulsing wall of television monitors — children will likely be entranced by the profusion of objects and the suitably non-stop media barrage at this museum of journalism. But younger kids may have difficulty tuning out the chatter and concentrating on the story at hand. The story is the story of news itself: what it is, how it's reported and why it matters that it's reported accurately. Famous news stories are recounted, and the nuts-and-bolts of journalism are explored. The place is rabidly interactive, with computers that allow you to try your hand at putting together a story and to address the ethical questions journalists face. Most impressive are three tiny TV studios where visitors can do their own stand-ups. TelePrompTers reel off the script, so kids who already read well will be most comfortable, though natural-born anchors can just take the microphone and do their own thing. (You can buy a tape of your child's performance for $10.)

> **Words to the wise:** *Images of war and violence (Holocaust victims, charred Iraqi troops) show up in TV footage and in photographs during the introductory "What Is News?" movie. Skip that film if you have little kids in tow or don't feel like explaining some tough issues.*

Nearby: Marine Corps War Memorial, Arlington Cemetery.

NEWSPAPERS

If you think your kids would enjoy visiting a real newsroom, try one of these area papers (even if reservations aren't required, it's wise to call to make an appointment). And if you visit *The Washington Post*, be sure to wave to us.

District of Columbia

THE WASHINGTON POST. 1150 15th St. NW. **Tours:** M 10-3 (ages 11 and up). **Reservations:** Required. **Phone:** 202/334-7969. **Metro:** Farragut North, McPherson Square. ♿

THE WASHINGTON INFORMER. 3117 Martin Luther King Ave. SE. **Tours:** W (ages 6 and up). **Phone:** 202/561-4100.

Maryland

THE CAPITAL. 2000 Capital Dr., Annapolis. **Tours:** W, Th at 6 pm. **Reservations:** Required. **Phone:** 410/268-5000. No strollers or babies in arms permitted. ♿

MARYLAND INDEPENDENT. 7 Industrial Park, Waldorf. **Tours:** F 10:30-2 (ages 6 and up). **Reservations:** Required. **Phone:** 301/843-9600, ext. 260. ♿

Virginia

LOUDOUN TIMES-MIRROR. 9 E. Market St., Leesburg. **Tours:** M-Th (ages 5 and up). **Phone:** 703/777-1111.

TELEVISION

WJLA-TV. 3007 Tilden St. NW. **Tours:** Weekdays 10 am. **Reservations:** Required. **Phone:** 202/364-7766. **Metro:** Van Ness/UDC. Channel 7's hour-long tours show kids the studios, the newsroom, the news edit suite and the control room. The children must be "older elementary school" age, since the tour is technical in nature. ♿

FOOD for THOUGHT

GIANT AND SAFEWAY have seen the value in instilling brand loyalty in future customers. They, along with most Shoppers Food Warehouse, Magruder's, Super Fresh and Fresh Fields stores, offer tours. Your best bet is to call the store of your choice (probably the one you frequent most often) and ask to speak with the manager. (Set up tours for groups of 10 or more at Shoppers Food Warehouse by calling the main office: 301/306-8608.) Stores require about a week's notice. You'll be asked the size of your group and the ages of the children. Most stores prefer that visitors come in groups of at least six, though some will add smaller groups to other tours.

ET CETERA

YOU COULD CALL this a chapter of stuff that didn't fit neatly elsewhere. Some attractions here may not at first glance seem that appealing to children, and yet there are things about them — a massive scale, an engaging design — that can be captivating. Among other things, we also note two places ideal for practicing a big child milestone: learning to walk.

NATIONAL BUILDING MUSEUM
401 F Street NW

HOURS: M-Sat 10-4, Sun noon-4; closed major holidays. **COST:** Free. **PHONE:** 202/272-2448. **WEB:** www.nbm.org. **METRO STOP:** Judiciary Square.   ♿

Yes, this is a museum dedicated to the building trades, and older kids interested in architecture and construction may find it interesting. But the real value here, especially for smaller kids, is the colossal scale of the interior space. The Great Hall, nearly as big as a football field, is studded with fat, 75-foot-tall Corinthian-style columns (actually towers of brick covered with smooth faux marble finish). It's one of the few places in Washington where kids can run around and just sort of fill up space in relative safety and calm. On the outside, there's a bit of Civil War history, in the form of a frieze depicting Union military troops. One kid-friendly permanent exhibit inside is devoted to the building of Washington, including touchable models of the Capitol, the White House and other local landmarks. However, the information provided — including in push-button question-and-answer games — is likely to appeal largely to the 10-and-up crowd.

If you have kids of that age who are interested in building history, guided tours are offered nearly continuously. Some exhibitions, like a recent one on how bridges and trusses support things, also can be intriguing to children. Two nice touches: the courtyard cafe is a great out-of-the-way spot to grab a meal or snack, and grown-ups may enjoy the stylish (but not cheap) architectural stuff in the gift shop. In short, a visit here offers a nice side trip on days when the big-draw museums are packed or it's raining outside.

NOTES: For wheelchair access, use the entrance on Fourth and G streets. Some displays are in Braille. **Nearby:** National Portrait Gallery, MCI Center, Chinatown, National Police Memorial.

OLD POST OFFICE TOWER
Pennsylvania Avenue and 12th Street NW

HOURS: Mid-Apr.-Labor Day daily 8 am-10:45 pm, other times 10 -5:45. **COST:** Free. **PHONE:** 202-606-8691 (TTD: 202-606-8694) **WEB:** www.nps.gov/opot. **METRO STOP:** Federal Triangle, Metro Center. ♿

It takes two elevator rides to reach the 270-foot-high observation gallery of this 1899 tower, which affords some of the best views available of the downtown Washington skyline and the Mall. The first ride, in a glass-walled elevator, whisks you up through the ornate, nine-story (160-foot-tall) atrium, which once served as the city's major mail depot and is now lined with offices of federal agencies dedicated to the arts and humanities. Then you take a dogleg through a hallway to a second, enclosed elevator, where you're carried up three stories more to the tower's observation deck. Two sides are enclosed in Plexiglas, but two sides are strung with protective wires, so you can feel the breeze and enjoy a sense of really being "up there." (The view is in some ways superior to what you get at the Washington Monument, and the lines at the Post Office are rarely long. Expect no wait at all midday on a winter weekend.) Make sure you take the narrow staircase down a few flights to visit the bell chamber, where you can get a close view of the Congress Bells, a gift from Great Britain for our national bicentennial in 1976. The bells are replicas of the 400-year-old set in London's Westminster Abbey. The largest bell, placed in the center of the arrangement and weighing in at 2,953 pounds, is big enough to accommodate an entire family of four. The bells are rung only for state and other special occasions, but you can press a button to hear a rather unconvincing recorded rendition. Note the extended evening summer hours — a great chance to beat seasonal crowds.

Words to the wise: *If you drive, expect to pay $5 or $6 to park for the day on weekends. Otherwise, you'll have to cruise a long time for the few unrestricted on-street parking places.*

NOTES: Wheelchair access to bell area can be arranged. There are a few shops; kids have a hard time resisting the one featuring magic, juggling and other toys. **Food:** The food court in the middle of the Post Office is an easy place to grab a snack, but Planet Hollywood, Hard Rock Cafe and other restaurants are in the area if you prefer. **Nearby:** FBI Building, White House, National Archives, Navy Memorial, Ford's Theater, National Aquarium, Mall museums.

THE FRANCISCAN MONASTERY
1400 Quincy Street NE

HOURS: M-Sat 9-5, Sun 10-5; tours: M-Sat 9, 10, & 11, Sun 1-4. **COST:** Free. **PHONE:** 202/526-6800. **WEB:** www.pressroom.com/~franciscan. ♿

You don't need to be Catholic to enjoy a trip to this captivating church in Washington's "Catholic Quarter." Patterned after the monasteries of Europe, the site is maintained by members of the Order of St. Francis, a.k.a. the Franciscans. A brown-robed, rope-belted Franciscan brother will lead you on a tour of the church, past replicas of

WALKIN' the WALK

WHEN YOUR CHILD is just starting to walk, your house or apartment can seem like a dangerous obstacle course. Despite moving the hard-edged coffee table and pushing the furniture out of the way, some kids still seems to find ways to bonk their heads. What you need is a wide-open carpeted space with lots of room to roam. Someplace like the . . . KENNEDY CENTER. Or the NATIONAL BUILDING MUSEUM.

Both of these cultural landmarks offer cavernous spaces where toddlers-in-training can plant their pudgy feet one in front of the other for yard after yard after yard, getting up a good head of steam. The Kennedy Center's red-carpeted main lobby stretches the building's entire length and is illuminated by shiny chandeliers. Outside is a terrace overlooking the Potomac where, in good weather, you can watch the planes fly to Reagan National Airport. Visit during the daytime (to avoid the intermission crowds), or get there early for one of the free Millennium Stage concerts (see p. 72).

The Great Hall of the National Building Museum is similarly open and even less crowded. Tall columns soar to the ceiling, dwarfing everyone. Children can career around the sprawling space, ambling from column to column like little pinballs.

A few visits to these two places and you'll have your little one walking in no time. And then you'll wonder how to get them to slow down.

---

various holy shrines — the anointing stone, the tomb of Christ — and down steps into a re-creation of the catacombs of ancient Rome. The catacombs are pretty neat (short, narrow hallways with body-sized niches carved in the walls — but no bodies), though you can access them only on the 45-minute tour. Signs remind you that this is a church, so decide whether your kids can behave. If they are rambunctious, a tour of the grounds alone — covered walkways, the stations of the cross, little hidden grottoes and a huge collection of rose bushes — might be better.

Words to the wise: *Some of the artwork is a little graphic: Christ on the cross, souls licked by the flames of Hell, St. Sebastian pierced by arrows, etc.*

NOTES: The tour includes some stair climbing, so the mobility-impaired may find some parts difficult. There is no restaurant nearby.

DISCOVERY CHANNEL DESTINATION STORE
601 F Street NW (in the MCI Center)

HOURS: M-Sat 10-10, Sun 10-6; closed Christmas Day. **COST:** Free; film is $2.50 adults, $1.50 ages 6-17 and seniors. **PHONE:** 202/639-0908. **WEB:** www.discovery.com. **METRO STOP:** Gallery Place/Chinatown. 🔥

This is the only retail store included in this book, and it's no mistake. While this four-story complex is essentially a high-end educational toy store and promotional device for Discovery Channel products, it offers enough other materials and activities — a 40-foot replica of the biggest T. Rex skeleton ever unearthed, a high-definition film about D.C.; scientific demonstrations, interactive kiosks everywhere — to justify a visit as an educational experience. Between floor one (Paleo World) and floor four (Sky and Space Science Frontiers) you'll find areas devoted to the ocean, wild animals and many other areas of interest. Our kids loved the staff demonstrations (a magnetic top that appears to float), the Hubble telescope pictures, the live anthill and the cockpit of the B-52 bomber. Each area, of course, offers related books, toys, videos, games and artifacts, some astonishingly expensive. The kids will also love the space capsule-like elevator, which makes thematically appropriate noises for each floor (mission control communiqués for the top floor, animal noises for the animal area).

Words to the wise: *Agree on a spending limit before going. Kids will have a fine time just exploring, but it's a rare child who will not want to take something home. You can get out for $1 a kid (a rock sample), but if your guard is down the Visa charges can pile up.*

NOTES: Except during major events at the MCI Center, several parking lots nearby will cost around $5. **Food:** Service at the MCI Center's Velocity Grill was an embarrassment during our two visits; if it seems at all slow, go elsewhere. If your kids like Chinese food, several moderately priced Chinese restaurants are in nearby Chinatown. **Nearby:** National Portrait Gallery, National Museum of American Art, FBI Building, Navy Memorial.

WASHINGTON NATIONAL CATHEDRAL
Wisconsin and Massachusetts avenues NW

HOURS: Daily 10-4:30; weekdays Memorial Day -Labor Day until 9. **COST:** $2 adults, $1 child donation; tours (30-45 minutes) M-Sat about hourly, opening-3:15; Sun 12:30-2:45. No tours during services. **PHONE:** 202/364-6616 (recording); 202/537-6200 (weekdays) **WEB:** www.cathedral.org/cathedral. 🔥

Many people travel to Europe to see the great cathedrals. But it's easy to overlook the fact that the world's sixth largest cathedral — one built mostly according to the style and methods of the great Gothic cathedrals of the 14th Century — is in northwest Washington. Kids of practically any age or religion often find this place awesome. Tots in backpacks can be mesmerized by the light splashing through the stained-glass windows and by the way footsteps and voices bounce off the vaulted ceilings. Elementary school kids often are intrigued by the stone gargoyles and grotesques (the former spew water from their mouths, the latter are merely decorative) the flying buttresses and the spooky crypts beneath the main floor. Older kids can appreciate the magnitude of the project (the cathedral, which was under construction from 1907 to 1990, was one of the last places in America to employ European-trained stonecutters) and the remarkable details, from the piece of moon rock embedded in Space Window to the 96 stone-faced angels surrounding the main tower to the 50 state seals embedded in the floor near the west entrance. Other highlights: Woodrow Wilson's tomb, his sarcophagus topped with a sword (he's the only U.S. president interred in Washington); the Darth Vader grotesque designed by a school kid as part of a contest (you'll need binoculars to see it from the east parking lot); the children's chapel (everything, including kneelers, is scaled down to kid-size, and the upholstery is decorated with animals); and the main nave, where Martin Luther King Jr. preached his last Sunday sermon before being assassinated. You can take a docent-led tour, but kids under 8 are better off touring with you. Don't miss the Pilgrim Observation Gallery (accessible by elevator) for a spectacular view of the Washington skyline and close-up looks at some stonework. The extraordinary 57-acre grounds feature the Pilgrim Garden (one of the most pleasant in Washington), a popular greenhouse, an herb garden and an herb shop.

Words to the wise: *The Observation gallery closes at 3:30 daily. Also, the Web page is a super way to prepare for a visit.*

Notes: Those with wheelchairs should use the north entrance (wheelchairs also are available inside the nave). However, the crypt level and a gift shop on the lower level, as well as some outside buildings, are not accessible.

NATIONAL FIREARMS MUSEUM
National Rifle Association Building, 1250 Waples Mill Road, Fairfax, Va.

HOURS: Daily 10-4, except major holidays. **COST:** Free. **PHONE:** 703/267-1600. **WEB:** www.nra.org/museum/museum1.html. &

Like the National Rifle Association that sustains it at its headquarters here, this museum views American life primarily through the lens of guns and their owners. The resulting exhibits present an intriguing, if narrow, view of U.S. history and culture. The tale they tell starts in the 14th Century with the discovery of gunpowder (and its earliest delivery mechanisms, crossbows and slingshots) and proceeds quickly to the firearms of

America's earliest settlers and its victorious revolutionaries. Displays highlight the weapons of each major U.S. conflict through the Persian Gulf War, those devoted to law enforcement, competition shooting, domestic hunting, safari hunting and more. Dioramas depict a boy's bedroom circa 1950, loaded with toy guns and cowboy and hunting paraphernalia, a group of World War II U.S. soldiers securing a Normandy town in 1944, and a fully operational, belt-driven, shoot-the-ducky carnival display from early in this century. More than 2,000 guns bristle for attention in cases (more than the Smithsonian has, the NRA points out). Among them is an ingenious single-bullet shooter handmade from scrounged parts by a prisoner, a genuine Mayflower musket, a pair of ornate Turkish pistols, a bona-fide Teddy Roosevelt safari gun and several Tommy guns.

While the museum is state-of-the-art — 14 computerized kiosks planted throughout the exhibit areas provide detailed information on most items — it can be annoying to take in with small kids, who inevitably ask questions about the biggest, strangest and most awesome items. To answer them, you'll need to type in the display case and item numbers via the kiosk keyboard (kids 8 and up will enjoy doing this themselves, at least for a while). A brief video is shown in a small theater zone, apparently designed as a fund-raising and promotional tool rather than a museum introduction, so feel free to skip it. The gift shop, essentially a NRA "team" store, has little to interest kids.

Words to the wise: *If you've read the above, you probably already know whether you want to take your kids. Any parent ambivalent about or hostile to private gun ownership will find no moderation or comfort here. The exhibits have a subtle but persistent pro-Second Amendment tone, implying that gun ownership is, and ought to be, insinuated fully into the fabric of American culture. If you're not comfortable with this message for your kids, don't go. If you are, you may love the place.*

NOTES: There's no food concession here and none immediately nearby.

Directions: *From the Beltway, take I-66 west to Exit 57A (Route 50 east). Bear left off the ramp and turn left at the first traffic light (Waples Mill Rd.). The NRA building is about a half a mile down on the right.*

THE AWAKENING
Ohio Drive SW off Independence Avenue (Hains Point)
PHONE: 202/426-6841 (Park Service).

J. Seward Johnson's "life castings"— bronze statutes designed to be alarmingly lifelike — are scattered all over Washington and other U.S. cities. But this 1980 work, depicting a giant struggling to emerge from the earth, is a knockout, one your kids are unlikely to forget. Certain body parts protrude

Continued on p. 202

WHERE'S the SMITHSONIAN?

SMITHSONIAN CASTLE AND VISITOR INFORMATION CENTER
1000 Jefferson Drive SW

HOURS: Daily 9-5:30. **COST:** Free. **PHONE:** 202/357-2700 (TDD: 202/357-1729). **METRO:** Smithsonian. **WEB:** www.si.edu.

The Smithsonian Institution is a bit like Elvis: It's everywhere, from the National Zoo in Woodley Park to the Naturalist Center in Leesburg, Va. It's everywhere in this book, too, since we haven't corralled it elsewhere under one heading. (See the array of Smithsonian attractions below.) For a full understanding of what the Smithsonian has to offer, head for its Castle — which children with visions of knights in shining armor may feel is a mandatory visit anyway — and check the Smithsonian Visitor Information Center. The center opens an hour before other Smithsonian attractions, giving you time to get your bearings and plan your attack. A video overview of the world's largest museum organization is shown continuously in two theaters, but at 24 minutes long it's beyond the attention span of many kids. The family can pick up free brochures in several languages and leave fingerprints on "touch-screen" computers that highlight various Washington attractions and events (both Smithsonian and non-Smithsonian). Even better, you can ask real live people for advice on what to see. The scale models of the city's monumental core are neat, and though you probably won't need the electronic wall maps, kids may get a kick out of pressing the button that illuminates the Metro: The map lights up like the body's circulatory system. There's also an automatic teller machine and a gift shop with modest selections from the more fully stocked museum stores you'll find around the Mall. This also is the place to pay your respects to James Smithson. The Smithsonian benefactor's crypt is just inside the door to the Castle.

THE SMITHSONIAN

- Anacostia Museum
- Arts and Industries Building
- Discovery Theatre
- Freer Gallery of Art
- Hirshhorn Museum and Sculpture Garden
- National Air and Space Museum
- National Museum of African Art
- National Museum of American Art
- National Museum of American History
- National Museum of Natural History
- National Portrait Gallery
- National Postal Museum
- National Zoo
- Naturalist Center
- Renwick Gallery
- Sackler Gallery
- Smithsonian Castle and Visitor Information Center

from the earth — a screaming face, a 17-foot arm, a knee, a foot — with the rest presumably just below the surface and ready to emerge any second. The effect is startling, kind of funny and kind of scary. It's also a great family photo op and a good climbing opportunity.

The Awakening is reason enough to head for Hains Point, a stub of an island facing the city's waterfront and the Potomac River, but there are other reasons as well: great open places to walk around and view the water, a miniature golf course, a full-sized golf course, tennis courts, playing fields and more. Close to the city's monumental action but a step more natural and less crowded, Hains Point is an ideal frisbee-and-snack-after-the-museum sort of place.

NOTES: Wheelchair access can be treacherous if the grounds are wet.

EINSTEIN STATUE
Constitution Avenue and 22st Street NW

PHONE: 202/334-2000 (National Academy of Sciences).

This often overlooked bronze sculpture of physicist Albert Einstein is one of our favorite Washington "secrets." Unlike most tributes to great men in Washington, this bronze casting is utterly accessible and invites intimacy — in fact it's designed so kids (and adults) can sit right on the grand man's lap. Set in a small grove of trees that keeps it half-hidden from the traffic on Constitution Avenue, the 1979 work delights kids, perhaps because it makes a man held in such high esteem seem so sweet, even warm. He's even dressed casually, in a sweater and sandals. Albert is also one of Washington's best family photo ops.

WHERE THEY ARE

DISTRICT OF COLUMBIA

African American Civil War Memorial
Anacostia Museum
Art Museum of the Americas
Arts and Industries Building
Awakening statue
B'nai B'rith Klutznick Museum
Bethune Council House
Bureau of Engraving and Printing
C&O Canal National Historical Park
Capital Children's Museum
Capital Crescent Trail
Capitol Building
Capitol River Cruises
Circus Mini Golf Putt-4-Fun
Corcoran Gallery of Art
DC Ducks
DC United
DAR Museum
Department of the Interior Museum
Discovery Channel Destination Store
Discovery Creek Children's Museum
Discovery Theatre
Dumbarton Oaks
Einstein Planetarium
Einstein statue
FDR Memorial
Federal Bureau of Investigation
Ford's Theatre
Fort Dupont Ice Arena
Franciscan Monastery
Frederick Douglass Home
Freer Gallery of Art
Holocaust Memorial Museum
Hirshhorn Museum and Sculpture
   Garden
Jefferson Memorial
Kenilworth Aquatic Gardens
Kennedy Center
Kidshop
Korean War Veterans Memorial
Library of Congress
Lincoln Memorial
Made By You
MCI Center/National Sports Gallery
Mexican Cultural Institute
Montrose Park
National Air and Space Museum

National Aquarium
National Arboretum
National Archives
National Building Museum
National Cathedral
National Gallery of Art
National Geographic Explorers Hall
National Museum of African Art
National Museum of American Art
National Museum of American History
National Museum of Health and
   Medicine
National Museum of Jewish Military
   History
National Museum of Natural History
National Museum of Women in the
   Arts
National Portrait Gallery
National Postal Museum
National Theatre
National Zoo
Naval Observatory
Navy Memorial and Naval Heritage
   Center
Navy Museum
Navy Yard
Old Post Office Tower
Pershing Park Ice Rink
Phillips Collection
Pierce Mill
Renwick Gallery
Rock Creek Regional Park
Sackler Gallery
Sculpture Garden Ice Rink
ShoreShot
Smithsonian Castle and Visitor
   Information Center
Smithsonian Castle carousel
Spirit Cruises
Tidal Basin pedal boats
Union Station
U.S.S. Barry
Vietnam Veterans Memorial
Washington Capitals
Washington Dolls' House and Toy
   Museum
Washington Informer
Washington Post

Washington Mail Processing and
   Distribution Center
Washington Monument
Washington Mystics
Washington Wizards
White House
WJLA-TV

MARYLAND

Montgomery County
Adventure Theatre
ARC Ice Skating Rink
Audubon Naturalist Society
Bankshot basketball
Becraft's Farm
Bethesda Academy of Performing Arts
Bethesda Metro Ice Center
Black Hill Regional Park
Bowl America Westwood
Brookside Gardens
Butler's Orchard
C&O Canal National Historical Park
Cabin John Regional Park
Capital Crescent Trail
Clara Barton House
Dave & Buster's
Discovery Zone (Germantown, North
   Bethesda)
Glen Echo Park
Glen Echo Park carousel
Great Falls Tavern
Homestead Farm
Imagine That!
Jeeper's
Lake Needwood
Locust Grove Nature Center
Made By You (Bethesda)
Meadowside Nature Center
Montgomery County Aquatic Center
National Capital Trolley Museum
National Railway Historical Society,
   Potomac Chapter
National Weather Service Science and
   History Center
Now This!
Puppet Company Playhouse
Putt-Putt Golf & Games

Rock Hill Orchard
Rockville Climbing Gym
Rockville Roller Skating Center
Seneca Creek State Park
Sportland
Sportrock (Rockville)
Suburban Maryland Mail Processing and
   Distribution Center
Summit Hall Farm Park
SuperStar Studios
The Track
Tuffy Leemans Glenmont Bowl
Wheaton Regional Park
White Flint Golf Park
White Oak Bowling Center
White's Ferry

Prince George's County
Allen Pond Park
AMF Bowie
AMF College Park
Beltsville Agricultural Research Center
Bowie Baysox
Bowie Ice Arena
Calvert Road Park
Cherry Hill Farm
Chesapeake Icebreakers
Clearwater Nature Center
Clinton Skating Center
College Park Aviation Museum
Cosca Regional Park
Fort Washington
Gardens Ice House
Goddard Space Flight Center
Herbert Wells Ice Rink
Howard B. Owens Science Center
   Planetarium
Jack Kent Cooke Stadium
Jeeper's
Johnson's Berry Farm
Lake Artemesia
Laurel Golf and Recreation
Laurel Skating Center
Miller Farms
Monte Miniature Golf
Mount Rainier Nature and Recreation
   Center
National Colonial Farm

National Wildlife Visitors Center
Old Maryland Farm
Oxon Cove Park
Parker Farms
Patuxent River Park/Jug Bay Natural Area
Piscataway Horse Farm
Rollingcrest-Chillum Splash Pool
Seabrook Skating Center
Six Flags America
Skate Palace
Skelterama Go-Kart Track
Sweet Spot Miniature Golf
Tucker Road Ice Rink
University of Maryland astronomy skywatching
Watkins Regional Park

Anne Arundel County

AMF Southwest
Banneker-Douglass Museum
Baltimore-Washington Int'l Airport Observation Gallery
The Capitol newspaper
Capitol Raceway
Chesapeake Children's Museum
City Dock Boat Tours
Discovery Zone (Annapolis, Glen Burnie)
Glen Burnie Bowling Center
Go-Kart Raceway
Lake Waterford Park
Made By You (Annapolis)
Naval Observatory
Pasadena Skating Center
Riviera Bowl
Skate Zone

Howard County

Centennial Park
Cider Mill Farm
Columbia Ice Rink
Columbia Mall carousel
Earth Treks Climbing Center
Ellicott City B&O Railroad Station Museum
ExploraWorld
Lake Kittimaqundi

Larriland Farms
Rocky Gorge Driving Range
Sharp's Farm
Supreme Sports Club

Baltimore and Vicinity

American Visionary Art Museum
B&O Railroad Museum
Babe Ruth Birthplace/ Orioles Museum
Baltimore Maritime Museum
Baltimore Museum of Art
Baltimore Museum of Industry
Baltimore Public Works Museum
Baltimore Ravens
Baltimore Society of Model Engineers
Baltimore Zoo
Cecil County Dragway
Cedarvale Farms
Clipper City Boat Tours
Davis Planetarium
Fire Museum of Maryland
Fort McHenry
Great Blacks in Wax Museum
Huber's Farm
Inner Harbor carousel
Inner Harbor Ice Rink
Maryland Science Center
Moore's Orchard
National Aquarium in Baltimore
Oriole Park at Camden Yards
Samuel D. Harris National Museum of Dentistry
Walters Art Gallery
Washington Monument, Baltimore
Weber's Cider Mill Farm

Frederick County

Antietam National Battlefield
Braddock Roller Rink
Catoctin Mountain Orchard
Catoctin Mountain Park
Catoctin Wildlife Preserve and Zoo
Children's Museum of Rose Hill Manor Park
Crystal Grottoes Caverns
Cunningham Falls State Park
Discovery Zone
Fast Track Raceways
Frederick Keys

Frederick Sport and Ice Arena
Glade-Link Farms
Greenbrier State Park
Laser Storm
Maynes Farm
75/80 Dragway
Sugarloaf Mountain
Thurmont Bowling Center
Village Lanes Bowling Center
Walkersville Bowling Center
Walkersville Southern Railroad
Way Off Broadway Dinner Theater

Southern Maryland

Battle Creek Cypress Swamp Sanctuary
Calvert Cliffs State Park
Calvert Marine Museum
Calvert Roller Skating Center
Cedarville Hatchery/Joseph Manning
    Fish Hatchery
Chesapeake Beach Railway Museum
Fantasy World Family Entertainment
    Center
Maryland Independent newspaper
Maryland International Raceway
Owen's Berry Farm
Rose Hill Farm
Seidel Farm
Talbot County Community Center
    Ice Rink
Waldorf 500 Go-Kart Track
Waldorf Roller Skating Center

Eastern Shore

Delmarva Shorebirds
Salisbury Zoological Park
Wye Grist Mill

Central/Western Maryland

Albert Powell Trout Hatchery
Baugher's Orchard
Carroll County Farm Museum
Hagerstown Speedway
Hagerstown Suns
Mason-Dixon Dragway
Sewell's Farm
Union Mills

VIRGINIA

Fairfax County

Bull Run Regional Park
Burke Lake Park
Centreville Mini Golf & Games
Chantilly Golf Center
Claude Moore Colonial Farm
Colvin Run Mill Historic Site
Discovery Zone (Fairfax, Falls Church)
Dug Out Batting Cages
Ellanor C. Lawrence Park
Fairfax Ice Arena
Fairfax Station Railroad Museum
Falls Church Bowling Center
Fountainhead Regional Park
Geological Survey
Great Falls Park
Gunston Hall
Hartland Orchard
Hidden Oaks Nature Center
Hidden Pond Nature Center
Huntley Meadows
Jeeper's
Jefferson District Park
Kidwell Farm
Lake Accotink Park
Lake Fairfax Park
Lee District Park
Linden Vineyards
Mason Neck State Park
McLean Central Park
Meadowlark Gardens Regional Park
Mount Vernon
National Firearms Museum
National Wildlife Federation
Northern Virginia Baseball Academy
    (Chantilly, Springfield)
Occoquan Regional Park Batting Cage
Paint Your Own Pottery
Planet Play (Reston, Springfield, Burke)
Pohick Bay Regional Park
Potomac Vegetable Farms
Reston Animal Park
Reston Skating Pavilion
Riverbend Park
Skatenation of Reston
South Run Rec Center
Stribling Orchard

Sully Historic Site
Vienna Railroad Station
W&OD Trail
Wakefield Recreation Center
  Climbing Wall
Willow Oaks Blueberry Farm
Wolf Trap
Woodlawn Plantation
Woody's Golf Range

Alexandria

Alexandria Black History Resource
  Center
Alexandria Go-Kart Raceway
Buddie Ford Nature Center
Cameron Run Regional Park
Carlyle House
Fort Ward Museum
Franconia Skating Center
Gadsby's Tavern Museum
George Washington Masonic National
  Memorial
Green Spring Gardens Park
Huntley Meadows Park
The Lyceum
Mount Vernon Recreation Center
  Ice Rink
Potomac Riverboat Company
Robert E. Lee boyhood home
Sportrock II
Stabler-Leadbeater Apothecary Shop
Torpedo Factory Art Center
West End Dinner Theatre

Arlington County

Arlington House
Arlington National Cemetery
Arlington Planetarium
Bluemont Park Disc Golf
Children's Theatre, Inc.
Classika Theatre for Youth
Gravelly Point Park
Gulf Branch Nature Center
Long Branch Nature Center
Made By You (Arlington)
Marine Corps Memorial
Newseum
Patent and Trademark Museum

Potomac Overlook Nature Center
Theodore Roosevelt Island
Tuckahoe Park and Playground
Upton Hill Regional Park
Women in Military Service to America
  Memorial

Loudoun County

Aldie Mill
Algonkian Regional Park
Ball's Bluff Regional Park
Crooked Run Orchard
Dulles International Mail Facility
Loudoun Times-Mirror
Luckett's Berry Farm
Merrifield Mail Processing and
  Distribution Center
National Weather Service, Sterling
Purcellville Roller Rink
Putter's Paradise
Smithsonian Naturalist Center
  (Leesburg)
W&OD Trail

Prince William County

Champions
Discovery Zone
Harbor River Cruises
Lake Ridge Park
Laser Quest
Locust Shade Regional Park
Magic Putting Course
Manassas Museum
Manassas National Battlefield Park
Old Dominion Speedway
Old Mine Ranch
Prince William Cannons
Prince William Forest Park
Prince William Ice Forum
Skate and Fun Zone
Splash Down
Water Works

Shenandoah Valley/ Skyline Drive

Burwell-Morgan Mill
Elk Mountain Trails
Endless Caverns

Fort Valley Stables
Front Royal Fish Cultural Station
Luray Caverns
Marriott Ranch
Mountain Top Ranch
Muskrat Haven
On the Wild Side Zoological Park
Shenandoah Caverns
Skyline Caverns
Stonewall Jackson Monument at
    Hupp's Hill
Summit Point

Virginia Countryside
Belvedere Plantation
Busch Gardens
Colonial Beach Dragway
Double B Farms
Finnegan's Berry Farm
Flying Circus Aerodrome
Moormont Orchards
Paramount Kings Dominion
Rick & Van's farm
Snead's Asparagus Farm
Spotsylvania Mall Carousel
Summerduck Dragway
Water Country USA

Pennsylvania
Chocolate World
Crayola Factory
Gettysburg National Military Park
Harley-Davidson Factory
Herr's Foods
HersheyPark
Land of Little Horses
Sesame Place

CROSS-PREFERENCES

To help you decide where to take your children, we've organized the attractions in *Kid-O-Rama* by some useful categories, from those that are free to others that are expensive but worth a splurge. Have a 3-year-old *and* a 10-year-old? Consider "Good for Mixed Age Groups." Interested in the best bets for birthday parties or for grandparent trips? For disabled children or for rainy days? For avoiding crowds or for catching the Metro? You'll find those and more. The listings, most of which include both individual attractions and broader sections to check, are of course suggestions, not guarantees that all will meet your needs.

FREE

GOOD FOR KIDS IN BACKPACKS

GOOD FOR TODDLERS

GOOD FOR STROLLERS

GOOD FOR
PRE-READERS

GOOD FOR MIXED
AGE GROUPS

GOOD FOR
OLDER KIDS

GOOD FOR BIRTHDAY PARTIES

GOOD FOR GRANDPARENT TRIPS

GOOD FOR
DISABLED CHILDREN

RAINY DAY CHOICES

SUNNY DAY CHOICES

LEAST
CROWDED PLACES

GOOD EXCUSES
FOR A COUNTRY DRIVE

EXPENSIVE BUT WORTH
A SPLURGE

INDEX

A

B

W

ACKNOWLEDGMENTS

This book would not have been possible without the expert and occasionally even uncomplaining assistance of my daughters, Gwyneth and Beatrice. They performed the admirable role of Everykid, while their mother — and, not coincidentally, my wife, Ruth — posed as Everymom. All three have my bottomless thanks.

Being an editor is a bit like being a parent, except the refrigerator art is a little better. My colleagues in the WEEKEND section, with whom I worked for nine years, created wonderful work every week, making me look better than I had any right to expect. I'd also like to thank the many freelance contributors to WEEKEND during my stint, especially the many scribbling moms upon whom I depended for Saturday's Child columns.

Finally, I'd like to thank Craig Stoltz not only for joining me in this endeavor and improving it at every turn, but for not punching me in the face when I swanned off to Cambridge, Mass., just as the book was entering its crucial final stages.

— John F. Kelly

The irony of writing a book about doing things with your children is that you spend a great deal of time sitting in front of the computer, talking on the phone and studying maps or other documents while the kids are . . . off playing somewhere, probably. My wife, Pamela Luttig, has been a loyal and persistent supporter of my writing this work and has contributed substantially to the reporting and to various assessments in it. Sometimes she took the kids places while I stayed home and wrote. I'll put it here in writing, for all to see. Pam: I owe you big time.

Caleb and Jordan, our two boys, were willing and (usually) enthusiastic laboratory subjects for an alarming number of experiments in entertainment and education. Many evaluations in this book reflect their increasingly expert, and utterly unforgiving, responses. I owe them, too, and promise to let them choose, for a while at least, which places our family goes for fun.

I owe a huge debt to my co-author, John F. Kelly, not only for inviting me to share in this book project but for bringing me into the warm fold of *The Washington Post* in the first place. For this I offer both gratitude and absolution.

— Craig Stoltz

Noel Epstein, our publisher, helped conceive, shape, pare and burnish the book. Like all great editors, he prevented nearly all of the authors' excesses and vanities from appearing in print. His assistant, Susan Breitkopf, also contributed valuable suggestions and edits. We know we should bow to grand *Washington Post* tradition and thank our superiors, mentors, pod-fellows and friends in the newsroom for their help and support. There are too many to name, and Epstein wouldn't give us any more space. You know who you are. Many thanks.

— John F. Kelly and Craig Stoltz